CLASSICS OF IRISH HISTORY

*General Editor:* Tom Garvin

Original publication dates of reprinted titles are given in brackets

P. S. O'Hegarty, *The Victory of Sinn Féin* (1924)
Walter McDonald, *Some Ethical Questions of Peace and War* (1919)
Joseph Johnston, *Civil War in Ulster* (1913)
James Mullin, *The Story of a Toiler's Life* (1921)
Robert Brennan, *Ireland Standing Firm* and *Eamon de Valera* (1958)
Mossie Harnett, *Victory and Woe: The West Limerick Brigade in the War of Independence*
Padraig de Burca and John F. Boyle, *Free State or Republic? Pen Pictures of the Historic Treaty Session of Dáil Éireann* (1922)
Arthur Clery, *The Idea of a Nation* (1907)
Standish James O'Grady, *To the Leaders of Our Working People*
Michael Davitt, *Jottings in Solitary*
Oliver MacDonagh, *Ireland: The Union and its Aftermath* (1977)
Thomas Fennell, *The Royal Irish Constabulary: A History and Personal Memoir*
Arthur Griffith, *The Resurrection of Hungary* (1918)
William McComb, *The Repealer Repulsed* (1841)
George Moore, *Parnell and His Island* (1887)
Charlotte Elizabeth Tonna, *Irish Recollections* (1841/47 as *Personal Recollections*)
Standish James O'Grady, *Sun and Wind*
John Sarsfield Casey, *The Galtee Boy: A Fenian Prison Narrative*
William and Mary Ann Hanbidge, *Memories of West Wicklow: 1813–1939* (1939)
A. P. A. O'Gara, *The Green Republic* (1902)
William Cooke Taylor, *Reminiscences of Daniel O'Connell* (1847)
William Bruce and Henry Joy, *Belfast Politics* (1794)
Annie O'Donnell, *Your Fondest Annie*
Joseph Keating, *My Struggle for Life* (1916)
John Mitchel, *The Last Conquest of Ireland (Perhaps)* (1858/9)
Harold Begbie, *The Lady Next Door* (1914)
Eugene Davis, *Souvenirs of Footprints Over Europe* (1889)

# *The Lady Next Door*

✦

**HAROLD BEGBIE**

*with an introduction by*
*Patrick Maume*

UNIVERSITY COLLEGE DUBLIN PRESS
Preas Choláiste Ollscoile Bhaile Átha Cliath

First published 1914
This edition first published by
University College Dublin Press 2006


ISBN 1-904558-52-6
ISSN 1393-6883

University College Dublin Press
Newman House, 86 St Stephen's Green
Dublin 2, Ireland
*www.ucdpress.ie*



Cataloguing in Publication data available
from the British Library

Typeset in Ireland in Ehrhardt by Elaine Shiels, Bantry, Co. Cork
Text design by Lyn Davies, Frome, Somerset, England
Printed in England on acid-free paper by Athenæum Press Ltd

CONTENTS

# INTRODUCTION

*Patrick Maume*



## BIOGRAPHICAL NOTE[1]

Harold Begbie was born in St Martin, Suffolk, in 1871, fifth and youngest son of an Anglican clergyman, Rev. Mars Hamilton Begbie. (The family had a strong military tradition.) After unsuccessfully attempting to establish himself as a Devon dairy-farmer and a poet, he worked in the 1890s on the *Globe* (a London Conservative newspaper renowned for producing satirists), eventually acquiring his own column. Begbie came to share the fears of the 'national efficiency' movement which saw the setbacks of the Boer War and the persistence of urban poverty as reflecting complacent and incompetent aristocratic leadership. Arthur Balfour, whom Begbie pilloried as effeminate and incompetent in a series of political nursery rhymes, developed a lasting detestation for him. Some practitioners of 'national efficiency' took up the cause of Joseph Chamberlain and social imperialism; Begbie regarded Chamberlain as a blustering demagogue and pinned his hopes on the Liberals. In 1904 Begbie became a freelance, and was subsequently well known as a practitioner of the celebrity interview on the Liberal *Daily Chronicle*. (The celebrated editor Robert Donald – who had rescued the paper from damage inflicted by internal Liberal Party conflicts over the Boer War – is the dedicatee of *The Lady Next Door*.)

Begbie had abandoned orthodox Christianity for a worldview based on the neo-Hegelian Idealist philosophy popular in the years before the First World War. He drew on his contacts with contemporary scientists such as Sir William Crookes to argue that the new physics had refuted materialism by showing that the apparent solidity of the material world was an illusion imposed by the limitations of the senses. He believed evolution was not random but directed towards higher ends and advanced by the individual human will. He appears to have believed in the existence of an *anima mundi* linking all living beings, which were reabsorbed into it on death and, insofar as they had improved themselves by exerting their willpower, helped to raise it towards higher levels of being. This underlay Begbie's belief in telepathy. He was a member of the Psychic Research Society, though he expressed scepticism about the showier séance phenomena pursued by such figures as W. T. Stead (whom he otherwise greatly admired). He has a minor niche in the history of fantasy fiction as the first author to imagine a detective who solves crimes through visions received in dreams. This form of philosophical Idealism had attractions for a journalist speculating on his influence over a mass readership.

The English neo-Hegelian school also encouraged those 'New Liberals' who argued that Victorian Individualism was outmoded, that society as a whole should take more responsibility for its poorer and weaker members, and that an interventionist state could represent the collective higher self in promoting the common good. Begbie wrote extensively on the hideous poverty of the East End of London; in his extensive fictional œuvre light comedy coexisted with (often pseudonymous) exposés of prostitution and child abuse. He was a zealous promoter of charities, alleged to have raised more for good causes than any of his contemporaries. Begbie produced several books of anonymous case-studies (supplied by the Salvation Army, whose social work he ceaselessly eulogised), arguing that developing willpower through religious regeneration was the key to the rehabilitation of alcoholics and outcasts; he was on friendly terms with the Army's founder General William Booth (whose biography he wrote) and his son and successor Bramwell Booth. In the years before the First World War Begbie was closely associated with Lloyd George, whom he hailed in such works as *Safety, Honour and Welfare: A Conversation with Lloyd George* (1911) as a prophet whose social legislation promised a brighter and fairer world.

Begbie had advocated peace, but on the outbreak of war he became a fervent reviler of German militarism. His 1914 verse 'Fall In!' achieved lasting notoriety as exemplifying emotional blackmail in wartime recruiting. In the first weeks of the war rumours circulated that British troops retreating before the main German offensive had been protected by heavenly figures. In 1915 the writer Arthur Machen disclosed that he had inadvertently started these 'Angel of Mons' rumours by publishing a short story which many readers mistook for a factual account. Begbie responded with *On the Side of the Angels* (1915) which collected second-hand accounts as 'proof' of a real miracle, suggested Machen's story was unconsciously inspired by telepathic messages from dying soldiers and met Machen's continued protests with accusations of concealing the truth for some nefarious purpose. (Machen was an occultist turned High Anglican Ritualist – a worldview Begbie particularly disliked.) Many of Begbie's witnesses were rapidly and humiliatingly exposed as fakes without apparently diminishing his credulity. Machen privately claimed Begbie had undertaken the task as a publishers' commission and was too intelligent to believe it.[2] It has been suggested that Begbie was acting on behalf of a semi-official war propaganda agency run by the former Liberal MP C. F. G. Masterman; on the other hand, Begbie's whole career shows considerable ability for wishful thinking and self-deception. His worldview generally discounted the possibility of external intervention by transcendent supernatural beings; he may, however, have seen them as some sort of collective telepathic manifestation.

As the war progressed, Begbie's predictions of a bright new world grew uneasy. His mentor Robert Donald was removed from the *Daily Chronicle* in September 1918 at the behest of his erstwhile hero Lloyd George for criticising aspects of the conduct of the war. (Donald ended as an adviser to Ramsay MacDonald.)[3] Begbie came to see conscientious objectors as hapless victims of inhuman bureaucracy (he had previously gloated over their imprisonment in his verse 'A Christian to a Quaker'), and clashed with wartime censorship when he attempted to publish a novel about their mistreatment (which appeared in 1919 as *Mr Sterling Sticks it Out*). Although Begbie continued to believe that the struggle against German militarism had been justified, he decided the conduct of the war had been grossly incompetent.

In the years after the war, while publishing light fiction under his own name, Begbie wrote extensively under the pseudonym 'A Gentleman with a Duster'. The earliest of these books, critical profiles of selected political leaders,[4] Society figures,[5] and religious leaders,[6] caused a sensation and were widely attributed to some prominent political insider. Their authorship became widely known on Fleet Street, though it was not officially revealed until Begbie's death. Begbie mourned that the post-war settlement had been mishandled by little men. He now regarded Lloyd George as a lost prophet grown cynical, unable to sustain the high moral vision by which a Gladstone might have produced a just and lasting peace; he bitterly criticised the limitations of Kitchener (whom he eulogised during the war).

Begbie produced Carlylean jeremiads denouncing all classes of society as decadent and corrupt, and proclaiming that their blindness was leaving Britain vulnerable to Soviet-inspired revolution and a resurgent Germany. The rich are attacked for setting a bad example to the poor by pursuing sensual gratification rather than social and intellectual improvement. (In some respects Begbie's style resembles that of the Belfast-born *Daily Express* journalist James Douglas, author of a pre-war sensationalist novel about a sympathetic though sexually frail modernist minister of religion from 'Bigotsborough' [Belfast]; Douglas's 1928 attack on Radclyffe Hall's lesbian novel *The Well of Loneliness* led to its successful prosecution as obscene.) Begbie raged against jazz, the plays of Noel Coward and the erotic paintings of Norman Lindsay as abominable and vicious self-indulgence which betrayed the deepest purpose of life; he stated that modernist art only escaped being ridiculous because it was evil.[7] He believed in teleological evolution; now it seemed to him the process was reversed.

The poor, on the other hand, are accused of following the upper classes into materialism and hearkening to socialist demagogues without realising that they will have to work just as hard – for more oppressive and less competent masters – under socialism, and that all alike, rich and poor, will suffer if the empire is lost. Neo-Hegelian exaltation of the reforming State as representing the General Will could easily turn authoritarian. By 1925 Begbie decided Chamberlain had been right in attempting 'to co-ordinate the Empire and protect our foreign trade' and regretted the defeat of Tariff Reform by 'the oratorical evacuations of Mr Asquith'.[8]

*Declension*, written after the General Strike, denounces the miners' leader A. J. Cook as a conscious traitor, praises Mussolini, claims that Carlyle's critique of the Second Reform Act has been vindicated by experience, and calls for democracy to be restricted by replacing the House of Lords with a vocationalist Senate elected by professional organisations whose members would choose the government of the day. Begbie's view of Irish affairs also darkened. In 1922 he ridiculed those who attributed the Treaty to the alleged 'statesmanship' of Lloyd George. 'Statesmanship was defeated in the eighties [i.e. with the defeat of Gladstonian Home Rule] and those who defeated it, those who exalted prejudice and racialism above rationality and foresight, are now among those whom the world hails as immortal statesmen. In truth, they have bowed the knee to violence.'[9] By 1925 he was lamenting that 'England had surrendered to the forces of anarchy in Ireland . . . if Ireland had been allowed to break away and its loyalists betrayed, why not India?' He did, however, praise Ireland for its stringent film censorship and regret that matters were handled differently in Britain. Begbie was involved with the Moral Rearmers of the neo-Evangelical Oxford Group, and his views on addiction influenced the founders of Alcoholics Anonymous. He was a strong supporter of Marie Stopes's birth control campaigns from a mixture of social concerns, anti-Catholicism, and eugenics. He married Gertrude Seale; they had three daughters. The anger of his later years may have been sharpened by a long illness which caused his death at his home in Ringwood, Hampshire on 8 October 1929.[10]

## THE LADY NEXT DOOR

*The Lady Next Door* belongs to a genre developed after Gladstone's first Home Rule Bill in 1886: tours of Ireland by journalists and other political partisans aimed at supporting or opposing Home Rule. Begbie was sent to Ireland by Robert Donald; the later chapters of the book (which respond to criticisms of the earlier chapters provoked by their appearance as newspaper articles in the *Daily Chronicle*) show how Begbie's interventions fed directly into contemporary debates about the position of Ulster in relation to Home Rule.

Such tours usually followed itineraries carefully shaped by their respective sponsors. Begbie omits to mention the role of the Protestant nationalist Stephen Gwynn (MP for Galway City 1906–18 and head of the Irish Parliamentary Party's propagandist

Irish News Agency) in arranging introductions for him.[11] The house where Begbie stayed in Cork belonged to the Irish Party activist J. J. Horgan, who recalled him as 'an amiable person' and his book as 'good of its kind but its kind is not usually good'. It is also likely that his presence at Sheephaven/Port-na-blah in Donegal was sponsored by the local landlord, Hugh Law (Catholic convert and Home Rule MP for West Donegal 1902–18; later Cumann na nGaedheal TD for Donegal 1927–32).

This sponsorship raises the question of the exact mix of propaganda, self-deception, and genuine belief in Begbie's writings. This is probably unknowable. Begbie can indeed be quite stunningly impercipient. His claim that there were no prostitutes in Dublin completely ignores the red-light district which flourished in Montgomery Street [now Seán MacDermott Street]. (His claim that Irish schools displayed a complete absence of snobbery is perhaps not quite so blatantly ridiculous since he is describing very young children less conscious of social divisions than their elders.) However, even if Begbie were entirely insincere (this does not seem to have been the case) the book would still be of interest as showing how the Home Rule question was presented for a particular British Liberal audience.

The book can be examined under three central headings. The first concerns the nature and limitations of the Liberal-Nationalist alliance; the second concerns the value of Begbie's interviews as a guide to some aspects of the nationalist project at the time of the Third Home Rule Bill; the third concerns his treatment of Belfast and Ulster Unionism.

*The Lady Next Door* has to be seen in relation to the theologico-political divagations of the British Liberal Party over the two preceding decades. The last years of the nineteenth century and the first of the twentieth saw the last politically significant wave of British hostility towards Catholicism and Anglo-Catholic 'ritualism' within the Church of England. This combined older strains of Protestant populism (exemplified by John Kensit, founder of the Protestant Truth Society, who habitually disrupted 'ritualist' services; after he was killed by a Catholic rioter in Liverpool in 1900 his work was continued by his son and namesake) and the growing social and political confidence of the Nonconformist churches with the 'national efficiency' movement which arose in reaction to the growing military and economic strength of America and the bigger Continental states and was boosted by British military setbacks in the Boer War. Exponents of national efficiency could join Protestant populists in decrying the aristocratic nepotism and amateurism of the Conservative governments led by the High Churchmen Salisbury and Balfour, and in claiming that Ritualism, like aestheticism, was seducing upper-class young men away from modernity and family life into unnatural and perverse lifestyles. Evangelicals joined secularists in hailing the formal separation of Church and State in France (on the grounds that it would clear the way for Protestant evangelisation) while High Church Anglicans allied with Catholics in declaring that the French Government was engaged in a general assault on religion and that such measures as the suppression of religious orders represented outright tyranny. The Protestant Crusade was intensified by the dispute over the 1902 Education Act, which subsidised denominational (including Catholic) schools; Nonconformists protested that they were being forced to pay for the propagation of religious doctrines of which they conscientiously disapproved, and embarked on protests which included concerted non-payment of education rates. This split the Conservatives; many Nonconformists who had deserted Gladstone over Home Rule reverted to Liberalism, while Protestant populist Tories accused the official leadership of fondness for ritualism as part of a wider complaint that Salisbury and Balfour were too complacently aristocratic. (These defections were particularly noticeable in

Liverpool, with its Protestant populist tradition,[12] and in Ulster where the Dublin-based Lindsay Crawford joined the independent Unionist MP and anti-ritualist agitator T. H. Sloan in founding an Independent Orange Order which accused official Unionism of appeasing Catholicism.) New waves of Evangelical street-preachers appeared in Irish towns throughout the 1890s, and were subjected to violence by Catholic mobs. The medical mission founded by Dr Joseph J. Long in Limerick in 1899 (and subjected to an aggressive boycott by the local Redemptorist-led Confraternity) was part of this trend.[13]

This development strained the residual Irish nationalist alliance with the Liberal Party, already in serious disrepair after the Parnell Split and Gladstone's final retirement. Nonconformity provided one of the central sources of Liberal popular support, and the Liberal Party was traditionally suspicious of the role of the State Church. Many Liberals saw 'priestcraft', the idea that a sacerdotal caste had privileged access to the truth and that ritual observance was indispensable to the soul, as inherently incompatible with reason and freedom. This view could be shared by secularists, Evangelical believers in the principle that individual interpretation of Scripture should provide the only rule of faith, and religious modernists who believed Christian doctrine could never be definitively codified but must be revised to meet the needs of every age. Begbie belonged to the last of these categories.

While leading figures within the Irish Parliamentary Party (such as John Dillon) believed the maintenance of the Liberal Alliance was indispensable if there was to be any hope of obtaining Home Rule in the near future, the IPP was pressurised by accusations of anti-clericalism from Catholic bishops and clericalist dissidents led by T. M. Healy to support Conservative education policy against Liberal opposition. Hostile commentators (including 'Liberal Imperialists' who believed Home Rule should be abandoned as an electoral liability) alleged that nationalist temporisations on this issue showed that Home Rule would indeed be Rome Rule. Liberal MPs (including Radical trade unionists) joined with Orangemen in publicising French reports of harsh treatment of inmates in 'Magdalen' institutions for ex-prostitutes and demanded official investigation of similar institutions within the United Kingdom; Irish Nationalists denounced such proposals as bigoted intrusion on the peace of the cloister, and the ex-Parnellites Edmund Leamy and William Redmond delivered particularly eloquent speeches in defence of these institutions.[14] (The secession of T. H. Sloan's Independent Orange Order was partly inspired by claims that the official Orange leadership had been lukewarm on the issue.)

Nonconformists like Rev. Silvester Horne (subsequently a Liberal MP) and the Methodist minister Joseph Hocking (whose novels were later reprinted by Ian Paisley)[15] cited Ireland as a terrible example of the ignorance and poverty fostered by priestly power; Horne invited the ex-Catholic publicist Michael McCarthy to address his congregation on the subject. Begbie himself produced a novel, *The Priest* (1906), depicting a crypto-Catholic conspiracy within the Church of England.

The effects of this last 'Protestant crusade' dissipated after 1906, when traditional party divisions asserted themselves (though clericalist critics within Ireland publicised such incidents as the 1907 prohibition of a Eucharistic procession at a Catholic congress in Westminster when Kensitites invoked an obscure law on the subject). After 1910 Ulster Presbyterians and members of other Nonconformist churches appealed to their British co-religionists not to abandon them, and accused British Nonconformists of handing over Irish Protestants to be persecuted in return for the removal of Irish Catholic influence from Westminster.[16] McCarthy commented indignantly on Horne's rediscovered enthusiasm for Home Rule.[17] Hocking travelled to Ireland and produced a book suggesting that Home Rule, by removing the association of Catholicism with patriotism, would clear the ground for eventual Protestant evangelisation; in the meantime Irish Protestants could always emigrate to Britain.[18]

Begbie's apologia for Home Rule is noticeably more enthusiastic than those of Horne and Hocking. He repeatedly emphasises that he is not an orthodox religious believer (cf. his comments that theology is an irrelevant imposition on faith; he repeatedly refers to arguments with priests over the Athanasian Creed, the implication being that Begbie spoke against it. William O'Brien's remark that theological Modernism had not gained the smallest foothold among the people of Munster probably responds to an unreported question by Begbie.) At the same time he retains a hunger for religious experience, and thus concludes that if Irish Catholicism makes its followers religious, contented and moral it is good whatever its doctrinal deficiencies. (Begbie's description of teaching nuns in Skibbereen as kind and motherly is clearly aimed at readers who think of all nuns as demented by frustration, just as his praise for nuns' work as nurses is meant to counter the view that such activities represented clerical domination of society and usurpation of jobs from lay professionals.) Begbie similarly mixes his eulogies for the Salvation Army founder William Booth and his son and successor Bramwell Booth with explicit dissociations from their evangelical theology.

Admirers of Begbie's earlier works did not take his praise for Irish Catholicism lying down. An anonymous work attributed to the Church of Ireland Archdeacon Hackett of St Michael's, Limerick devotes several chapters to attacking Begbie: 'I have read some of his books with pleasure, but I do not care to read any more . . . He has sacrificed truth to become a self-serving politician'. Hackett counters Begbie's denials that Catholics ever persecute Protestants by providing a list of attacks on street-preachers, proselytisers, and converts to Protestantism; although some of his sources are anonymous and he does not distinguish between attacks on Protestants as such and on Unionists who happen to be Protestant (Hackett had been pelted while attending an Unionist public meeting at Limerick in October 1912), he does establish that Begbie's views on Irish Catholic tolerance are excessively rosy. Hackett defends Dr Long against Begbie's charge that he caused his own problems by needless provocation: 'It is true he used strong language about Romanism, but not a bit stronger than Mr Begbie himself'. At the same time Hackett reinforces Begbie's point about Irish ultra-Protestant intransigence by denying that Catholicism is Christian in any sense, and thereby implying that its adherents are outside the pale of legitimate discourse or equal citizenship: 'I am sure [Begbie] would have made out quite as good a case for the heathen Chinese as he does for the Roman Catholic Irishman, as there is a good deal of similarity in their religions, only less idolatry in China'.[19]

Begbie's willingness to turn on his former allies and his enthusiasm for the prospect of a Catholic peasant state under Home Rule reflects the hostility to British landlordism and the aristocracy which was still a significant issue in Liberal politics in the years before the First World War. Begbie's laments that the British aristocracy created urban congestion by driving smallholders off the land and hindered slum clearance by extorting prohibitive prices for housing land on the city outskirts are directly related to contemporary British political debates. Lloyd George's 'People's Budget' and 1910 election campaigns were expressly directed against the landed aristocracy, who were directly affected by his increases in direct taxation; Lloyd George hoped that once Home Rule was enacted he could make a 'land campaign', increasing land taxes to break up large estates and encourage smallholdings, the central issue in the next general election. (The distributism of the English

Catholic publicists G. K. Chesterton and Hilaire Belloc, whose advocacy of a society of smallholders was admired by a generation of Irish Catholic activists, also arose in this context; both men were Liberals – albeit of an increasingly maverick and discontented variety – up to 1914.) In the years before the First World War, Liberals saw themselves engaged in a race against a dangerous alternative social model – the social imperialism associated with Joseph Chamberlain and the Tariff Reform movement, which claimed social reform and national defence should not be funded by direct taxation but by tariffs on imported goods.[20] (Begbie seizes on eighteenth-century British mercantilist attacks on Irish industry as paralleling Tariff Reform). Lloyd George and his admirers presented his social reforms as a quasi-religious crusade for the common good against a dangerous coalition of self-serving vested interests; tariff reform would not only benefit the privileged at the expense of the poor, but by setting up fresh barriers between nations would increase the risk of wars which no one really wanted.

Begbie's denunciations of Irish landlordism should be seen as designed to rouse echoes of British political struggles. Begbie expressly declares himself a supporter of Henry George's Single Tax (or 'land nationalisation') and regrets that it was not adopted in preference to peasant proprietorship. Much Liberalism looked back nostalgically to an idealised small-town community such as that depicted in contemporary Scottish kailyard literature; Begbie's evocations of the kindliness and solidarity of the Irish poor, his detailed descriptions of the place and person of his interviewees (complete with dialect conversations) are meant to inculcate a similar sense of intimacy and identification.

One of the chief points of interest in *The Lady Next Door* for present-day readers is its use of interview material – both because some of his interviewees are identifiable and because of Begbie's own skills as interviewer and profiler. (Despite his extensive reliance on memorial reconstruction it is possible to develop significant understanding of his techniques and concerns.)

The town where Begbie begins his inquiries is Skibbereen in West Cork, and the bishop is Denis Kelly (1852–1924; Bishop of Ross 1897–1924). Begbie gives an excessively rosy picture of Kelly; despite significant work in developing technical education facilities and assisting the relief of distress, the bishop is remembered in the Skibbereen area as a cold, distant figure who thought Ross too small a stage for his talents and was preoccupied with attempts to secure a more prestigious see such as his native Killaloe.[21] Kelly had been brought in by the Ross clergy because his main local rival – who had been prominent in the Land League and virtually ran the diocese under the previous bishop – was considered excessively autocratic. Kelly's career as a bishop had included successfully campaigning against a county council candidate in 1899 on the grounds that he was 'a bad Catholic' (i.e. a Parnellite) and having a public house denied the renewal of its licence amid accusations that he was influenced by its business relationship with a Protestant-owned brewery. (Kelly's publicly stated rationale here was that it employed female rather than male bar staff, a practice which he regarded as dangerous to morals.)

Kelly served on the 1899 Intermediate Education Commission, on the 1906 Poor Law Commission (he co-authored the Irish section of its report), and on the 1911 Cabinet Committee dealing with Home Rule finance (where he suggested old age pensions should be cut under Home Rule). He was a member of the Congested Districts Board and the Council of Agriculture, which advised the Department of Agriculture and Technical Instruction. Cynics suggested his service on commissions was prompted by desire to spend as little time as possible in Skibbereen. Kelly advised the Home Rule party on financial questions, and spoke on the subject in the 1917–18 Irish Convention; he denounced the

Easter Rising as 'murder pure and simple' (adding that it would make Britain less likely to grant financial concessions to a Home Rule Ireland). He supported the Irish Parliamentary Party even after 1918, declaring that the IRA were bringing down the curse of Cain on the country, comparing Sinn Féin to the Bolsheviks, and describing the socialism of Countess Markievicz as a threat to the faith of St Patrick. He allegedly blocked a proposal that the Bishops should recognise the Dáil government in June 1921.

Kelly's remarks to Begbie are in accordance with views he constantly expressed elsewhere. In discussing the case for Home Rule, Kelly tells Begbie that the Liberal tendency to shift the fiscal burden from indirect to direct taxes (hence the slogan of the 'free breakfast table') and the introduction of old age pensions means that if the Union continues Britain will run Ireland at a loss. (Nationalists had previously treated the 1896 report of the Childers Commission, which held that Ireland was overtaxed, as a major plank in the case for Home Rule.) While some Home Rule commentators such as T. M. Kettle suggested that the deficit was illusory and Ireland was still being overtaxed, Kelly admits that the subsidy is genuine; he opposes its continuance on the grounds that personal and national self-reliance is more important than material welfare. Kelly claims that the Irish people are not materialists like the British and will be content with a lower standard of living; he also argues that since Ireland has few wealthy people, the British trend away from taxes on consumption (affecting the poor more than the rich) to progressive direct taxation is unsuitable for Irish circumstances. Kelly's views were maintained to the end of his life (in 1919 he was still discoursing on the undesirability of the factory system for Ireland) and were widely shared by Irish Catholic clergy at the time. (Even his obsession with the evil effects of stewed tea finds an echo in an t-Athair Peadar Ó Laoghaire.)[22]

These views were actually carried into account in the first decades of the new state, with tariffs fulfilling the function of indirect taxation. There were two versions of this arcadianist economics. One advocated total autarky; Kelly's view that a repopulated rural society can be achieved by turning Ireland into England's market garden places him in the other tradition (represented by figures such as James Dillon), which held that Ireland's primary industry must remain export agriculture (with industry relegated to a supportive role) and that an Irish state should focus on reducing taxation and expenditure to keep down the cost of capital. Kelly saw no contradiction between this and his attempts to develop technical education locally. He organised technical classes in Skibbereen; when a technical school opened in the town after his death it was given his name. (He also tried to develop opportunities for the inmates of the Baltimore Fisheries industrial school, though he shares responsibility for the abominable conditions endured by them.) Advocates of autarky could point out that this involved continued dependence on Britain and did little or nothing to address the continuing depopulation of rural Ireland. Both versions evaded the extent to which Ireland was integrated in a wider labour market, and the extent to which emigration showed the Irish peasantry were dissatisfied with the sort of frugal comfort prescribed by the different varieties of arcadianist. (Kelly, like others of similar inclinations, was reduced to denouncing emigrants as irrational and as wilfully endangering their souls.)

The two interviews with Famine survivors have not so far been cited by students of the Famine's role in Irish memory. It is noticeable that both involve intermediaries. Kelly rather than Begbie interviews the Skibbereen survivor, who is notably reluctant to dwell on his own experiences – presumably the old man felt obliged to reply to the Bishop, whom he repeatedly addresses as 'me lord', as he would not have to an English outsider like Begbie; Kelly has to intervene repeatedly to keep him from sidling off into a general account of the Famine. (Given Begbie's incorporation of this interview in an anti-landlord narrative, it is ironic that Kelly had publicly defended the 'quarter-acre clause' responsible for many Famine evictions on the grounds that it encouraged self-reliance and kept poverty from becoming pauperism.)[23] The Donegal survivor goes into greater detail about her own experiences of suffering and hunger; this may be because of her more marginal position (as a beggar-storyteller), partly because her interlocutor was not an authority figure but a local woman able to supplement her life-story from personal knowledge.

The two MPs interviewed by Begbie in Chapter VI are the solicitor J. J. O'Shee (MP for East Waterford 1895–1918) and the old Fenian Thomas Condon (1850–1943; MP for East Tipperary 1885–1918) and the town in question is Clonmel. Condon was a former butcher, son of Jeremiah Condon (*c.*1825–1908) who had been arrested in 1848 and 1867; Condon himself had been imprisoned during the land agitations of the 1880s; he was Mayor of Clonmel nine times between 1889 and 1916 and was frequently accused of 'bossing' the town in the interests of his relatives and political allies.[24] Although it is quite possible that Condon could have personally witnessed floggings and hangings (there was a barracks in Clonmel and public executions took place outside the jail until the 1860s) it is also possible that Begbie, noting Condon's remarks from memory, confused his personal recollections with accounts of events before his birth (such as the floggings carried out in 1798 by the notorious magistrate Sir Thomas Judkin Fitzgerald). O'Shee, a solicitor, was the leader of the section of the Land and Labour Association (an agricultural labourers' union) which followed Redmond (a rival faction under D. D. Sheehan, MP for Mid-Cork, followed William O'Brien). His prediction that under Home Rule Irish politics would be divided between a reformist minority led by Devlin and a conservative majority under Redmond was widely shared at the time. Redmond himself expressed the view (made by Begbie's Quaker interviewee) that, under Home Rule, the business classes would take a much greater role in politics than they did at that time.[25]

The 'internecine conflict' between Home Rulers to which Begbie refers (p. 14) does not involve the incipient Sinn Féin movement (which he completely ignores – although one of his interviewees, the Capuchin Provincial Fr Aloysius Travers, was to administer the last rites to some of the 1916 leaders and was later known for his pro-IRA views), but the dissident All-for-Ireland League (AFIL) of William O'Brien and T. M. Healy. William O'Brien (1852–1928), one of Parnell's principal lieutenants in the 1880s (when he achieved fame through his leadership of the Plan of Campaign and refusal to wear prison clothing), had broken with the Irish Party in 1903 after adopting the view that Home Rule could be secured gradually by co-operating with moderate Unionists such as Lord Dunraven to secure limited devolution measures. After several years in which O'Brien and his allies (primarily based in Cork) had remained semi-detached members of the Party, the general election of January 1910 saw all-out electoral conflict between O'Brienites and Redmondites; O'Brienite electoral successes (especially in County Cork) temporarily made him seem the coming force in Irish politics, but reverses in the December 1910 general election began a decline from which the AFIL never recovered. Begbie presents the AFIL's alliance with Dunraven (and Dunraven's own attempts to promote economic development around his estate town of Adare in East Limerick) as proof that Protestants who co-operate with the nationalist movement can expect to play a significant role in Irish life under Home Rule. His interview with O'Brien is one of the most memorable sections of the book; his description of the AFIL leader catches the almost schizoid division between geniality and autocratic egotism which Davitt indicated in nicknaming O'Brien 'the Czar'. O'Brien combined a fervent devotional Catholicism with a long history of political disputes with priests; his conversation with Begbie characteristically combines praise for priestly zeal and chastity, and indiscretions about clerical alcoholism.[26]

Begbie's journalistic portrayal of Belfast produced indignant protests from Unionists – some of which, with Begbie's responses, are incorporated in the book. (Hackett's response is worth noting as exemplifying the cruder type of Unionist polemic. He claims the slums of Belfast are solely inhabited by Catholics, whose condition is due to their resistance to Protestant charity as a cover for proselytism: 'The Lady [on Begbie's cover] . . . is a Protestant lady, dressed in fancy costume, as an Irish peasant, and the three Belfast factory girls are Roman Catholics, and his pictures of Belfast slums are taken from the Roman Catholic quarter of Belfast'.) At a later date the Belfast-born playwright St John Ervine (a supporter of Home Rule before the Second World War who subsequently reverted to Ulster Unionism) singled out *The Lady Next Door* as proof that English Liberal and Leftist commentators on Northern Ireland were 'incurably addicted to drivel'.

> Grass . . . was never far from any doorstep in my childhood in Belfast, where infants smiled at least as often as infants anywhere else, and were sometimes known, especially when English Liberals were about, to laugh aloud . . . The easy tears of English journalists, who wept over our unsmiling faces and our ignorance of green grass, would have excited our derision had we become aware of them; for we had greater knowledge of sheep and cattle, horses and pigs, crops and chickens, though we lived in little streets, than all the massed authors of lachrymose articles in national newspapers put together.[27]

Here again Begbie blends his own habitual treatment of urban poverty in the East End (some of whose inhabitants might have found him equally condescending even as they benefited from his advocacy) with a widespread nationalist discourse which pointed to the Belfast slums as proof that the industrial development of the North-East under the Union was a very equivocal blessing, and that most Ulster Protestant supporters of the Union were dupes gulled by their exploiters.[28] It is notable that Begbie does not interview a single Ulster Unionist or inhabitant of Belfast, apart from the one Labour activist (described in the preface) who takes the 'Walkerite' view that the Union is necessary so that British-led and financed reforms can deal with Belfast's problems in a manner which would never be attempted under a conservative, rural-dominated Irish Parliament. Neither Begbie's Unionist critics nor his nationalist admirers appear to have noticed that he implicitly endorses this view. If the rest of Ireland is irreformably un-British, the problems of Belfast are all too familiar to British urban reformers. The book can thus be read as implicitly partitionist; it would be interesting to know whether Begbie drew inspiration from that section of the Liberal leadership (notably Lloyd George and Churchill) who already privately advocated partition in 1912.

To the social reformer's horror at urban slums Begbie adds the suburban arts and crafts mentality (initially inspired by social reformers who believed the aesthetic ugliness of Victorian society reflected a blunted social conscience, and to address one was to address the other) which took a more stridently reactionary turn in his post-war writings. Here the poverty and degradation of urban slums (of which Begbie was so acutely aware) are contrasted with an idealised image of pre-industrial 'Merrie England' to suggest that industrialisation and urbanisation may have been a ghastly though irreversible mistake.

Thus Begbie provides a reminder of how far the stereotyped pastoral image of Ireland was reinforced by the yearnings and discontents of Britain. His feminised image of Ireland is contrasted with London Society women who refuse to bear children and with militant suffragettes, whom he regards as a disgrace to their sex. He regards the dullness of Irish life as positively virtuous because it shows that Irish social life is still centred on the home (rather than restaurants and places of public entertainment; the Irish pub completely escapes his notice). His Irish apologia can be seen in retrospect as a form of condescending exoticisation; in reaction against the failure of older attempts to turn Ireland into an extension of Britain by the reckless application of political economy, he presents Ireland as a Glocca Morra or Brigadoon desiring only to exempt itself from the historical forces to which he and his [British] readers are painfully subject.

The supreme value of *The Lady Next Door* lies in its presentation of contemporary expectations, soon to be swept away by events; in so doing, it not only provides glimpses of Liberal and Redmondite self-presentations, but inadvertently displays the Edwardian escapist deliquescence of the Victorian moralist rhetoric once wielded with such force by Begbie's heroes Gladstone and Stead.

## Notes to Introduction

1 This note is based on several of Begbie's works and on 'The Furious Mr Begbie', Jack Adrian's introduction to his edition of Begbie's story collection, *The Amazing Dreams of Andrew Latter* (Ashcroft, British Columbia: Ash-Tree Press, 2002). The overall interpretation of Begbie's worldview is, however, my own.

2 David Clarke, *The Angel of Mons: Phantom Soldiers and Ghostly Guardians* (Chichester, 2004), pp. 160–4.

3 For Donald's career and worldview see Alan J. Lee, *The Origins of the Popular Press 1855–1914* (London, 1976) pp. 164, 214, 216–17; Stephen Koss, *The Rise and Fall of the Political Press in Britain* (London, 1981–4) as well as the *Oxford DNB* entry on Donald (by A. J. A. Morris).
4 *The Mirrors of Downing Street* (London, 1921).
5 *The Glass of Fashion* (London, 1921).
6 *Painted Windows* (London, 1922).
7 *Declension* (London, 1925), p. 88.
8 *Declension*, p. 30.
9 *Painted Windows*, p. 211.
10 Begbie's publications of Irish interest include *Shackleton: A Memory* (London, 1922) (Begbie advised the explorer on his book *South*), which contains some interesting comments on the fluctuations of the great man's Irish accent, and *Albert, Earl Grey: A Last Word* (London, 1917), which has extensive extracts from a letter by AE discussing Grey's work for the co-operative movement.
11 J. J. Horgan, *Parnell to Pearse* (Dublin, 1948), pp. 163–4.
12 P. J. Waller, *Democracy and Sectarianism: A Political and Social History of Liverpool 1868-1939* (Liverpool, 1981), pp. 167–248.
13 Joseph John Long, *Medical Missions in Ireland: The Story of Limerick* (3rd edn, London, 1925: updated by R. Mercer-Wilson).
14 *Weekly Irish Independent & Nation* 29 November 1902, p. 11.
15 Ed Moloney and Andy Pollak, *Paisley* (Dublin, 1986) p. 125 [wrongly identifies Hocking as American]. His career is outlined in John Sutherland, *The Longman Companion to Victorian Fiction* (London, 1988), pp. 300–1.
16 Paul Bew, *Ideology and the Irish Question* (Oxford, 1998) touches on this literature in its discussion of the Ulster Unionist case against Home Rule.
17 Michael J. F. McCarthy, *The Nonconformist Treason* (Edinburgh, 1912).
18 Joseph Hocking, *Is Home Rule Rome Rule?* (London, 1912).
19 'An Irishman', *Intolerance in Ireland: Facts not Fiction* (London, 1913), pp. 178–90. The attribution to Rev. Hackett rests on a manuscript annotation in the Queen's University, Belfast, library copy; internal evidence suggests a Limerick-based author. For Hackett's involvement in an 1898 dispute over the destruction of a flag at the grave of a Fenian in the Kilmallock churchyard when Hackett was incumbent of the parish, see *Leader*, 17 December 1910, pp. 446–7. For Hackett's experience at the Unionist meeting, see Long, *Medical Missions*, p. 107.
20 G. K. Peatling, *British Opinion and Irish Self-government: From Unionism to Liberal Commonwealth* (Dublin, 2001).
21 The most accessible account of Kelly's career is Liam O'Regan, 'The "Imperialistic Bishop of Ross" and his political influence', *Mizen Journal* no. 5

(1997), pp. 43–64. The article is marked by an undisguised antipathy towards Kelly's Redmondism (which O'Regan regards as so self-evidently wrong that it does not require refutation); there may be more to be said for Kelly on some points at issue. Contemporary newspaper obituaries are inevitably more laudatory: *Irish Independent*, 18, 19 April 1924; *The Irish Times*, 19 April 1924; *Freeman's Journal*, 18, 19 April 1924.

22 For general discussions of this Catholic arcadianism and its implications see Patrick O'Farrell, *Ireland's English Question* (New York, 1971); Tom Garvin, *Nationalist Revolutionaries in Ireland, 1858–1928* (Oxford, 1987); Tom Garvin, *Preventing the Future: Why was Ireland so Poor for so Long?* (Dublin, 2004).

23 Diarmaid Ferriter, *The Transformation of Ireland 1900–2000* (London, 2004), p. 45.

24 Seán O'Donnell, *Clonmel 1840–1900: Anatomy of an Irish Town* (Dublin, n.d. [1999])

25 Bew, *Ideology and the Irish Question.*

26 For a fuller analysis of O'Brien's religious views see Patrick Maume, 'In the Fenians' wake: the crises of fin de siècle Ireland in the sentimental rhetoric of Canon Sheehan and William O'Brien M.P.', *Bullán: Journal of Irish Studies* 4: 1 (Autumn 1998), pp. 59–80.

27 St John Ervine, *Craigavon – Ulsterman* (London, 1949), pp. 6–7. Ironically, Ervine's own intellectual trajectory as a self-made journalist-author who moved from a provincial fundamentalist background to an egoistic form of Protestant religious Modernism turning sharply to the Right after the First World War, has much in common with Begbie's own development. One of Begbie's post-war jeremiads praises Ervine's *Observer* theatre criticism for upholding moral and artistic values against the decadence of the Bright Young Things; both men wrote eulogistic biographies of General Booth, and Ervine spent his later life in Devon. (Patrick Maume, 'Three Ulstermen of letters: the Unionism of Frank Frankfort Moore, Shan Bullock, and St John Ervine' in Richard English and Graham Walker (eds), *Unionism in Modern Ireland* (London and Dublin, 1996), pp. 63–80.)

28 David Miller, *Queen's Rebels* (Dublin & New York, 1978); James Loughlin, *Gladstone, Home Rule and the Ulster Question 1882–93* (Dublin, 1986).

*Note on the Text*

*The Lady Next Door* is printed as a facsimile of the 1914 popular edition published by Hodder & Stoughton.

# THE LADY NEXT DOOR

BY

HARAROLD BEGBIE

AUTHOR OF "BROKEN EARTHENWARE"

"There dwells sweet love, and constant chastity,
Unspotted faith, and comely womanhood,
Regard of honour, and mild modesty."

SPENSER.

POPULAR EDITION

HODDER AND STOUGHTON
LONDON NEW YORK TORONTO

TO MY FRIEND

ROBERT DONALD

A POLITICIAN WITHOUT BITTERNESS

A JOURNALIST WITHOUT MALICE

A MAN WITHOUT ENEMIES

I AM indebted to the Editor of the *Daily Chronicle,* at whose suggestion I went to Ireland, for his kind permission to incorporate into this book certain chapters or parts of chapters which appeared as articles in his newspaper.

# FOREWORD

As if a guiding Providence had so ordered it, the indestructible soul of Ireland emerges from the smoke and ruin of an upheaval in the labour world which has shaken England to her very foundations.

It is a climax, a coincidence, luminous with meaning for mankind.

Ireland enters upon the strewn and trembling stage of British politics with a significance, not only for England, not only for the British Empire, but for all the foremost nations of the earth now regarding each other from the outposts of civilization, from the fortified and haunted frontiers of progress, with a dolorous apprehension.

She does not arraign the ambitions of these civilized nations—many of whom learned the alphabet of their first pure culture from her own heroic sons—but she asks to disentangle herself from the confusions of an industrialism, the violence of a materialism, and the brutalizing ugliness of a false civilization, into which she has been dragged, harshly and tyrannously dragged, against her judgment and her will.

In making this claim for liberty, Ireland must surely dispose the conscience of England to reflect upon the character of English civilization, the course and purpose of English progress. To the troubled nations of the earth, but in particular to England, Ireland now puts the question which her missionaries asked of heathen Europe in the sixth century, What shall it profit a man if he gain the whole world, and lose his soul alive?

It is a question of arithmetic. England, long accustomed to the logic of the ledger, long versed in the grammar of Profit and Loss, should be able to give an intelligent answer.

What shall it profit a nation if it become the clearing-house of the whole world, and miss the way to peace? What shall it profit a democracy if it gain the whole Wages of Mammon, and lose the Joy of Life?

Are we not at least inclined to forget, both politically and individually, that nothing which belongs to peace, nothing which tells "in making up the main account" can be bought with money?

# CONTENTS

# PREFACE

AN honest man, going to Ireland with no pre-judgments in his mind, might easily return from his study with inspiration, arguments, citations, and economical data for two distinct books. One book would persuade the world to call for Home Rule. The other book would convince the world to maintain the Union. I can conceive of a perfectly just and righteous man writing both these books.

A Frenchman once said of a certain critic that this ingenious gentleman had three ways of making an article: *to assert, to re-assert, and to contradict himself.* But in the two books for which I can imagine a single writer there would be no violence of contradiction, no confession of conversion, no casuistry, shuffling, explanatory apologetics, and peevish vindications of a changed mind. Each work would blow into the air the steam of a distinct thesis, would travel if on parallel then on separate lines, and not side by side, racing to left and right of the same platform at a single terminus, but in clean contrary directions, passing each other only for a single moment, looking all the way for different signals, and reaching ultimately the other's antipodes.

And neither of these two books—this is interesting and full of encouragement for the bored reader of political speeches and factioneering pamphlets—would make use of arguments employed by the rival protagonists of Irish politics. Both books would belong to humanity rather than to faction, and the two covers might be dyed with any colour in the milliner's window save orange and green.

It is all a question of definition, purpose, and point of view. What is life? What is the object of existence? What is the conscious direction of your own spiritual progress? Until one has come to a more or less reasonable conclusion on these matters, it is idle to entertain a definite, rigid, and exclusive opinion on the subject of Ireland; and, since the scope of these matters is so wide and so uncertainly mapped, the same man, in different moods, looking at the identical question from two distinct points of view, may come with equal honesty to conclusions at variance with each other, so entirely at variance that they are not really in conflict. "*Corot disait que pour saisir l'âme et la beauté d'un paysage, il fallait savoir s'asseoir.*"

I mean this: that a man perfectly satisfied with civilization, convinced that social evolution is pursuing the right road, and persuaded that competitive commercialism is the predestined way of the human species, would come to an opinion about Ireland different from the conclusion of a man who suspected civilization and felt himself inclined to call a halt to the progress of disorderly materialism. Or, the very same man, feeling at one moment that he could do nothing to arrest the movement of democracy and at another moment inspired to believe that the only hope of salvation lay in a violent antagonism to this power, would come honestly and righteously to two different decisions.

For myself, I went to Ireland with the leaning towards Home Rule of a man who knows the Imperial Parliament to be congested and who has the loose inherited faith of the average modern in the usefulness of local government. Beginning at the south I worked my way zigzag through the villages and little towns of rural Ireland till I came to the north, and I arrived in the north with no more definite idea in my mind than this conviction, that the Irish people are charming, delightful, virtuous, and sagacious. The industrial north filled me with depression. I can think of few sharper contrasts in the world than to go from some beautiful village on the coast of Donegal straight to the squalor, the poverty, the desperate ugliness and the deadening depravity of Belfast. This was my experience. I came from the rugged grandeur of Port-na-blah, from the society and gracious hospitality of happy peasants and kindly fishermen, into the mud and destitution, into the noise and vulgarity, into the shabbiness and disquiet of Belfast. I am no stranger to slums, I am acquainted with the poverty of big cities in many countries both East and West, but I was overwhelmed by this particular contrast. I felt in Belfast that industrialism was the enemy of the human race. I compared the beautiful faces and the noble manners of those primitive people with whom I had stayed on the shores of Sheep Haven with the hard looks, the stunted bodies, the anæmic faces, and the rough manners of these thousands of human beings crowding the streets of Belfast. And I felt that civilization had taken a wrong turning, that progress was hurrying along a road that led only to destruction, that life as industrialism had made it was something harsh and detestable, something for which humanity owed no laudamus to the heavens.

One night I sat in my hotel at Belfast with a singularly enlightened member of the working-class, a local leader of the Socialist party. We discussed for some time the wages paid in Belfast factories, the conditions of labour, housing, and the Insurance Act, of which he is an enthusiastic supporter. Then we turned to the general question of Socialism. Towards the end of our colloquy I said to him, " Are you quite sure that you will get all the social reforms you require in Belfast out of an Irish Parliament ? "

His eyes expressed surprise, he regarded me for a moment with astonishment, then, laughing as one who sees his way out of perplexity, he demanded with amusement, " You don't think I'm a Home Ruler, do you ? "

The incredulity of his tone surprised me, for it expressed a far greater contempt of Home Rule than ever I had heard on the lips of perfervid Orangemen.

" Are you not ? " I inquired.

He replied, with decision : " I should think not ! No ; I'm a Unionist, out and out. England is absolutely essential to us. An Irish Parliament would be entirely Tory. It would do nothing in the direction of Socialism, quite the reverse ; it would be the most Conservative Government in the world. But we can screw out of England all we want, bit by bit, and she can help us to pay the bill ! "

Then I saw an argument for the Union which the professional agitators of the Orange Party in their devotion to religious animosities have excluded from their oratory ; and I saw also an argument for Home Rule which the Liberals of England in their enthusiasm for social reform have omitted from their dialectic. Here at my side was a Socialist, a man of great intelligence devoted to the betterment of working-class existence, a man for whom Mr. Lloyd George does not move fast enough, and who condemns the manual labourer for trusting to his trade union instead of using, with an absolute force and with an uncompromising energy, the political instrument —and he was a Unionist !

Penetrate to the soul of political contention, and there is always perplexity. The Tory defends the Indian Government, the Socialist attacks it ; and yet the Indian Government owns the railways and the land of India, and uses public funds for the purpose of developing national trade. What the Socialist wants in England he attacks in India, and what the Tory condemns in England he passionately defends in India. Lord Curzon is a Tory in England, a Socialist in India ; and Mr. Keir Hardie is a Socialist in England, a Tory in India. " The world's heroes have room for all positive qualities, even those which are disreputable, in the capacious theatre of their dispositions."

But the perplexity is even greater in the case of Ireland. English Conservatives and Ulster Socialists are of one mind about the Union ; English Socialists and Irish Conservatives are of one mind about Home Rule. The English Conservative condemns Home

Rule, and the Irish Conservative clamours for it. The Irish Radical fights for the Union, and the English Radical condemns it. Sir Edward Carson commands the regiments of Irish Socialism in the army of British Conservatism, and Mr. John Redmond leads in the army of Irish Conservatism the regiments of English Socialism.

Such chaos and confusion may seem incredible, but it is true; and, indeed, it is this very confusion which puts into a man's hand the veritable thread which he must follow if he would emerge into the light and sanity of open air from the labyrinth of Irish politics.

There are two Irelands—not as they are known to English people as Catholic and Protestant Ireland, as Home Rule and Unionist Ireland, but Conservative Ireland and Democratic Ireland. Conservative Ireland regards Home Rule as the one way of escape from the industrial anarchy, the commercial brutality, the ultimate bankruptcy, which she holds must be the inevitable fate of union with England; and Democratic Ireland, filled with the Futurist's enthusiasm for machinery and modernity, and utterly reckless of agriculture, regards the Union as her one means of marching abreast with the civilized nations to the goal of Socialism.

It requires profound thinking and a prudent judgment to decide which of these Irelands has the truer vision. I am persuaded, for instance, that a mere pressure of atmosphere, a little change in the weather, even a slight difference in the digestive organs, might turn the judgment of so nice a philosopher as Mr. Arthur Balfour from one decision to the other. Are we not all the victims of our moods, and do not our moods largely control for us the judgments of our intellects? Does not life fluctuate for all of us, as once for Bishop Blougram, between faith diversified by doubt and doubt diversified by faith? But let a man settle once and for all his definitions of life, and hold to them, if he can, throughout his reflections on Ireland, and then he may possibly reach a conclusion to which he can give the energy of his voice and the solemn affirmation of his vote.

# CHAPTER I

## BY WAY OF INTRODUCTION

### I

To fall in with popular notions is the wisdom of most transitory writing. One thing the self-respecting reader resents with energy, and that is disturbance of his prejudices, upheaval in his preconceptions.

Thus it is that a distinguished writer recently began a book on Paris with the charming avowal that no sooner had he detrained than he felt a sparkling tide of festive gaiety surge up against him from the pavements of Paris and bear him smiling and radiant away into the sunlight of that brilliant city's incomparable joy. The driver of his cab, he tells us, sang all the way from the station to the hotel. Whether the distinguished author, infected by this gaiety, pushed his hat to the back of his head and joined in the chorus, we are not informed; nor is it stated that the hall porter executed a *pas seul* at his entrance into the hotel, that the lift boys broke into song, and that the clerks at the office pledged him in champagne. But enough was said, and with the first stroke of the pen, to set the self-respecting reader entirely at his ease, and we may fancy how he straightway settled himself down in his arm-chair, stretched his legs, pulled complacently at his pipe, and gave himself completely into the safe-keeping of this jolly and confirmatory author.

But consider the state of that reader's feelings if the book had opened with a reference to the mental fatigue of streets too long and rigid, to the lugubrious melancholy of fat cab-drivers, to the listless, fagged, weary, and bored expression of pale-faced, goggle-eyed gentlemen gathered round tin tables at dusty boulevard restaurants, like mourners at a wake, to the blasé and cynical aspect of a music-hall audience, to the poverty and wretchedness of Parisian miserables, to the dullness and torpor of overdressed children in the Bois—in fact, to that total sensation of ennui and exhaustion which strikes the mind of many travellers in their peregrinations of the French capital. No; such a beginning would be fatal to a cheerful progress. Paris, by the common consent of universal ignorance, is the gayest city in the world. . . .

Now, the popular notion of Ireland is the reverse of all this. Ireland is a distressful country, a savage and dreary country populated, except in a brilliant north, by assassins and dynamitards who sleep with a pig in their beds, and spend the day either in tearing holes in their own coats, or treading on the tails of somebody else's coat. Of late a body of writers has arisen with the gospel of another Ireland, but it is still a melancholy Ireland. According to these mystical authors there is something sad and tragic in the very atmosphere of Ireland, a spirit of wistful reverie broods upon Irish life with the pensive sorrow of an immemorial grief. In the tender manner of Pierre Loti, and with the elegant gestures of Rossetti, they breathe into our susceptible souls the feeling that Ireland is gloomed with some unearthly woe and tortured by an everlasting spiritual unrest. To deny the gospel of these mystics, to say that potatoes flourish in the soil and little boys go sliding on the frozen ponds, is to confess oneself dull of soul and lacking in refinement of spirit.

And, again, there is the popular notion that Irish life is consumed in the fiery furnace of political controversy. It was bad enough, we are told, when the Catholics warred against the Protestants, and when the Home Rulers took arms against the Unionists ; but now, when the Home Rule camp is the scene of an internecine conflict so fierce and implacable that no man's life is safe from Portrush to Skibbereen—the country has become unpardonably tiresome.

And so the average Englishman, who has his garden to plant, who is worrying over a chess problem, who suffers from indigestion, and who has just received a troublesome letter from his aunt in the country, puts Ireland out of his head and wishes that confounded country, if not ten thousand leagues under the sea, at least three thousand miles away from English shores.

But if the inquirer can manage to exist for a few weeks without confirmation of his prejudices, and can accustom himself for the same period to the mental disturbance of receiving illumination, he will surely find that a journey in Ireland is as delightful and interesting an occupation as anything to which he has ever addressed his affections and intelligence. He will be refreshed by the contradictions of his prejudices, and exhilarated by the enlightenment of his ignorance. In a word, he will find that there is nothing in life half so beguiling and half so amusing as sober truth. The truth about Ireland—the social, political and religious truth—is perhaps the most interesting romance in the world.

Therefore, if I cannot secure the confidence of my reader by beginning with the customary sigh, at least let me stimulate his curiosity by this hint of something strange and amusing. He will find himself, if he be so good as to follow me, in the stimulating and agreeable company of noble landlords, sitting in the cabins of

Donegal peasants over a peat fire on the stone hearth, listening to the thunders of a Fenian, supping and sitting up to all hours in the night with a Catholic bishop, chatting to a sharp Quaker, standing in a snow blizzard on the rugged cliffs that front the Atlantic, wandering in glens as beautiful as fairyland, talking to lovely maidens who blush and hang the head before a stranger, hearing the tales of old men who remember the great famine, visiting a hospital, examining a school, penetrating slums, moralizing in a monastery, and discussing without fear of fire-arms or shillelaghs some of the most delicate problems which agitate the Hibernian bosom. And as he makes the journey, he will find, if my conceit does not mislead me, that the tangle of Irish politics is a very simple and human matter, that the great rock of difficulty, known as the Irish question, is but a pleasant hill for a morning's walk, and that the chief thing to become acquainted with in Ireland is the Irish heart, which is as kindly and gracious and patient a centre of human affections as the heart of the woman he loves best in the world.

"No man," said Parnell, and created a false impression, "has a right to fix the boundary of the march of a nation." One does not hear in Ireland the tramp of a multitude marching through the night, does not see stern and exalted faces lifted to the dawn, does not discern the moving of dark banners in the gloom of the upper air. Rather one beholds a young and capable matron seated at her fireside, who raises her grey eyes to the visitor, and says without apology, but with a whimsical and ingratiating play of laughter at her lips, "I wish to do my own housekeeping; I think I can do it in a better way, and more cheaply, than other people can do it for me. I have no desire to fall out with my neighbours, no inclination to remember old scores against them. I simply want to be left alone to attend to my own business and bring up my own family in my own way."

The old gentleman next door may be alarmed by this ambition, but the lady has really no more evil intent against his prosperity than to sell him the surplus of her butter and eggs.

## II

### THE OFFENCES OF OUR FOREFATHERS

Before we set out to visit our neighbour, it is well to have in mind some knowledge of the temper which characterized our past relations, if only to avoid a *faux pas*.

To begin with, then, it is a fact acknowledged by every historian, high and low, that England, having set herself to subdue the Irish, without success, screwed herself to the point of attempting to exterminate these irrepressible neighbours. This is a most important matter to keep in mind. All the pother of these present days has flowed from England's blundered policy of extermination. Our forefathers endeavoured to wipe the Irish slate clean of Irishmen. They did not succeed. The remnant which survived the bloody sponge refused to kiss the hand which had clenched itself to erase them.

The poet Spenser has described one after-effect of this policy: "Out of every corner of the woods and glens, they came creeping forth upon their hands, for their legs could not bear them; they looked like anatomies of death; they spake like ghosts crying out of their graves; they did eat of the dead carrions, happy were they if they could find them, yea, and one another soon after, insomuch as the very carcases they spared not to scrape out of their graves. . . . In short space there were none almost left, and a most populous and plentiful country suddenly made void of man or beast."

Sir Arthur Chichester saw some children gnawing at the flesh of their starved mother. Lecky tells how old women lighted fires to attract children, whom they slew and devoured. The English soldiery put to the sword "blind and feeble men, women, boys, and girls, rich persons, idiots, and old people." M. Paul Dubois narrates: "In the Desmond country, when all resistance was at an end, the soldiers forced the people into old barns, which they then set on fire, putting to the sword any who sought to escape; . . . soldiers were seen to catch up children on the points of their swords, making them squirm in the air in their death agony; . . . women were found hanged from trees, with the children at their bosoms strangled in the hair of their mothers."

Not only did the English destroy crops and drive cattle into their own camps that the Irish might be starved, not only this, but they deliberately and with cunning purpose made a great slaughter of infants. The terrible phrase, almost the most terrible phrase in human recrods, "Nits will be lice," was the laughing, murderous, and devilish justification for this slaughter of babes. The steel of England's might ran red with the blood of Irish infancy. Lips that had not learned to speak a human word, lips that knew nothing more than to hang contented at the circle of the mother's breast, were twitched with agony, uttered screams of desperate pain, and grew purple in the wrench of violent death. Little feet that had but lately got the trick of balance ran, stumbled, and fell before the smoking swords of most inhuman murderers. Little hands that had but lately learned to fold themselves in prayer were raised in clamorous appeal for mercy to men who smote them down, and set their heels upon those stricken faces. "Nits will be lice," cried these slaughtering devils, and the beautiful flower of Irish childhood was crushed into the bloody ooze of a land that was like hell.

Most men who have abandoned the idea of eternal torment reserve some special place of agony and torture in the next world for Philip the Second of Spain, the Duke of Alva, and Cardinal Granvelle. They could not meet those souls in heaven without murderous thoughts and instincts only fit for Gehenna. But the atrocities in the Low Countries, those atrocities out of which the spirit of William the Silent rose godlike and sublime, can be matched step by step, and inch by inch in the records of England's dealing with Ireland. No just Englishman can read that history without a shudder, without an overwhelming sense of shame, without uttering the prayer, "Remember not, Lord, our offences, nor the offences of our forefathers."

On the evening of Dettingen, George the Second exclaimed, "God curse the laws that made these men my enemies!" And M. Paul Dubois pronounces true judgment when he says, "It was England herself, it was the English in Ireland, that made the Irish rebels." Mr. John M. Robertson has justly summarized our dealings with Ireland in these few sentences: "Seven centuries of rapine and violence. Carelessness alternating with ferocity. Not a gleam of humanity, nor of political wisdom. Not even the wisdom of the peasant, who takes care of his beast, lest it perish."

In vain did England plant out in Ireland people from her own shires, and people from the neighbour land of Scotland. In vain to these aliens did she give the rich pastures of Ireland, and forbid them either to speak Irish or to marry with Irish women. The rightful children of the soil, the little remnant that had escaped extermination, absorbed these invaders into the mysterious spirit of Irish existence. Depressed, broken, crushed, degraded, and impoverished, the faithful remnant did, nevertheless, in some most marvellous manner conquer without force of arms these foreign masters, and make them more Irish than the Irish. They clung to one thing, these aliens, one thing which marks their children to this present day—an arrogant conviction of superiority, a determination to maintain a social, political, and religious ascendancy; but in all else they became Irish, as different from the people of England and Scotland as the people of Glamorganshire are different from the people of Norfolk. Spenser exclaimed, "Lord, how quickly doth that country alter men's natures!"

To a rightful appreciation of modern Ireland, it is essential that the English mind should possess, at least, this knowledge of the past. England's policy was first to subdue, then to exterminate, afterwards to overwhelm with an alien population. For seven centuries she showed to Ireland neither mercy nor wisdom, neither kindness nor intelligence. For seven centuries she was tyrant, oppressor, and panic-minded coward. Never once did she employ righteousness and peace, justice and conciliation. And it was not until famine had driven Ireland to transitory crime, and transitory crime had driven England to fear, that the thought of responsibility, the idea of justice and reparation occurred to a few just and noble Englishmen.

"Your oppressions," said Lord John Russell, "have taught the Irish to hate, your concessions to brave you. You have exhibited to them how scanty was the stream of your bounty, how full the tribute of your fear."

England's whole policy towards Ireland may be expressed in two words: A crime and a blunder. This is a judgment with which Unionists and Home Rulers, every honest man in every nation under the sun, cannot help but concur. A crime and a blunder.

## III

### CROMWELLIAN COMMERCE

This also is a thing to bear in mind :—

When England had beaten the poor Irish to their knees, had laid waste that lovely land, and planted out her own subsidized people in every quarter of the country, one thing remained vital and unsubdued—the indestructible soul of the Irish nation. Practical people in England guffaw at this indestructible soul; gentlemen with money in the stocks, and a considerable stake in the country, ridicule any reference to the matter as a piece of stupid sentimentalism. Nationality, they say, butters no parsnips. An indestructible soul is not so useful as a balance at the bank. But these practical people are more versed in affairs of the Money Market than in the steadfast lessons of history.

A sense of Nationality is the life-blood of a people. It is the quickening power which animates their action, enlarges their vision, and directs their hopes. And in Ireland, crushed and broken Ireland, even in her darkest hour, this conviction of an indestructible soul, this sense of sacred and affectionate Nationality, has kept alive all that is noble, all that is glorious, all that is beautiful and pure in Irish character. Nor was this passion of the spirit wasted in the region of sentiment or confined to the tubs and barrels of political agitation. It became a force in commerce. The practical people who now scoff at the idea of Irish Nationality cannot know that the inspiration of Nationality drove the suffering Irish from their knees, lifted them from the morass of destruction, and set them to the task of forging a destiny. Ireland became rich and prosperous. If she had stopped at that—if the spirit of Irish Nationality had arrested its pressure at that point—all might now be well with her. But rich, prosperous and rejoicing, this happy people set no boundary to their ambition. They became in their impious progress the rivals of England. And England—not with the sword, but with those instruments which Tariff Reformers would again place in her cleansed hands—once more reduced Ireland to beggary and ruin.

"One by one," said Lord Dufferin, "each of our nascent industries was either strangled in its birth, or handed over, gagged and bound, to the jealous custody of the rival interests of England, until at last every fountain of wealth was hermetically sealed, and even the traditions of commercial enterprise have perished through desuetude." Irish ships, laden with beef, mutton, tallow, hides, leather, and wool, sailed every week to Dunkirk, Ostend, Naples, La Rochelle, and the West Indies, till England began to quake for her trade. And then came Navigation Acts which broke this growing trade upon the sea, and reduced Ireland to direst want. "The conveniency," cried Swift, "of ports and harbours which Nature bestowed so liberally upon this kingdom, is of no more use to us than to a man shut up in a dungeon." Ireland turned her attention to wool. "A real industrial enthusiasm," says Lecky, "had arisen in the nation. Great numbers of English, Scotch and even foreign manufacturers came over. Many thousands of men were employed in the trade, and all the signs of a great rising industry were visible." But frightened England stepped in and forbade the exportation. Commerce produced its Cromwell, the Bible in one hand, a tariff in the other. "So ended," says Lecky, "the fairest promise Ireland had ever known of becoming a prosperous and happy country."

In 1798 Lord Clare made this statement: "There is not a nation on the face of the habitable globe which has advanced in cultivation, in manufactures, with the same rapidity in the same period as Ireland." In the same year the bankers of Dublin passed the resolution "that since the renunciation of the power of Great Britain in 1782 to legislate for Ireland, the commerce and prosperity of this kingdom have eminently increased." "From the concession of free trade in 1779," says Lecky, "to the Rebellion of 1798, the national progress of Ireland was rapid and uninterrupted. In ten years from 1782 the exports more than trebled."

Then England saw that to conquer Ireland was but a small thing in comparison with destroying her sense of Nationality. And to destroy her Nationality she brought about the chief scandal and the blackest crime of her legislative history—the Act of Union. Gentlemen in Ulster profess loyalty to this Act of Union, they threatened to kick Queen Victoria's crown into the Boyne if it were repealed, to fight for it they have advertised for rifles in German newspapers, to uphold it Lord Londonderry has lavishly devoted his intellect and wealth, and Sir Edward Carson has practised the oratory of a stage rebel. But what in very truth is this Act of Union which Orangemen would have us hold as something sacrosanct and pure? It is something to shudder the soul of an honest man.

Hear what Lecky has to say: "The years between 1779 and 1798 were probably the most prosperous in Irish history, and the generation which followed the Union was one of the most miserable. The sacrifice of Nationality was extorted by the most enormous corruption in the history of representative institutions. It was demanded by no considerable portion of the Irish people. . . . As it was carried, it was a crime of the deepest turpitude, which, by imposing with every circumstance of infamy a new form of government on a reluctant and protesting nation, has vitiated the whole course of Irish opinion." Professor Dicey declares that if the Act of Union could have been referred to a court of law, it must at once have been cancelled "as a contract hopelessly tainted with fraud and corruption." Gladstone said: "I know no blacker or fouler transaction in the history of man than the making of the Union between England and Ireland." Ireland, indeed, was swindled out of her national independence; and the traitors in her own camp were either rewarded with titles or paid, like cash tradesmen, with enormous sums of money, which a shameless England did not scruple to charge upon Ireland.

This is the great Act for which Lord Londonderry, Sir Edward Carson, and the Orangemen of Belfast, with a well-advertised piety, are ready to lay down their lives, for which they are willing to perish in metaphor on the banks of the Boyne, the sacred document with which they make piteous and theatrical appeal to the loyalty of ignorant Englishmen. England, that first set herself to conquer, then to exterminate, and afterwards to beggar the inhabitants of Ireland, by this Act of Union, like a common scoundrel on Epsom Heath, deliberately swindled Ireland out of her national independence. And ever since that day, an impoverished, dispirited, and vanishing Ireland has struggled by every means in her failing power to recover that without which she can neither lift up her head nor restore her broken fortunes—struggled heroically, desperately, violently, and for a little space criminally, to recover her spirit of Nationality.

When you consider the history of Ireland, are you not amazed that any man in England can be found to sneer at that tide of almost holy money which the expatriated children of Ireland save and send home every year for the recovery of their country's freedom ?

## IV

### WITHIN LIVING MEMORY

The old man sat forward in his chair, holding a black felt hat in his hands which he swung nervously between his legs. His pale face was clean-shaven and thin, the features refined, the dark eyes, set deep under the brows, appeared dim and blurred. His hair, of which he had plenty, was the colour of snow.

The Bishop, in biretta and soutane, leaned against the mantelpiece, and questioned the old man : " You remember the great famine, don't you—the famine of '47 and '48 ? "

In slow and deliberate fashion, speaking in a deep voice, the old man made answer : " I do, me lord ; I remember it very well."

" Tell us something about it, something that you yourself saw and knew. You understand me ? "

" Perfectly, me lord. I understand you very well."

" Come, then, let us hear what you have to say."

" Well, me lord "—sitting back, opening the top button of his frieze coat, and assuming the grave expression of a national historian—" I remember the day, just as if it was only last week, when me father come home and said that the taties were specked. There were little black spots all over them. That, me lord, was the beginning of the great famine. The seed pertaties, do you see, were . . ."

" Yes, but tell us what you yourself saw and suffered."

" I will, me lord." After a pause, shifting in his chair, and moistening his lips : " Well, me lord, I remember very well that all round the country hereabouts the tatie crop was a failure. The ground gave nothing but little, poor things no bigger than marbles, and all specked with the disease . . ."

" Yes, yes ; but tell us about the people, about yourself ; tell us how you lived during the famine."

" How we lived, me lord ! God knows we lived very poorly. There was nothing for us, don't you see, but the little specked taties, and not many of them. I remember how me mother gave most of that food to me father, saying that he had to do the work in the fields, and needed the food more than the rest of us. She herself, good soul, took just enough to help her through the day's work ; and we little ones got what was left, which was sometimes only the water in which the taties had been boiled. It was hungry times, me lord. Ah, and it got worse. Soon there were no taties at all. I can mind how we went out to hunt for turnips in the field. Turnips are good food, but the starving sheep were of the same opinion!—they left little of them for us at all. We used to pull up the roots, the little tail of the roots, which the sheep had left in the earth after eating down the turnips level with the ground. There was not much nourishment in that, me lord, but we were terribly grateful to find them roots. Then it came to chewing nettles and docks, and even grass. I've seen people nearly mad for food chewing a handful of rank grass. Ah, me lord, they were bad times, bad times they were."

"And the people died?"

"Like flies, me lord; and particular the little children. They died so fast there was no time for decent burial. A big box was made; it was driven round on a car; the poor dead bodies were picked up in the road or taken out of the houses, put in the box, and then carted to the burying-ground. A great pit was dug there, and into that pit the dead bodies were tumbled out of the box, one atop of the other. Terrible times! It was wonderful, me lord, how people died in them times. They died standing, died leaning against doors, dropped down sudden in the road. I remember me father coming on a man who was resting against a wall. Me father was a terrible man for his pipe, and he offers his pipe to that poor fellow, and ses he, 'Take a pull, man, it will warm you,' he ses. Then he went off to get a car for the man; but when he got back the poor fellow was leaning in the same position, dead as dead."

"And you were turned out of your houses, weren't you?"

"That is so, me lord. You must understand that some time before the Government had made the landlords responsible for all rates and taxes. Instead of collecting from the tenants, the Government collected from the landlords, and the landlords added the taxes to the rents. Well, do you see, me lord, when the poor starving people had no money, and couldn't pay their rents, the landlords still had to pay the rates and taxes. So they thought they would be ruined, and it seemed to them better to have the houses empty, because then they wouldn't have to pay the taxes. That was how it was, me lord."

"Well, what did they do?"

"When the tenants wouldn't turn out, me lord, the agent came with a party of men, and they swung a great rope under the eave of the thatch, and then, with a kind of a jerk and a run backwards, they ripped the roofs clean off the little cabins. If that didn't do, they set fire to the house. We were burned out, me lord, like rats. Ah, it was a sight to see the roads filled with men, women, and children, all starving and dying, with no home at all, and no shelter from the rain. It was a sight I shall never forget, me lord—never. Hundreds and hundreds of men, women, and children. . . ."

The Bishop turned to me. In a whisper he said: " One of the landlords in the neighbourhood was a Church of England clergyman. He kept a yacht, which he used to fill with disreputable women, and then go cruising in the Mediterranean!" He added: " What made the famine so hard for the people to bear was their knowledge that food existed in Ireland plentiful enough to supply their needs. But it was sent to England. It was sent where money could be got for it. And the money was required to pay the landlords' rents."

" Ah, that is true, me lord," exclaimed the old man, smiting his knee with a clenched fist. " There was plenty of good food in the country, plenty; but we weren't allowed to touch it. . . ."

In another part of the country you may see a magnificent house standing in a great demesne and surrounded by a wall. To make the demesne, farmers were turned out of their holdings, and given miserable land on the hillside; to lay the roads, to build the mansion, and to erect the wall, tenants were ordered to give so many days' work—" duty days "—for which they received no wages.

A lady belonging to what is called the " English garrison " said to me: " I blame the landlords for everything bad that has happened in Ireland. They had the greatest chance in the world." They were not all bad; some were good men; but among them were monsters, tyrants, and petty thieves.

The patience, the submissiveness, the loyalty, the devotion, and the courtesy of the Irish peasant—even now, after centuries of tyranny and brutality—fill the mind with admiration and with wonder. And, remember, they have heard with their ears the story of our past oppressions, and there are still living old people who tell how landlords burned them like rats out of their wretched hovels when the land was wasted by famine. " Och, but sure that was in the old times, your honour," says the peasant; " thim was terrible times; but, glory be to God, it's a different time now altogether."

## CHAPTER II

### THE BISHOP'S DREAM

It was my good fortune to spend a few days in the beautiful and happy south of Ireland with a very remarkable Roman Catholic Bishop. This brilliant and engaging man is chiefly famous as an authority on the financial relations between Great Britain and Ireland. Blue Books are the staple of his reading, as statistics are the passion of his life. In a moment, with a pinch of snuff between thumb and index, his biretta at the back of his head, he can tell you the exports and imports in a given year, quote you the latest figures from the Board of Trade, give you the population of Belgium or Poland, analyse the entire revenue returns of Great Britain, and marshal the legions of humanity in three orderly columns of pounds, shillings and pence.

But he is something more than auditor to the human race and financial expert of the United Kingdom. He is a man who holds that life must be controlled and directed, that it can be made happy and secure, that it is wholly in the hands of men to decide whether it shall flow peacefully, broadly, and beautifully to its destined end. He does not believe in a Time Spirit that urges mortality forward. He does not believe that man is powerless in the winds of fate. He does not believe that we are driven like a flock of sheep. No; he believes that the same choice is presented to nations as to individual men, and that by its deliberate choice a nation may walk quietly towards God, as by its deliberate choice, or the mere absence of decision one way or the other, it may go headlong to the devil. He argues that everything depends upon this choice.

One night, after dinner, we sat up till past three in the morning discussing this aspect of the Irish question. The table remained uncleared; the housekeeper, who cooks and waits and does everything else in the house, was sent to bed. At the appointed hour the Bishop withdrew to say his Office, leaving me to my cigarette and my reflections, and then returned to his seat at the head of the table. And the night ended—but I do not propose to keep the reader up so late—with a discussion on the Athanasian Creed!

With one arm, clothed in the sleeve of his purple-edged soutane, laid across a corner of the disordered table, his buckled shoes tucked under his chair, the biretta pushed far back on his head so that the thick grey hair was visible, the little Bishop leaned towards me, his red face wreathed with smiles, his small, deep-sunken eyes bright with animation, his large mouth cheerful with good-humour, and rolled me out his mind.

So far as I can remember it, this was the soul of what he said:

"People in England do not understand what is at the back of our demand for Home Rule, what is the spirit that animates the Irish movement. They remember some extravagant utterance of a Fenian, or some rather flamboyant piece of rhetoric ejaculated by a heated politician in the excitement of debate; and they think that we are inspired by hatred of England—the whole movement of Irish nationality inspired by hatred of England! Of course there are in Ireland people who hate England, and of course there are many more people who persuade themselves that they ought to hate England; but that is not the spirit of the Irish movement. In England you have people who say feverish and reckless things about Germany, and I suppose a man who thought it worth while might form a collection of extracts from speeches and newspaper articles which would make it seem that the whole spirit of English Imperialism was hatred and jealousy of Germany. But would it be true? Would it not be very foolish to assert that the whole policy and diplomacy of the English people are inspired by enmity towards Germany?

"Well, it is equally foolish, equally untrue and unjust, to say that the great movement of the Irish people towards freedom and self-government is urged forward by antagonism to England. There is antagonism between the two countries, a real, unalterable, and inevitable antagonism, but that is the work of nature. Politicians have nothing to do with it. Have you ever thought what that antagonism is? It is one of the main arguments for Irish self-government, traced back to its source, it is the spirit which animates, and has ever animated, the movement of Irish nationality. Let us talk about it.

"England is a rich, industrial, and conquering nation. Ireland is a poor, agricultural, and domesticated nation. England's population has increased by leaps and bounds, and has flooded across the habitable globe, taking countries, colonizing countries, establishing an empire of enormous extent. Ireland's population—since the Union with England—has dwindled in a desperate degree. Her revenue has fallen. Her trade has almost vanished. Her sons do not go forth to conquer and to colonize, but as poor emigrants, weeping bitterly and loth to go.

"What is the antagonism? It is economic. There is nothing here of Celtic hatred for the Saxon, or of Saxon contempt for the Celt. It is the natural, the inevitable antagonism which separates a rich industrial nation from a poor agricultural nation. Unionist politicians maintain that the wholly antagonistic interests of the two countries can be combined, can be made one. They declare that the British Parliament can budget and legislate for two countries whose interests, talents, and resources are entirely different. They might as well argue that the legislation and the budgets of Westminster are equally suitable for Denmark or India! How can a rich industrial nation legislate and budget for a poor agricultural nation? Who would not smile if a politician suggested that a rich man should order a poor man to keep house on the same scale as his own? Must not the two houses be separate in finance and management, even as they are separate in bricks and mortar?

"Let me give you two or three instances of the blunders which come from this discordant union. Take Old Age Pensions. In England five shillings a week is only just sufficient for the needs of an old person; in Ireland it is too much. In England it is hard to get a cottage under two shillings a week; in Ireland rents are as low as a shilling, ninepence, even sixpence a week. Two old people in England, a man and wife, with five shillings a week each can manage to live; in Ireland such a couple are unnecessarily rich. Not only are commodities cheaper in Ireland, but the manner of living is simpler, very much simpler. Our pensions ought to be three-and-sixpence a week at the most. But Ireland has to run at the side of galloping England, and we are saddled with your harness and pull at your load.

"Then, again, take the question of Income Tax. In England you place no tax on incomes of £160 a year, and you deduct this sum from all moderate incomes before you begin to take your toll. Well, this is perhaps a suitable method for a rich country, a country where there is a vast population and a very considerable number of extremely well-off people. But it is unsuitable for a poor country in which the numbers of very wealthy people can be reckoned in two or three minutes. This objection applies equally to Death Duties. Ireland keeps fairly abreast of England and Scotland among the smaller sums contributed by moderate estates, but directly we come to very considerable estates she contributes nothing at all. Those blanks in the columns of the statistical table are extremely significant.

"Once more: the tendency of taxation in England is towards wealth, and wealth alone. Your phrase the 'Free Breakfast Table' means that you want to relieve the poor of every single tax in your budgets. You seek to take off the toll on tea, on sugar, on coffee, on currants, perhaps on tobacco. Well, that is very good, it is excellent—for a rich country. But do you see what that means? It means this: that if the Union continue, if the enactments of your Chancellors of Exchequer are to apply to Ireland equally with England, Ireland will be a dead unprofitable loss of many millions a year to the British Treasury. Do you see? That is inevitable. You will get a little from Income Tax, something from Excise, almost nothing from Death Duties, and absolutely nothing at all from Customs. Are you prepared for that loss? Do the people of England care to pay all the bill, are they prepared to fill Ireland's purse and leave her free to enjoy herself?

"Consider, on the other hand, how much more reasonable it is that Ireland should keep house for herself. We should economize, because we are poor. We should simplify, because we are not ambitious. And we should arrange our taxes to suit the means of our own people. We should tax small incomes, levy death duties on small estates, keep the taxes on tea, coffee, sugar, and tobacco; in short, the direction and tendency of our taxation would be towards that mark from which yours is every year moving further away. We should keep house as Denmark keeps house, or as Belgium keeps house; instead of having our house kept for us by the wealthiest and most extravagant housekeeper in the whole community of nations!

"Now, you may say, How foolish of you to cut adrift from us, when by your own showing we shall soon be paying the whole cost of your national existence, while, by cutting adrift, you will have to shoulder yourselves the entire burden of that existence! Well, it sounds absurd, it sounds rather simple and stupid. But consider a moment.

"In England you think of patriotism in a wide discursive and extended manner. Your patriotism is spread over a vast empire. The term for you connotes imperial grandeur and colonial expansion. You hardly think of England when you speak of patriotism; you think of India, Canada, South Africa, Australia, and some hundreds of little islands scattered you hardly know where! It is difficult for you to think of patriotism as something local, racial, and circumscribed. If you so thought of it, you might be tempted to despise it. But there is such a patriotism. Denmark has it—Switzerland has it—Ireland has it. And this national, racial, and local patriotism is a spirit that makes for independence. It is a spirit that dislikes dictation from outside, that cannot be content to sponge on other nations. And so this little, simple, and poor Ireland, instead of wishing to sponge upon rich England, desires to stand on her own feet, to shoulder her own burden, to pay her own way, to be a self-supporting, self-respecting, and self-reliant nation.

"Why? Is it only the obstinacy of conceit?—is it only the braggart self-assertion of independence? A little of that, perhaps, here and there. We are very much tarred with human nature! But, believe me, this spirit of Irish patriotism, taken all in all, is a righteous and a noble spirit. John Bright saw far into the soul of Ireland when he said, *Throw the Irish upon themselves; make them forget England.* We want to be thrown upon ourselves; we want to forget the long enmity with England; we want to feel ourselves responsible and free. It is our conviction that the more you pay our bills, and the more we hang upon you for our support, and the more you take our destiny out of our own hands, the more swift, the more searching, the more pervasive, will be the decay of our Irish manhood. And that is something we do not wish to see decay.

We are ready to pay for it, as our fathers were ready to die for it. We say to England, Trust us : leave us to look after ourselves : we have a business to do in which you cannot take a part, the achievement of which instead of being a danger to you will be a source of strength—it is the preservation of Irish character.

" And now we come to a subject which will interest you more than any commercial chatter about budgets and taxation.

" I do not say that every Irish politician realizes the truth of what I am going to say to you, nor do I assert that every Irish politician will agree with my sentiments. But I am pretty certain that at the back of the Irish movement, consciously or unconsciously, the ideas that I am now going to set before you are the driving force, the animating, vitalizing spirit.

" Let me tell you my ideas in the shape of an aspiration, an ambition—if you like, a dream. I hold that the most precious thing in Ireland is neither the shipbuilding of the north nor the agriculture of the south, but Irish character. Irish character is to me, being a local patriot, a very precious and a most beautiful thing. The tenderness of Irish character, the purity, the chastity, the domestic virtues of that character, the simple faith, the unquestioning content and the wonderful self-reliance of Irish character, are for me the sovran values of Irish nationality. I want to preserve them. I want to develop them. And so I ask for Home Rule. My ambition is that Ireland shall live in the midst of the nations, as it was at the beginning of its history, a people that places God first, a people that does not seek to be rich, arrogant, and conquering, but devoted to beauty, consecrated to holiness, content with simple things. And this does not seem to me a wild or an unpractical ambition. Nature, indeed, has ordained that this shall be our destiny. We have little but our fields and gardens to support us ; our inclination is almost solely towards agriculture ; we have little or no taste for the excitements and excesses of a civilization founded upon industrialism. We are a people who love family life and who believe earnestly and sincerely the Christian religion.

" I love to dream that Ireland may live isolated and yet in the midst of those tumultuous nations who are abandoned to commercialism, a place where men may come from other lands, as it were to a retreat—a place where they may refresh themselves with faith and establish in quiet the central touch of the soul with God. I love to think of Ireland peopled by a humble and satisfied humanity, the villages extending through the valleys, the towns never out of contact with the fields, the cities famous for learning and piety, the whole nation using life for its greatest end, its ultimate and eternal purpose. It would be surely a good thing for the British Empire to have such a sanctuary at its heart. Might not such an Ireland be of service to England, if only in reminding your democracy that no wages can buy happiness? Are you not in some danger in this respect?

"My dream for Ireland is not quixotic. We can never be, except in the north, an industrial nation. We have no coal to speak of, we are too far from markets, and our genius is not in that direction. On the other hand, we are by nature and by inclination husbandmen. We can get a living where an Englishman would starve. We grow wheat where an Englishman would feed sheep. We are attached to the soil by a love which all the tyranny and madness of a very wicked landlordism has not been able to destroy. And we are rich on little.

"The strength of our national life is the chastity of our women. All the beauty of family life in Ireland flows from the purity of Irish mothers. You have seen some of the cabins in which our people live; not very long ago almost the whole peasantry of Ireland was housed in that way—one wretched room for the existence of a family—for eating, sleeping, everything. Well, in spite of such a dreadful environment, the purity of the people has persisted. Our women are chaste, our men are chivalrous, our children are virtuous. Nothing seems able to brutalize them. Here and there, of course, evil manifests itself; we are not perfect; but rare are the cases of seduction, almost unknown are the cases of adultery, and when such things occur they are met by the censure and the opposition of a virtuous public opinion. We can justly boast that our people are chaste. Now, with a nation so minded, and left to develop its own way of life, is it not certain that Ireland might become the sanctuary, the holy place, of my ambition? What is to prevent it? Our women breathe into the souls of their children a love for family life, our men teach their sons to cultivate the land and to turn the temper of the sulkiest soil on the side of a hill; and father, mother, and children believe in God. Is there not here everything that makes for the beauty of life and the sanctity of social existence?

"I do not mean that there will be no progress, that we shall remain cultivators and nothing but cultivators. We hope to raise our population to at least ten millions, and agriculture must therefore be fortified by industries. But we shall seek to develop village industries. Instead of factory towns, with their horrible slums, their poverty, and spiritual degradation, we shall add little workshops and little factories to our villages. We shall always be, in the first place, cultivators. We shall be the market-garden of England, perhaps one of its wheat-fields, and this will be our chief employment. But we shall seek to supply our own needs in the way of manufactures; so far as we can, we shall endeavour to make locally some at least of our chief necessities. It will never be our objective to export these manufactures, never our ambition to come into commercial conflict with great manufacturing nations like England and Germany; no, we shall be content to make what we can for ourselves, and to support ourselves firstly and chiefly by the fruit of our fields.

"Why cannot we do all this under the Union? Because we have no incentive of enthusiasm; because we are spoon-fed and debilitated with one of England's hands, let, hindered, and obstructed with the other; because our intellect is absorbed by politics; because we have a passion for freedom; because we cannot rest while we are governed by another; because the form of government under which we live has impoverished our industries and drained our population. It will take years before we can recover the lost ground, but with the first beating of enthusiasm in the blood of Ireland's freedom that recovery will begin.

"Have I made you feel, have I convinced you, that the Irish question is a spiritual question, a religious question? Our movement in its soul is that, nothing but that. We do not believe in the strife of industrialism. We do not believe in the struggle for existence. We seek to disengage ourselves from all that strife and struggle, into which the Union has dragged us, in order that we may follow our own way of life, which is quiet, simple, and modest. We are quite certain that materialism is wrong. What is more important, we are quite certain that idealism is right. We make the conscious choice of beauty and peace, rather than ugliness and contention. We deliberately elect for God, and as deliberately we reject Mammon.

"You hear people say that Home Rule will be the death-blow of Rome in Ireland. That is not true. Ireland is religious, and Ireland is Catholic. At first, perhaps, the strong wine of freedom may tempt the younger generation to resent the paternal interference of the priest; at first there may be an unreckoning enthusiasm for secular education, leading to agnosticism; but the habit of religion will assert itself again. I welcome Home Rule for one thing in this respect, that it will deliver the parish priest from the sphere of politics, and set him free for his purely spiritual duties. Remember that the priest has been driven into politics. In the bad times, before recent legislation, the peasants had no one else to whom they could carry their complaints against the landlord or his agent. The priest was the witness of barbarous cruelties. He saw his people defrauded, starved, ill-treated, sometimes debased and demoralized, driven into exile. Do you wonder that he became a politician? Would not English clergymen become politicians in a like circumstance? But with Irish freedom, the excuse, the justification, for this political interference will go. And then the parish priest will devote himself solely to the spiritual needs of his people, he will instruct them exclusively how to live, and leave them to vote as they will.

"You have seen something of the influence of the Irish priest. You are not a Catholic, but do you see anything in that influence which is evil or dangerous? Does not the parish priest, whatever be his dogmas, teach virtue and the love of God? Do you know of any country in the world where the priest is more closely and intimately associated with the family life of the nation, where his influence is more powerful for beauty, kindness, and chastity? Again, do you know of any clergy in the world with fewer black sheep among them than the clergy of Ireland?

"I am not afraid. Time will bring changes, life will advance, knowledge will modify even those opinions which seem to us now of primary importance; but the essential characteristic of the Irish nature will endure, and that characteristic is the religious sense. Ireland will never be infidel.

"So it all comes to this: under the Union we are dragged against our will, we a poor and simple agricultural people, into the roaring machinery and the extravagant organization of a rich, complex, and industrial civilization. The more you bear our burdens, the more you paralyse our sense of responsibility. The more you advance along your difficult road, the more you drag us from our firesides and our fields. We do not desire a complex civilization. We do not want to become sophisticated. We dislike and we suspect the elaborate machinery of your social life. We say to you, Set us free: leave us to pursue our own path, to fulfil our own destiny. We feel that something more than our fortunes are bound up in this plea for self-government; it is our character. You destroy our independence, you paralyse our self-reliance, you take away from us what God gives as a chief blessing to a nation, our sense of responsibility. We tend under the Union to become the parasites of your wealth, the hangers-on of your imperial greatness, the sponging toadies of your bounty. That, to us, is more than intolerable, more than perilous; it is fatal to body, soul, and spirit. Canada could not advance in such shackles, Australia could not advance in such bonds, South Africa in such a case would be a constant danger to your peace. Your genius is to preside over a brotherhood of free nations, to leave the component parts of your empire to develop along their own lines ; the greater the freedom you grant them, the greater their loyalty, the greater your security. Why cannot you treat Ireland in the same way ? For how many centuries have you tried in vain to govern her from London, to destroy her nationality, and to suppress the spirit of her independence ? Why make of this little island the single dark exception to the brilliant success of your genius for empire ?

" Believe me, Ireland will never be at rest until she is free. Until you set her free she will be a thorn in your side. There will always be Irishmen—even if the dwindling mass should become slothful and apathetic—who, for the sake of Irish character, will preach the ancient gospel of freedom, will rouse the undying spirit of her independence. You would surely do the same in England, if some power were at work which threatened your English character, which sapped and ruined the foundations of English manhood. You would fight, then, not for empire, but for character, for life. It is the same with us. Again and again I tell you that we are at war with you for the spirit of Irish nationality. We do not criticize your civilization, we admire many of your splendid qualities, we envy you much of your energy, your grit, your sterling common sense ; but we think that your civilization is not suitable to Ireland, we believe that we have qualities that are of value to mankind, and we believe that only by exercising the functions of self-government can we develop our kind of energy, our kind of grit, and our kind of common sense. You must go forward on the road of industrial progress, creating new problems as fast as you solve old, treading down and obliterating landmarks as fast as you set up new ones ; but we must live our own life of pastoral simplicity, moving more slowly, content to see fresh horizons when God reveals them, attempting to solve only those ancient problems which frustrate the growth and mar the beauty of man's soul. Leave us to that. We shall be then no hindrance to your progress. And perhaps some of the statesmen of your new democracy may occasionally pay us a visit to see how an old-fashioned people, following in the footsteps of its ancestors, manages the business of human life.

" Believe me, we wish you no harm. Most cheerfully shall we send you our milk and butter, our eggs and bacon, our cabbages and potatoes ; and always most delightfully shall we welcome you to our shores when you are in need of quiet and repose !

" Am I a dreamer ? Well, when you are in Belfast perhaps you may think so. But go among our peasants ; sit by their peat-fires, stand in their gardens, visit their cowsheds, walk through their fields, and you will find that I do not dream. And do remember, when you are in Belfast, that something like 70 per cent of Ireland's population is engaged, directly or indirectly, in agriculture, and that only 30 per cent is industrial. My dream is the aspiration of the Irish people."

## CHAPTER III

### THE LIFE OF A TOWN

"So many people in England," said the little Bishop, "believe the legend of Roman Catholic intolerance, that I should like you to take a walk through this town and make your own inquiries of the shopkeepers. You will find that all the principal shops are kept by Protestants."

The town is Catholic; it is situated in the centre of an agricultural district which is almost entirely Catholic. The Protestants are numbered by tens, the Catholics by thousands.

It is one of those half-sleepy and half-dreamy towns which a man in a motor-car regards with lifted eyebrows and a bored contempt—only interested if he has to lunch there, and then mightily depressed. Except on market-days, when picturesque peasants throng its narrow pavements and crowd its little shops, when every conceivable kind of vehicle and every possible specimen of horse and donkey get themselves into inextricable confusion in the one long curving street, when old women, with old baskets over their arms and old hooded cloaks over their heads, tramp in from far-away villages to do their week's marketing, and when fox-like looking men, long-lipped, small-eyed, and whiskered, flourishing long sticks and shouting unintelligible maledictions, urge cows, sheep, pigs, and goats through the crowd—only then does the town open its eyes quite wide, raise its nodding head, pull down its waistcoat, settle its collar, and realize the existence of mankind.

Not beautiful, not ancient, and not really picturesque, there is nevertheless something ingratiating and restful in this drowsy town. It is of a size which makes for human intercourse. Everybody knows everybody, and as there are two of everybody in particular, existence is saved from dullness and stagnation. One is conscious of a ruffle of competition. There are certainly two doctors, as certainly two solicitors, as certainly two bank-managers, as certainly two priests, and if not two bishops at least a sufficiency of clerical aggressiveness on the part of Protestants to temper the episcopal monopoly of the Catholic bishop.

Moreover, there are certain representatives of the English "garrison" living tea-party, gardening, and Diana lives in villages close at hand, so that the little town is not without a touch of aristocracy, a breath of culture. One likes to see the brougham of Sir Thomas pulled up before the poulterer's door, to see the Colonel's dog-cart and the Colonel's eyeglass come grandly round the corner, and to see Miss Priscilla and Master George walking their ponies over the cobbles, their eyes directed to the tuck-shops.

Now, will you believe it—will you believe it after all you have read in Orange pamphlets and Unionist newspapers—will you believe that all the chief shops of this market-town are kept by Protestants and are supported by Catholics ? A gentlemanly and blushing young Methodist, presiding over the counter of a flourishing grocery stores, informed me that he had the Bishop on his books, most of the Catholic priests, and a very satisfactory percentage of the Catholic population. He said the Catholics were by far his most numerous customers.

" Why do we deal with these Protestants, why don't we go to our own Catholic grocers ? " asked the Bishop. " The answer is very simple ; it is not in the least Satanic ! We go to the Protestant shops, because the Protestant shopkeepers are better men of business than the Catholic shopkeepers. They give us better value for our money. We are very glad indeed to have such excellent business-men serving the bodily needs of the community. We do not inquire to what church they belong or to which political party they give their votes ; we judge them by their prices, the quality of their goods, and the honesty of their dealings. They are a very estimable body of people. We like them and we respect them."

The true character of what is called the Religious Difficulty may be gathered from the following incident, which occurred in quite another town situated in quite another district of the south of Ireland.

This town, one might almost say, is exclusively Catholic, as it is hotly and overwhelmingly Home Rule. A manager of one of the two banks began to make his preparations for retirement, and the second-in-command began to make his dispositions for obtaining the managership. But he was in a difficulty. For he was not a Home Ruler, and he was not a Roman Catholic. It seemed impossible to suppose that the directors of the bank would appoint a manager so unlikely to prosper their business. But he took courage, knowing the kindness of his clients, and went among the chief people of the town asking if they would support his application. He met with not one single refusal. Everybody he asked signed his application, and he obtained the post.

Two Catholics in the town, speaking to me of this bank manager, used almost identical words. One of them said : " Mr. —— is a gentleman, a real gentleman ; there's nothing I wouldn't do to oblige him." The other : " We would all do anything for Mr. ——, because he's a true gentleman." Neither of them could tell me whether he was Home Ruler or Unionist.

The bank manager himself said to me : " It is quite certain I should never have got the post if I had been a Unionist politician ; but my religion made no difficulty at all. My experience of Catholics is this : they do not ask what a man believes in religion, but they object to a man, Catholic or Protestant, who is opposed to the national demand for Home Rule. I have never, in the whole course of my experience, come across one single instance of Catholic intolerance."

As I walked with the little Bishop beside the little shops of his little town, I told him of this bank manager, and he said to me, with a charming smile, taking my arm with an impulse of the friendliest goodwill : " We are really not monsters ! I assure you, whatever our shortcomings, we are not so black as we are painted ! What the bank manager said to you is probably true—he would not have got his comfortable house and his larger salary if he had been an active politician on the Unionist side. Whenever you hear of Catholics opposing the advancement of a Protestant to some more or less public position, you may be perfectly certain that the reason is political. They might oppose a Protestant who mocked and maligned their religion ; but never—in the case of an able and honest man—one who used charity to his religious neighbours and either supported Home Rule or kept his Unionism for his private life. I am perfectly certain that when Home Rule comes, a very large number of representatives from the south of Ireland will be Protestant men of business, Protestant men of position—in fact, that very class which would now be sitting in the House of Commons if they were Nationalists."

He suggested that I should see something of Catholic education in an agricultural town, and I was accordingly taken to the big school close to the modest house where his lordship lives with a single servant to look after his needs.

It was interesting to see the effect produced by his entrance. To begin with, at sight of him the scholars all dropped upon one knee, while the master, or mistress, hurriedly advanced, and, kneeling, kissed the episcopal ring. The Bishop, who is a democrat and a startling innovator, almost in the same breath as he gave his blessing, told the children to rise and began asking them questions. And one saw that the kneeling was but a ceremony, a mediæval courtesy which has altogether lost anything it may have once possessed of servility or fear. The children's faces were soon bright with smiles, the Bishop's loud laugh rang through the rooms, and master, or mistress, entered with accustomed pleasure, completely at their ease, but always respectful, into his badinage.

The children, with but very few exceptions, were fat and well-ooking, their bodies clothed with stubborn homespun and their feet excessively shod with lasting leather. Here and there a pale child, barefoot and ragged, struck a tragic note, told of drunken parents, and witnessed to the misery of poverty. But such children, I observed, were placed nearest to the stove, and seemed to be on perfectly good terms with the well-dressed children of prosperous tradesmen.

In these Catholic schools there is a refreshing absence of class-feeling, of money differences, of blighting snobbishness.

"Well, young giant," said the Bishop, tapping a little stump of a boy on the shoulder, "what are you going to be when you grow up?" "Soldier, sir." "Soldier! Why a soldier?" "So as I can fight the English," replied the boy, at which Bishop, schoolmaster, and class burst into bountiful laughter. "Fight the English!" I said reprovingly; "why, they're going to give you Home Rule. Why not fight the ——?" naming a most charming nation on the Continent. The little pugilist regarded me with perplexity; I was Double Dutch to his understanding. "Want to fight the English," he muttered stubbornly.

The Bishop said to me: "Properly dressed up, what a story for the Orange pamphleteer! A whole schoolful of tremendous big boys drilling to overthrow the British Empire!"

We visited the convent-school, where a beautiful Reverend Mother in voluminous garments of black that seemed to fizz and crackle as she knelt to kiss the Bishop's ring, guided us with a merry good-humour through the bright and speckless house.

In one of the class-rooms a Bible lesson was proceeding. "What!" cried the Bishop, wheeling round upon me with an expression of simulated shock; "teaching the Bible! and in the vernacular! How terrible! Did you ever know of such wickedness?" And then leaving me to my smiles, he whipped round to the class, and began asking questions suggested by the Bible lesson.

"All sin is wicked," he said; "that is so, is it not?" "Yes, my lord," in treble chorus, from young ladies with pinafores and hair-ribbons. "Yes, and all sin is distressing to God, *all sin:* isn't that so?" "Yes, my lord." "But there are degrees of sin: some sins are worse than other sins?" "Yes, my lord." "Now, stealing is a sin, but it is not so great a sin as murder: that is so, is it not?" "Yes, my lord." "Murder is a terrible sin?" "Yes, my lord." "A very terrible sin?" "Yes, my lord." "Now, is there any worse sin than murder?" Silence, hesitation among pinafores and hair-ribbons. " Think a moment ; is there any worse sin than killing a human being ? " One shy hand timidly lifted. " Well, you tell us ; come now, don't be shy, tell us what is a greater sin than murder." " Please, my lord, perjury." " Quite right, quite right ; and can you tell us why perjury is a greater sin than murder ? Speak up, now." After a tremendous moment of breath-drawing—" Because, my lord, murder is sin against man, but perjury is sin against God." The Bishop triumphantly : " Do you see, girls ? Perjury is a greater sin, because he who commits it tries to make God a partner of his sin. He calls God to witness to a lie. God is all truth. And the perjurer tries to make Him a liar. Perjury is a spiritual sin, the most awful sin we can commit. Very well, then. Good-bye, girls. God bless you."

And in the next room the Bishop demands : " Now how many girls had stirabout for breakfast this morning ? " Titters and confusion from this elegant class of young ladies almost marriageable. " What, only one ! Shameful ! Dreadful ! Well, now let us see : how many had tea ? " A general uprising of elegant hands and slender arms. " Appalling ! " cries the Bishop ; " oh, shocking, shocking ! " Laughter, simpering, and naughty whispering among the fillies. " Well," says the Bishop, " although tea cannot compare with good porridge it is a pardonable sin—but remember, only pardonable when it is freshly made. Now, who can tell me why stewed tea is bad ? " A blushing maid volunteers : " Because tea contains tannin." " And what is tannin used for ? " " For hardening leather." " Quite right ; so if you don't want to have stomachs as tough as leather you won't drink stewed tea, will you ? " Then he explains, smiling and gracious, that poor people in Ireland lose their teeth and their appetites, become wretched and feeble, because they destroy their digestions with horrid black stewed tea.

The Reverend Mother whispers to me with a tolerant smile . " The Bishop is always going on about stewed tea. It's one of his fads. But he really has made a great difference in the habits of the people—he is always telling them about open windows, milk, cleanliness, and proper cooking. He's a regular reformer ! "

Now I would like you to know that the Sisters teaching in this school were very nice and very cheerful people. Their eyes had that unfathomable depth of maternal kindness and that pleasing twinkle of quizzical amusement which is characteristic of the Irish woman ; and their bright faces shone as if a cake of soap had been used with the vigour of a housemaid's hearthstone ; and their linen was as white as snow, and their black garments had the shine and rustle of a Genevan gown in the evangelical pulpit of a wealthy congregation; and everything about them suggested alacrity, health, energy, enthusiasm, and contentment. Not one of them gave me the impression of the paid teacher who is bored by her task and regards her pupils as the guilty cause of her spinsterhood. Not one of them seemed likely to terrorize young children or to make religion detestable.

In these schools I had a feeling of the town's future, the nation's morrow. Outside the walls, in the pleasant sunshine and the drowsy hum of the morning, men and women were at work with worldly business—the peasant sowing, the shopkeeper selling, the housewife preparing dinner, the carpenter building, the cobbler hammering on his last, the smith making his anvil ring, and the merchant weighing a speculation. And here, provided with all the necessaries of existence, were those who some day would be bearing the burden of the town's prosperity, who would themselves be the money-getters and the corn-growers and the bootmakers, and the mothers of posterity. Something so sweet and tender and intelligent in these children seemed to assure me that the town's future and the nation's morrow, enlightened by education and consecrated by religion, would be happier and richer. . . .

One of the doctors in this town was kind enough to take me on a visit of inspection to the infirmary. Here, too, I found Sisters of Mercy in charge of the patients—gentle, merry, and tender-hearted women with whom it was a pleasure, almost a tonic, to come in contact. Need I say that the wards were wonderfully clean and bright?

I shall never forget as long as I live some of the patients in this hospital. We came to a bed on which a little human form turned upon its side was discernible by the humped shape of the huddled bed-clothes. Going round to the further side of the bed, I saw upon the pillow the oldest face I have ever seen—a skull covered with wasting wax-like skin, the lids of cavernous eyes fast closed, the line of the sunken mouth just visible in the midst of infinite wrinkles, the aquiline nose shrunken to the likeness of a bird's beak.

As if she were a mother speaking of her child, the Sister said to me: "He's such a dear old man!"

"How old is he?" I asked.

"Over ninety. And the poor old fellow has been lying like that for nearly five years. He is quite bed-ridden. He will never leave his bed. He just dozes and sleeps all the day, and all the night. And he never complains; he is just waiting for God to take him."

I felt a shock of horror, looking at the ancient in his sleep and striving to imagine such a doom for myself, five years in bed, five years in one position, five years of waiting for release.

There were very old women in these wards, and little children and men dying visibly and swiftly of consumption. And there were men about the place who bore no likeness to humanity; soulless creatures, misshapen, misfeatured, hideous to the eye, repellent to the mind—idiots and degenerates.

The doctor said to me: "There is a movement to have the Sisters supplanted by trained hospital nurses. But will all the training in the world give nurses to poor men like these, as kind, as gentle, and as sympathetic as the Sisters who now wait upon them for the love of God? For myself, I doubt it. Religion, it seems to me, ought to play a great part in the nursing of the poor."

I went a motor-drive with this doctor, and he told me among other things that Mr. Lloyd George was the most infamous man in the whole world. He made no exception, not even ——. As politely as I could, and as diplomatically—for it is never quite safe to defend the Chancellor of the Exchequer before his enemies, and on this occasion I was a Saxon in a Celtic motor-car—I hinted that Mr. George is really not so entirely devilish, so unreservedly in league with Satan, as the purest, most pious, and most cultured classes of the community are unfortunately disposed to imagine. But the doctor swept my feeble straw-works of defence to one side, and charged over the prostrate body of my debilitated loyalty with a sword-like flash of indignation and contempt.

"I will tell you what he has done," quoth he; "then, you shall judge for yourself. He has made my life a hell. He has made every doctor's life a hell. Since his eruption—the devil take his soul!—there is not a doctor in the land whose life——"

"You are speaking of the Insurance Act. Well, you must remem——"

"I am not speaking of the Insurance Act at all, at all! I'm speaking of Old Age Pensions."

And then the doctor, laughing delightedly at my discomfiture, proceeded to tell me how he is now sent for at every hour of the night, and called out of his motor at every mile of his way during the daytime, by people anxious and alarmed over nothing in the least serious which has happened, or is, they think, about to happen, to grandfather and grandmother.

"Where family affection did not exist before," said the doctor, "your Chancellor of the Exchequer has created it; and where it did exist, he has developed and intensified it to a degree which doctors find utterly insupportable. It is really inhuman! One might almost say that a main employment of the peasants nowadays is to keep their old people alive. That five shillings a week has worked a revolution. But, on my honour, the blessing has tremendously increased a country doctor's work."

He spoke of other revolutions.

"The change," said he, "made by the Land Act is little short of amazing. It used to be the hardest thing in the world to get the peasants to live in a sanitary way. I have brow-beaten them hundreds, thousands of times, for keeping animals in their cabins, for having their roofs out of repair, for leaving their broken windows unmended, for the general beastliness and horror of their homes. But it was always in vain. 'Och, dochter dear!' they would exclaim; 'sure, we are so poor we can't afford it!' And so the thing went on. Sickness, disease, epidemics, death. It simply broke one's heart. But now—God bless you, it's the hardest thing in the world to find a really disreputable cottage. The animals live outside; the thatch is kept in good order; the interiors are beautifully clean; and the people wear decent clothes. You would never know them for the same peasantry. And all this change is due to the Land Act. In the old days, if they built a pig-sty, if they mended their roofs, if they went to church in anything but shabby rags, the landlord's agent raised the rent. They simply could not afford to be self-respecting, sanitary, and ambitious. It was too expensive. English people don't realize that. All the dirt and squalor of the Irish peasant was literally created by insatiable landlords."

As the doctor told me of these matters I recalled one of the most striking, and one of the most terrible passages in Henry George's *Progress and Poverty*. Do you remember the words in which he imagines a universal cry of humanity to the Creator, and shows how the answer to that cry, the merciful and miraculous answer, would be of no avail?

> "In the very centre of our civilization to-day are want and suffering enough to make sick at heart whoever does not close his eyes and steel his nerves. Dare we turn to the Creator and ask Him to relieve it? Supposing the prayer were heard, and at the behest with which the universe sprang into being there should glow in the sun a greater power; new virtue fill the air; fresh vigour the soil; that for every blade of grass that now grows two should spring up, and the seed that now increases fiftyfold should increase a hundredfold! Would poverty be abated or want relieved? Manifestly no! . . . Landowners would alone be benefited. Rents would increase, but wages would still tend to the starvation point!"

The abolition of landlordism in Ireland—***without the miracle of a more bountiful earth***—has worked an absolute revolution in Ireland. It has transformed the peasantry. The simple pleasures of these kindly and industrious people have been increased, their joy in work has become intensified, and the beauty of their home-life is now glad and confident, without shadow, and without fear.

This Act, which is buying out the Irish landlords, commits an appalling blunder in conferring the land for all time upon the descendants of those who by mere accident are its present occupiers—a blunder so colossal that it sickens the brain to think that it was committed in the full light of day thirty years after Henry George had demonstrated the salvation of State Ownership; nevertheless, in getting rid of tyrannous landlords, in setting up a race of homesteaders, and in giving fixity of tenure to the peasants of an agricultural country, it has compassed a social revolution. The greatest credit is due to Lord Dunraven for his conception of this measure, and to Mr. George Wyndham for its conduct through the House of Commons. Modern Ireland dates from the passing of that Act.

"I must tell you an amusing story," said the doctor. "I was rung up pretty late one night by a peasant from an outlying village, fifteen miles away. It was in the days before I had a car. The wind was blowing horribly, the rain was sweeping against the house, and it was deadly cold. The peasant asked me, rather shamefacedly, if I would come and see his mother. I invited him to come in; I gave him a glass of whisky. 'Patrick,' I said, 'your mother is a very old woman.' 'I know that, doctor,' he admitted. 'She's over eighty, Patrick.' 'She is all that, doctor.' 'And nothing that I could do to-night would be of the smallest use to her.' 'Sure, doctor,' said he, 'I know very well it's the truth you're telling me; but me poor mother, do you see, would have me come and fetch you because she does not want to die a natural death.'"

Another story the doctor told me. One of his patients, brought to death's door, had a long talk with the priest. On the following day he said to the doctor with extraordinary animation, "Doctor dear, that Father Murphy's a very strange man; I'm thinking he's out of his mind altogether!" "Out of his mind!" exclaimed the doctor; "not at all! Father Murphy is a most able and sensible man. Why, whatever makes you think——" "Wait now, till I tell you, doctor dear. I was asking him, do you see, about the Protestants, asking him what would happen to them at the Judgment Day; and I said, said I, that it was a terrible lot of people to go all at once into hell. And what think you he said, doctor dear—this Father Murphy? Can you imagine it? Will you believe it? He said to me, and it's God's truth I'm telling you, doctor, that maybe Protestants wouldn't go to hell at all, at all, that many of them, to his certain knowledge, stood just as fine a chance of getting into heaven as Catholics! That's what he said, doctor. He said that. He did, doctor dear. If it's the last word I speak, that's what Father Murphy said to me. Doctor dear, the man's mad. To tell me that, and me a dying man! I said to him, 'Father Murphy,' says I, 'if it is possible for Protestants to go to heaven, can you tell me then, I says, why should I have been a Catholic all my life?' Och, but sure the man's out of his mind!"

While the doctor told these stories he steered his motor-car through some of the most beautiful and romantic scenery in Ireland. Our road lay far from the market-town: now winding with a wooded river through cool and gentle valleys; now climbing into heathered hills, over sandy moorland; now skirting the side of steadfast lakes dropped like mirrors on the earth by clouds so beautiful that they died to see themselves; now jolting over rugged tracks through fields of pasture and tillage to the creeper-covered dwelling of a farmer or the new rate-built cottage of a labourer, and now creeping quietly along the scarred and suffering face of the cliff, with the setting sun flashing a pilgrim's path of golden illusion to the land of dollars.

It was delightful to dismount from the car, and go with the doctor into the houses of the peasants. One obtained in this way memorable glimpses of little interiors where one seemed to see the very soul of Ireland smiling at the hearth of Irish life. The invincible neatness of these homes—these humble, human village shrines—their bewitching cheerfulness and content, the sweetness of the people, the air of prosperity and simple happiness, which came from all of them, made not only a most charming impression, but brought one into real and intimate communion with the Irish heart.

Nearly every modern cottage has now an acre, or half an acre, of land surrounding it, and—however plain the architecture, however relentless the red of the bricks—set in the midst of this ample kindly garden each cottage greets one with a graceful sense of Arcady. One knows that potatoes will soon be thrusting their dull green leaves and spreading their white and lilac-coloured flowers over the tilled earth; that the necks of excited hens will soon be thrust through the battens of the coops wriggling for sight of certain wandering balls of down on legs of gelatine; that orchestral squeakings will mingle from the sty with the deeper gruntings of content now sleepily audible; that canary creeper will be clambering over the lattice of the porch, and a hum of bees will sound above the buzzings of summer flies at the open cottage door through which the sun will be slanting.

But it is the older cottage, generally set by the roadside, the little, white-washed, one-storied, straw-thatched cottage that one most loves to penetrate. In these dim cabins, the peat seems to burn with a redder glow and to diffuse a warmer, richer incense: the smoky rafters seem to have a visible hospitality, a discernible spirit of shelter and protection: the humble walls, covered with pictures of the Saviour and St. Mary, seem as if they have caught a sense of blessing and consecration from a hundred years of family affection. And the cooking utensils look as if they have given joy on many a winter night to the tired half-frozen father returning from the fields; the china on the dresser looks as if it has been polished for centuries by little maids conscious of enormous responsibility and of intense pride in the work of helping mother; the chairs look as if they have been drawn to the fireside on a thousand occasions for happy gossip and domestic festivities; and the poor old sombre bed sprawling on the floor in a dark corner, very shapeless and depressed, and if truth be told rather spongy, grimy, and squalid, looks as if the new souls born upon it and the old souls parting from it, generation after generation, have touched it with the mysteries of birth and death.

One meets in these cottages very old, shrunken, bent-over people, toothless and inarticulate, middle-aged, disenchanted, but courageous people, and young girls so beautiful, so fresh, so innocent, so shy, that they lay, as it were, an awe upon the soul of a stranger. But one sees seldom in these cottage homes young men at the threshold of life.

What kindness we received on our visits! How glad the people were to see the doctor! How pretty it was to watch him in talk with wide-eyed, blushing girls, or bending over the pillow of some smiling patriarch! And when the dark fell, and we were delayed on the road with trouble to our lamps, how willingly, and with what gracious courtesy, help came from a wayside cottage!

We went to a corner of the coast, where a thousand little isles floated mist-wrapt on moonlit waves that scarcely seemed to move, and here we stood for a few minutes looking towards Cape Clear while the doctor recited poetry in a low voice and the car that we had left behind us purred in a low monotone to the innumerable stars.

And then, at a great pace, with the cold wind in our teeth, and the golden ring round the moon deepening to orange, we sped through silent and sylvan country back to the market-town.

The Bishop had been obliged to go away that morning, and a priest was to come in and act host for me at the dinner-table. I found him waiting for me, a short, fat, rigid, high-shouldered, low-necked, red-faced, top-heavy man, whose immense and massive head—with its two little staring brown eyes deep buried in hard-hammered bone, and its little button of a mouth squeezed up to nothing under a nose like a blob of putty—seemed as if it had been shaped, roughly and impatiently shaped, out of granite by some Titan sick of Grecian prettiness. I never saw head so solid, dense, thick, and neckless on the squared, high shoulders of a body so brief and rigid.

Now I must tell you that every Catholic bishop who entertained me provided in my honour Gargantuan meals and battalions of bottles. Poor, humble, and simple in their habits, these warm-hearted people delight to load and overload their tables for the entertainment of a stranger.

So it came about that when the door opened and the housekeeper, having removed an excellent soup, came in with a great dish of smoking beef, then with a fizzling pair of roast chickens, then with a steaming roll of boiled bacon, then with potatoes in their jackets, cabbages cooked to a turn, onions that filled the firelit room with the rich and genial odours of a kitchen, and finally with a bottle of champagne that looked as if it had been corked and labelled only that very morning—it came about, I repeat, that my little, fat, high-shouldered host, whose eyes had been gradually blazing, whose little round lips were literally smacking with delight, and who seemed, indeed, as he put a terrific edge upon a mighty knife, as if he were snorting and pawing the ground to be off, was swept to a very zenith of stupefaction.

It was, I think, the appearance of the bottle of champagne, brought so calmly to the table by the pale and perspiring housekeeper, that blew him finally clean into the empyrean.

He sat suddenly bolt upright, knife and sharpener paralysed in mid-air, raised his huge head, regarded the housekeeper with an absolute incredulity, and demanded: "What! Champagne! Julia, are we to have champagne?"

"Yes, Father; his lordship said so; and—the liqueurs as well."

His shoulders went with a great thump against the back of his chair. Then, coming to himself, he exclaimed with a most fervent gratitude, a most genuine piety, his extraordinary face almost rigid with solemnity: "Glory be to God!"

At the next moment carving-fork and carving-knife were plunged into the ribs of beef, and my host was puffing and blowing at his work in a manner that made conversation seem a trivial, foolish thing.

## CHAPTER IV

### TESTIMONIES

I WAS talking one day to a brisk and voluble woman of business who entertains the very clearest notions on the religious question. She spoke to me with a whispering suggestion of mystery, now tapping my arm, or affectionately fingering one of my coat buttons, and now stepping back to regard the effect of her words on my sympathetic face. Occasionally she almost threw herself upon my bosom in the excess of her confidence, or in the exuberance of her matchless verbosity; and occasionally she caught my forearm to support herself in a nip of laughter. A tubby, fat, elderly lady, shrewd and capable, famous for the success of a rather unique establishment.

"Och, sure, there's bigotry in the north of Ireland," she told me, "but it isn't religious bigotry at all. Look, sir, I'll tell you what it is; 'tis just black-hearted bigotry. Thim Protestants have any God's quantity of money, and they dispise thim that haven't it. 'Tis that, sir, and 'tis nothing more. Och, they're terrible! Look, sir!—they wouldn't spit on you, if you'll pardon the expression, even if you was on fire; no, they wouldn't. Och, they're a dirty, proud, black-hearted lot; and it's God's truth I'm telling you; och, but it's terrible. You ought to see thim Protestants, so you did, driving with their motor-cars into the big towns, making a kick-up and all, and staring at poor folks, my dear darling sir, with such a look as they'd be sorry to die with. And how do they do it? Och, sure, they couldn't do it all if it wasn't for paying the people who works for thim the wages of poverty. Ten shillings a week! Half a crown for girls! Och, but it's terrible. Glory be to God, but that's true. Me own husband, sir—he'll soon be eight months dead, poor man—how did they treat him then? Och, 'tis the devil's own shame. Sure, sir, they came to me, his poor widow, and him hardly cold in his coffin, and demanded six hundred pounds of repairs on the house if I wanted to go on with the lease. It was that, sir, or I had to go into the streets without a house to me head. And what sort of property do they own? Och, 'tis nothing but dirty slums with a smell to 'em, my dear darling sir, that would scratch the very bottom of a decent stomach, yes, it would. Me own sister's son, sir, look at him then. He caught diphtheria in a tramcar from a man they call Shamus Dwyer, who was just out of hospital; and he was in hospital, me poor nephew was, for six weeks; and when he came out of hospital, look you, sir, he passed a boy they call William McGifferty, and he caught the scarlet fever from him. Now, in the name of God, is that religion, then? Whist, there's no religion about it at all. Look, sir, I know one of thim Protestant families in the North, great folks, and I'll tell you what I've seen in their house with me own eyes as God is my Judge. There's a picture in the library, just at the side of the door as you go in, and 'tis a priest, sir, in his full vestments as I'm a living woman, saying the Mass It's there to this day, sir. Look at that now. It's God's truth I'm telling you. Och, but it's terrible. And phwat do you think of this ? One of their ladies, sir—such a poor and meagre soul ye niver saw since God made ye, and dressed up with her silk stockings that cost a fortune, and shoes and petticoats the saints would have blushed to see, a kind of a dandy woman, and ugly, my dear darling sir, you never saw an uglier, flat-chested, yellow-faced old harridan in your born days ; och, terrible ! told me, sir, she told me her very self as true as I'm a living woman that she was only waiting for her husband to die to have a real grand time of it—look at that now ! You must excuse me laughing ! Och, 'twould have split a herring to hear of it ! When her husband died, sir, the money was tied up as tight as a whelk ! She was worse off than when he was a living man ! Och, you should have seen her weeds, they was shameful for a virtuous woman.

"They talk of religion, but, my dear sir, the North's full of Home Rule. Faith, but it's the same all the world over. Och, sure ! You can't live in the country and not see the need of it. Thim Protestants are a hard people. Grasping people, they are. Faith, they'd squeeze the blood out of a brick. And the pride of thim, the sinful pride ! Maybe you saw it in the paper and maybe you didn't, but in one of the Ulster towns, just a little time ago, the Catholics made a J.P. of a bill-poster ! Och, you nivir heard such a cry-out ! I think his name was Jerry O'Meara—a decent, honest, well-liked sort of a fellow, but going round with his paste-pot and brush. The Resident Magistrate was a Protestant colonel, and one day he was sentencing a man for being drunk, when a little meek voice says at the side of him, 'I object to the sintince, it's too hard for the offince.' He was a very fierce-looking man, the magistrate, and he wore a glass that made him worse than he was, and he turns round of a sudden, and he scowls like the very divil himself, 'And who are you ?' he asks in a voice of thunder. And thin, smiling like a cherub, and speaking as meek as a lamb, Jerry says, 'A'm O'Meara, the Jah Pee !' Faith, sir, the whole court burst into a fit of laughter and the poor magistrate dropped his glass and looked as poor as a piece of bread on the end of a toasting-fork.

"Och, but there's good men among the Protestants. I'm not saying they're all given to the divil ; not at all. Look, sir, there's one or two of the sort up in County Derry who might have been sent by Heaven to help poor people. Good landlords, good Christian people. But why is it ? Faith, sir, they know there's a God above thim. That's how it is. And if they're not for Home Rule, they're not very far off of it, and you'll nivir hear of thim saying cruel things of the poor Catholics, and you'll nivir hear of thim oppressing any human creature on the earth, Protestant or Catholic.

"I say this, sir, Why can't people leave other people alone? Why should they always be wanting to interfere? Faith, a man's religion is born with him, and he can't help himself. And it isn't what a man says he believes that makes a pennyworth of difference; it's just how he lives. Do you think God spends all His time listening to the arguments of the Protestants. Not at all! Not at all! Sure, God Almighty doesn't care what we think; it's the heart of a man He'd have clean and sweet; and I say a Catholic may have a bad heart and a Protestant may have a good heart, and it's helping people, being kind to people, that gets a soul into heaven when all's said and done. So why do they always go arguing and sniffing at poor Catholics? Isn't it enough for thim that they've got the blood-money out of working people, and ride in their motor-cars, and go to a town I know very well, which 'tis nothing more than a bad place, a kind of a rendezvous, you understand me—och, 'tis a terrible place. Wouldn't it be better, my dear darling sir, if we had Home Rule, and a little peace and quiet, and all set about helping those that are poor and in the want of things? That's how I look at it. And as for religious bigotry, sure, sir, I tell ye, there's no such thing; 'tis nothing more than a proud stomach."

A less impassioned and perhaps a more informing presentation of this great matter was offered to me by a Protestant man of business in a pretty considerable town of the south of Ireland—such a town as the lady above would surely call "a kind of a rendezvous."

He is a man some sixty years of age, a spare, lithe, grey-headed figure, lean-faced, grey-eyed, grey-bearded, the colour of his skin a tinge of grey, the note of the whole man vigorous, alert, trenchant. All his live he has lived in Ireland, and all his life he has avoided politics. He is first and foremost a successful, keen, ambitious, and enterprising man of business.

He laughed away the suggestion that under Home Rule Ireland would become a difficult country for Protestants.

"I assure you," he told me, "the Catholics of Ireland are the kindest-hearted and the pleasantest people in the world. I prefer them infinitely, *infinitely*, to the people of my own religion. In fact, so narrow, and bigoted, and political are the Protestants of this town that I now very seldom go to church; I find myself every year more and more drawn towards the Catholics. I have often thought that I am in danger of seceding. But like a great many other people here, I'm drawn to Catholics and repelled by Catholic dogma. I like Catholics immensely, but I cannot bring myself to swallow what they teach. As for Catholic intolerance—that is the purest moonshine. I do not know anything that more disgusts me with our Protestants than their shameful use of this detestable invention.

There is excuse for you in England, but none for Protestants in Ireland. You in England might imagine the Catholics would try to pay off old scores under Home Rule, but the Protestants here know perfectly well that the Catholics are far more charitable, far more tolerant, far more courteous and well-behaved than themselves. When they talk about Catholic intolerance they say what they know to be untrue. I don't know how theologians would classify such statements, but in business we should call them lies.

"The truth is, our Protestant clergy are very second-rate people, they are really the fools of the family; not having any solid depth of character and precious little genuine enthusiasm for the life, they turn themselves into theologians, make themselves the violent pamphleteers of a fighting Protestantism. It sickens me, really sickens me, to go to church on Sunday and hear a sermon preached, not about the Life, but about the dogmas of Rome. That is what our sermons are, a perpetual attack on Roman dogma. It gives religion the narrow and un-Christlike spirit of party politics. How people stay for Communion after listening to these frothy, scornful, and embittered diatribes I cannot think; for myself, I come out of church in a thoroughly disgusted spirit.

"Some time ago a friend of mine was taken very ill and had to keep his bed. He was a Protestant, and a man of some importance. The rector of the parish called to see him. The first utterance of the reverend gentleman was an angry exclamation at sight of a picture on the bedroom wall. 'What!' said he; 'you have got a picture of a priest up here!' 'Not a priest,' said the invalid, 'but a Christian brother.' 'Humph! you must be very fond of him, he must be a very great friend, to have his picture in your bedroom.' 'Yes,' said the other, 'he was a very great friend of mine, but it isn't for that reason I keep his picture in my room; it is because he was the truest, noblest, simplest, and purest Christian I have ever known, and I like to see his face, like to think about his life, the last thing at night and the first thing in the morning.' This Christian brother, I must tell you, was the famous Brother Burke; the holy and beautiful old man who introduced science and technical instruction into schools long before anybody else, and who made the North Monastery in Cork one of the most famous schools in Europe. People came from all over the world to see his museum, his laboratory, and his technical rooms. And the poor worshipped him; they adored him. His funeral in Cork was like a king's. Every shop was closed. A multitude followed the hearse. Women and children from the slums cried as the procession passed.

"And yet that rector regarded it as a sin that the photograph of such a man—a man who lived the life of a Saint Francis, who so humbly, modestly, beautifully, and tenderly followed in the footsteps of his Master—should hang in a Protestant bedroom! That will give you some idea of the dismal abyss of Protestantism in the south of Ireland.

"Believe me, it is Protestants and only Protestants who make religion a part of politics. Catholics have no warmer welcome than for a Protestant who shares the national aspiration for Home Rule. I know myself the Protestant manager of a big shop in Cork, one of the biggest shops in the town, who gives up his private room to a Catholic bishop from the country when that gentleman visits the town and wants to see people on business. The bishop walks into the room with a smile, and says, 'Now, my friend, out you go: no more pounds, shillings, and pence: I want your room for the souls of people'; and the manager laughs and goes. He tells me that the bishop makes him realize the force of the Christian life more than any of his own clergy, who only come to see him when they want subscriptions.

"Cork, by the way, is a town you ought to see. The principal street, and a very handsome one too, Patrick Street, contains hardly a single Catholic shop. The Protestants, who are in an absolute minority, long ago collared all the best sites and laid the foundation of their trade; and their prosperity depends absolutely upon the custom of Catholics. There is not a Protestant in Cork who can deny that fact. The custom of Protestants would not pay the rents of those shops. Now is it not monstrous, with demonstrations of this kind before their eyes, not merely staring them in the face, but interwoven into the very commerce of their daily lives, is it not monstrous for Protestants to talk about Catholic intolerance?

"No; the cry of intolerance is a sham, and a very mean sham at that.

"I will tell you something more. In family life the Catholics are superior to the Protestants. The purity of their women is extraordinary. I am convinced that Catholicism is essential to morals in Ireland. I should look with horror on any decay of Catholic power. And I will tell you why I say that. We see in towns like this the return of a good many Irish emigrants. They come back with fine clothes, pretentious manners, a sort of drawling contempt for their own people, and with no rigid sense of purity. America gives them money with one hand, and takes away their moral code with the other. Of course there are exceptions. But what I tell you is strictly true of the average emigrant. And this is the proof of it. Precious few emigrants, however well off, remain in the country. They take a look round, leave a little money behind them, and go back to the States. Ireland is too dull. Why is it too dull? Because the women are pure, because the home is the centre of the national life, and because religion exercises a real authority. For a man with no moral code, Ireland is the dullest country in the world; for a man who believes in God, it is one of the most beautiful.

"This is a strange thing, which has often puzzled me: in works of philanthropy, in organized charity, the Catholics are far behind us, so far indeed that one might almost say they are indifferent to the matter. On the other hand, the Protestants think of hardly anything else. It is not only the spirit of their religion, but a part of their propaganda. Examine the accounts of our Protestant parishes and you would think they were nothing else but the scenes of benevolent activity, you would think that Protestantism was a living and victorious faith, that Catholicism was exhausted and dying. And yet, Protestantism is waning in Ireland. You never hear of Catholics becoming Protestants, but you do hear, and fairly frequently too, of Protestants becoming Catholics. I've told you that I myself should turn Catholic but for the impossible dogmas that drive me out of the idea. In spite of all the philanthropy of the Protestants and in spite of all the vigour and energy of their charities, I would become a Catholic to-morrow if it were not for dogmas that repel me. And why is that? Because no man can live in Ireland without feeling that Catholics—whatever they believe intellectually—are nearer to the life of Christ, while Protestants—however ardent their philanthropic activity—have failed to win the spirit of their Master. Protestant as I am in my intellect, I should regard it as the very greatest disaster that could overtake this nation were it to become Protestant. And much as I should regret from an intellectual point of view the total conversion of Irish Protestants to the Catholic religion, still I should not be able to deny the conviction that such a revolution would make for the moral grandeur and the sweeter manners of the nation.

"It will give you an idea of Protestant intolerance when I tell you, a man in my position, that I dare not, dare not, from a business point of view, declare myself a Home Ruler. If I did so I should certainly lose three-fourths of my Protestant clients. The Catholics come to me, knowing that I am a Protestant, and ignorant that I give my vote at every election for Home Rule. Now, does not this alone convince you that bigotry and intolerance are on the side of Protestants?"

He told me that very often he spends his holidays in bicycling through the west of Ireland, and that every experience of this kind deepens in his mind the sense of that beauty and purity of Irish life which must certainly strike the mind of every intelligent visitor from England. " I have been," he said, " in tiny hovels where the only decency in the sleeping arrangements was a pile of old biscuit tins between the beds of parents and children, of big boys and big girls ; and those people, I assure you, are more nice in their virtue, more exquisite in their chastity, than many better educated people with every advantage that wealth confers. It is this kind of thing which has made so deep an impression on my mind. It is unavoidable, and it is, at least I find it so, extraordinarily persuasive. The Catholics have the secret of the moral life."

It was my pleasure to have a conversation on this subject with Mr. William O'Brien, no great lover just now of the Irish priesthood.

Mr. O'Brien has something of the aspect of a prophet. His hair is long, his moustache and beard, I imagine, do not often go to the barber, and he is a little unorthodox in the matter of raiment.

You are tempted to think, while he is talking, that the man is one of the most genial, tolerant, and good-humoured enthusiasts that ever lived. The low voice is cordial and placating, the broad, heavy-featured, pale face is wrinkled into a smile that seems to have grown there from infancy, waxing sweeter and wider in its charity with the greying of his hair ; behind their spectacles his little twinkling eyes under their twitching long-haired brows overflow with the philanthropy and urbanity of a citizen of the world. No man could be nicer for a tea-party.

But with the last full-stop of his talking, instantaneously, just as if a string had been suddenly jerked from inside, the smile sweeps from the face, the features become set, the eyebrows stand rigid over eyes that have become hard as steel, the cordial waving hands fall to a grip on the knees, he regards you with a fixed stare that is inhuman, and with little impatient noises in the throat he sits like a statue, cold and motionless as stone, not so much hearing what you have to say, as obviously waiting to spring off with something fresh of his own. In these moments, in these brief pauses between the cascade of his smiling, tolerant, and philanthropic eloquence, you realize that the man is a true fanatic—if he will forgive me for saying so, a veritable Mad Mullah of Irish politics.

The reader must imagine in what follows that " William " is sitting politely on the edge of a little chair, leaning towards his visitor, speaking in a low and pleasant voice at great speed, with little hurrying gasps between the sentences, smiling cherubically, now spreading his nice white hands in the air, like a conjurer, and now rubbing them softly and purringly together as though he were giving everybody in the world £500 a year and was explaining how he has just concluded a most admirable contract for the refreshment tent in a millennial Paradise to be opened by himself at three clock this very afternoon.

He gives one no impression of a man fighting against most desperate odds, but rather of a man riding on the crest of a sunlit wave. You would never think that he has burned his boats, is in arms against a solid phalanx of his former friends, that he is in danger, perhaps imminent danger, of overwhelming disaster.

"I deplore disunion wherever it occurs," he declaims; "disunion in social life, in family life, in religion, in politics. Differences must always exist, but where those differences make for strife they are terrible, they should be removed. And I believe in a peaceable settlement of every difficulty in the world. I want peace to sweeten existence as well as to heal old wounds. I am an evolutionist in politics; I don't believe in keeping up old feuds and old hostilities; I believe in growing away from the past into something better. No one can say that I have not fought for the cause. I have fought and agitated with all my might. I have been in battles where we routed the enemy horse, foot, and artillery, in others where our forces were smashed into dust. In those days fighting was necessary. I remember very well when King Edward came to Ireland as Prince of Wales. The first row he ever saw in his life was here in Cork. We organized it on purpose. We wanted to show him our real feelings. We paid him the compliment of truth. There was such a shindy at the railway station that some of his friends wanted him to go back; it was, as I have told you, the very first row he had ever seen. But although he turned white and looked scared to death, he came bravely through the howling crowds at the station, and entered a carriage. What did he find? A complete absence of crowds in the streets; a frightful silence throughout the whole city; and all the windows draped in black. His procession was like a funeral. An old woman came from a court entry and hurled a potato at him—marvellous to relate, it hit him. That was the only incident. For the rest it was silence, emptiness, death—a city in mourning. Well, we converted him! Yes, I am told that Cork converted him. He went back to England convinced that the Irish people were sincere in their cry for freedom, and ever after he was a loyal friend of Home Rule.

"But days for that kind of thing have passed. Old methods give way to new methods. You would not send soldiers armed with bows and arrows to engage an enemy armed with rifles. My dear friends of former days apparently want to go on in the old way; they believe in the draped windows, the mourning, and the hurled potato. Now, I don't agree with them at all. I believe in drawing all classes together, in offering the warmest friendship to those moving in our direction. I think that Lord Dunraven has acted magnificently; I think the party ought to have given him their very heartiest gratitude. Why stand aloof? Why keep up the old estrangements? Why insist on the very letter of your demand? Why not try conciliation, a seeking of agreement, a give and take, an amicable undertaking? I am persuaded that if the Nationalists took up this position we should soon have the whole country pulling together, and both parties in England agreed about Home Rule.

"The religious question is a manufactured one. It is deplorable and disgraceful. I am simply amazed by Edward Carson's obscurantism. He is a man who despises more heartily than anybody else in the House of Commons Tory ignorance of Ireland; and yet he takes up this shameful cry, apparently he believes in it, and he stands out against a rational government. I cannot understand it. Amazing, amazing! Edward Carson is a very intelligent man. He is not a genuine bigot. I believe he is absolutely honest, and I know very well that he has a most thorough contempt for the English Tory's ignorance of Ireland. Is it not a most amazing position?

"But, you know, religious intolerance is the ruin of the North. They have splendid qualities up there, they develop some very fine sides of human character, but they are lacking in charm, in sweetness and light, in universality. Their narrowness and rigidity is most distressing—oh, most distressing! In the south of Ireland it is different. We lack a great many of their qualities, to our considerable loss, but we are more civilized, we are nicer people to live with, the least of our peasants has a touch of the grand manner in comparison with those insensate bigots of the North.

"You ask me about the priests. Well, to begin with, they are very bad politicians. Some of them are just awakening to that fact. We are teaching them the lesson here in Cork. They went against me, solid; but the people would take no ruling from them. I heard of one poor woman here who told a priest to his face that he was very good for her soul, but no use at all for her politics. Oh, the priests have immense power; but only in the moral sphere is that power unquestioned. It has always been questioned, and very often openly withstood, in politics; but never in morals. They are the very finest shepherds in the world, but sometimes precious bad politicians—oh, very bad!

"You must know that the rock of the Church in Ireland is the chastity of the priests. The Church would go to pieces to-morrow if the priests were immoral. There is one thing the Irish people, gifted with great imagination as they are, cannot understand—and that is an immoral priest. In the whole course of my long life I have only known of two cases of impurity among Irish priests—only two. And if those cases had not been summarily dealt with the whole country would have been in arms. No; they are a very wonderful body of men. I do not think there is a more honest priesthood in Christendom. They have failings. Some of them are rather ignorant, and rather lazy, and there is perhaps more drinking among some of them than is altogether good. But the Irish people, the most virtuous, can understand and forgive a priest who tipples. The worst could not forgive an immoral priest. You hear them say, 'Och, the poor Father, sure if he does take a drop too much now and again, isn't it a lonely life the poor man lives, with no wife, and no children, and him so far away from learned folk? dreary's the day for him, and God knows it.' The Irish peasant is more subtle than the English in his distinctions. He lays much more importance on qualities of the spirit than on abstinence from merely selfish or really dangerous habits. But chastity for them is the very bed-rock of all spiritual qualities. They cannot imagine how an immoral priest can possibly be sincere.

"People who do not live in Ireland find it very difficult to understand the Catholicism of the Irish nation. It is different from the Catholicism of Europe—more childlike, trusting, and satisfied. Liberal ideas have not touched the primitive faith of the Irish people; so far as the peasants are concerned neither science nor literature has had the smallest influence on their religious life. No; the New Theology is unknown; Modernism has not gained the smallest foothold. Christ, you may be quite certain, is accepted absolutely as God. There is no question about that. And everything taught by the Church is cherished and believed as utterly as if the Almighty Himself had spoken it.

"The rebellion of the Irish nation against the tyranny of England in ancient days was the natural outburst of a kind-hearted people to whom tyranny of any kind is unthinkable. That such people will ever become tyrants is not to be imagined. It is part of the very childlike character of their faith to be tender, warm-hearted, and loving. No man who knows the Catholics of Ireland can believe for a moment that they will exercise the power of their majority against the Protestants. Even if the priests should urge them to such wickedness—a thing beyond belief—they would resent the idea with the whole force and energy of their nature."

I have often said to Englishmen who fear Catholic intolerance under Home Rule: "The Irish people have been known throughout history as the kindest in the world; why should they become tyrants in the twentieth century?" The answer has been: "Oh, it isn't the people; the people have to do what the priests tell them." But the Irish priest is an Irishman, drawn almost invariably from the kind-hearted peasantry, and if the people have no seeds of tyranny in their blood neither have the priests.

## CHAPTER V

### A QUAKER'S PARLOUR

One night I arrived, a few minutes before the hour of dinner, at an old-fashioned hotel in a rather prosperous and awakening garrison town of Southern Ireland. Among the letters awaiting me was one that had not come through the post, a local letter, the address written in a thin, stiff, careful hand, the top of the envelope marked with elaborate instructions for immediate delivery.

This letter came from an eminent Quaker in the town, who had been advised by a friend of my arrival. It requested me, after I had dined and rested, to come and spend an hour with him at his house—the directions for finding this house occupying the greater part of the letter. Among other things, I was told that a street lamp stood opposite the door, so that I should have no difficulty in reading the name of the house, which was plainly lettered. A nice, kind, thoughtful, and considerate letter, but with something in it that rather chastened my natural good spirits.

I traced the house, advanced up a dark path, found myself confronted by a sombre big door, and timidly pulled the iron bell-handle. In a minute the door was opened by my host himself.

In the feeble gaslight of the hall he looked like a spectre, and even in the warm lamp-lighted parlour, into which he conducted me with a somewhat jerky and nervous hastiness, there seemed to me an aspect of inhumanity about this good and worthy man. Tall, thin, emaciated, of a cadaverous complexion, and with something vulture-like in the crouch of his neck, something inexorable and merciless in the curved rigidity of his spine, he made me feel at once that I must not sit at ease in my chair, that I certainly should not be asked to smoke, and that our conversation was like to be as stiff, dangerous, and mechanical as a cross-examination. He wore steel-rimmed spectacles; his greying brown beard descended to the third waist-coat button; his clothes were a worn black; on his feet were carpet-slippers.

There was another person in the room, my host's sister. He sat upon one side of the fireplace, I on the other, and behind us, seated at the table and close to the lamp, with a big basket of needlework before her, sat the sister, spectacled, silent, busy. I could hear, in the pauses of our conversation, the tiny griding of her needle against the thimble, the drawing of the thread through linen, and the crumpling of the material as she humped it into a fresh position.

The room was strictly Victorian. The solid chairs, the big table covered by a dull red cloth, the woollen antimacassars, the thick curtains drawn across the closed windows, the heavy mantelpiece, the big-framed story pictures, and the drilled rows of heavy volumes in the glass-panelled bookcase—these things, and the closeness of the atmosphere, the exceeding primness of the arrangements, the awful quiet and peace of the room, filled me with a sense of my own irreverence. I never knew a clock to tick so slowly, so sleepily, so eternally, as the square dark marble clock in the middle of the mantelpiece.

I longed for the door to burst open, for a child to come running in, for a dog to bark at me, even for a cat to curl itself up on the black hearthrug in front of the fire. But the fire burned steadily on, the curtains remained unruffled by a breath of air, my rigid host regarded me with the air of a vulture, and from over my shoulder came, with the warm lamplight, the scratching of needle and thimble.

It is not my purpose to give the reader a full account of our conversation ; I have merely dwelt upon the aspect of my host and the character of this Irish interior to suggest to his mind the spirit of Irish Quakerdom. I am sure the reader, had he been in my place, would have felt that here was a man, and here was an atmosphere, likely to be at discord with the national aspirations of Irish Catholics.

But on the contrary. Although sentiment, apparently, plays no part in the machinery of this gentleman's mind, he is altogether on the side of Home Rule ; and far from having anything to say against the Catholics of Ireland, he confesses with a grim humour, chuckling metallically, that he could wish his fellow-Protestants were a trifle more Catholic in their virtues.

He told me that Home Rule is a matter of business. As a man of business he criticizes and condemns the present system. There can be no substantial advance in Irish industry, he avers, while the capitalists of the country are subject to the uncertainty of Downing Street. A man is not going to invest money in Ireland while its government is tethered to a clerk's desk in London. There must be something settled and secure in the government of a country before men will embark in great enterprises. It will probably take fifteen years after Ireland has secured Home Rule before capital feels itself secure. But then the country will go ahead at a great rate. There is no doubt of that. The natural advantages are enormous. The character of the people is a guarantee of prosperity.

Before I knew where I was, he suddenly carried the battle into my own camp. With a malicious smile in his eyes, sardonic laughter under his beard, he demanded to know on what possible grounds England could refuse self-government to Ireland. He spoke of South Africa, and insisted that I should give a reasonable reply to his challenge. He quoted statistics to prove that Ireland was the most crimeless nation in Europe. On what ground, then, on what possible ground, could England refuse Home Rule to Ireland? Did England think the Irish were savages? Did she imagine they were not able to look after their own affairs—like a parcel of children? Did she truly believe that Ireland would cut herself out of the empire and one day appear at London Bridge in German cruisers?

My answer to this onslaught—it is a very terrible experience for a man in a Quaker's parlour to find himself suddenly called upon to defend the honour and intelligence of Mother England—drew from my host a very remarkable statement, a statement the truth and likelihood of which I have since confirmed all over Ireland.

I said to him: "You must remember that the Englishmen who have to decide this question are very ordinary people, poor men, for the most part, struggling to make two ends meet, exceedingly anxious for more pressing reforms at home, and entirely ignorant of Ireland. It would have been different, I think, if Irish members of Parliament had produced a different impression on those English people. The average Englishman in the matter of politics acts almost wholly by instinct. And his instinct concerning Ireland, got from the hurly-burly of Irish politicians at Westminster, has so far been against Home Rule."

The Quaker replied: "But does the average Englishman imagine that under Home Rule an Irish Parliament will be composed of the men now at Westminster?"

"I think he does. Is it not the case?"

The Quaker laughed. "There are some very able men," he replied, "among the Irish members, some very clever, shrewd, capable fellows; but the bulk is not representative of Ireland. Those men are our servants. We hire them, we employ them, and we send them to Westminster with one definite object, an object for which they are excellently fitted. We send them there to hold up your Parliamentary machine. We send them to do the rough-and-tumble work of making England sick of the Irish question. And when Home Rule is a fact, their work will be done, their job will be over; they will subside to their natural place in the body politic. No; the Irish Parliament will be composed almost solely of business and professional men. Throughout the country there are men of weight and position who will enter politics, men who will not be ashamed to become politicians when Irish politics is a science of government. You cannot expect such men to waste their time over work at Westminster which a second-rate person can do better than they could do it themselves. You must remember that the men of whom I am speaking are men of very real parts; Ireland is a civilized country; our merchants and our traders are rational creatures. We shall have a Parliament quite capable of looking after our affairs. You need have no misgiving on that head. Ireland will be governed in such a way as to encourage the investment of capital and to increase our commercial prosperity. The demand for Home Rule is chiefly for this purpose. The present arrangement is bad business, it is ruinous. As a business community we want something better."

He spoke with warm admiration of certain Irish members of Parliament, but he was emphatic in his affirmation that the ruck would have no place in the politics of a self-governing Ireland. He said that there were plenty of men connected with railways, with mills, with factories, with land, and with the learned professions who would only be too glad to enter an Irish Parliament and devote their powers to Irish prosperity.

As I have said, I found that other men in Ireland confirmed this statement. From one end of the country to the other I came across business men who told me with an equal emphasis of conviction that an Irish Parliament would be composed of the most capable and responsible citizens.

I asked the Quaker if he had no misgiving on the head of Catholic intolerance.

"There is no such thing," he answered, "except in the imagination of Orangemen."

"You think that Catholics will be fair and just?"

"They are fair and just now, why should they be anything else under Home Rule? They could boycott us now, they could make it impossible for us to live, without breaking the law in any way they could drive every one of us out of the south of Ireland. Our bread-and-butter, do you not see, depends upon them. We are only a handful, they are a multitude. But they trade with us, they show us consideration, and they manifest no resentment against our prosperity. I find them in business singularly straightforward and honest. I wish I could say the same thing of all the Protestants. Now, why should people who for centuries have lived with us on the most amicable terms, who might have ostracized us, who might have boycotted and ruined us without incurring the smallest danger, and who, by our ruin, might have gained our prosperity—why should they suddenly, just because Ireland manages her own affairs, put us to the sword? The idea is preposterous! In spite of the contempt shown to them by certain Protestants, they have always manifested to us a feeling of respect and friendliness. I have a great admiration for the virtue and honesty of Irish Catholics."

I am sure the average Englishman who has given little thought to Ireland will be impressed by the fact that there are Quakers living in that country who are in favour of Home Rule. I hope that what is written above may have weight with English Protestants. And to emphasize this striking fact of Quaker confidence in Irish Catholics, I will take leave to quote in conclusion of this chapter a letter written by a prominent and substantial Tipperary Quaker to the *Spectator* on the subject of Catholic intolerance. No just man, after reading this letter, can surely believe the wicked and shameful insinuations with which certain unscrupulous Protestants living peaceably in Catholic Ireland have sought to traduce, for the gross sake of social ascendancy, their fellow-Christians.

This is the letter, written by Mr. Ernest Grubb, of Carrick-on-Suir :—

"Sir,—My attention has been directed to a letter from Miss Anne W. Richardson, of Moyallah, Co. Down, in your issue of March 18th last, which contained statements as to the state of feeling existing between Roman Catholics and Protestants in the south of Ireland.

"Miss Richardson may be an authority as to the state of affairs in the north-east of Ireland, but she has not lived in the south of Ireland, and she has not had the experience of social life there that I have had.

"I must be somewhat egotistical in order to establish my claim to be a competent witness, one who can give reliable evidence on this question. I am a member of the Society of Friends, and have spent my life as a trader at Carrick-on-Suir, Clonmel, etc., in the south-east of Ireland. I have taken an active part in the public life of my neighbourhood. I am a Justice of the Peace for the counties of Tipperary and Waterford, and have been for many years an elected member (and Chairman) of the County Council of Tipperary South and the Urban Council of Carrick-on-Suir and other public bodies. Ninety to ninety-eight per cent. of my constituents are Roman Catholics, and if 'religious intolerance' existed I would not have been chosen for these positions. As regards the willingness of Roman Catholics to elect Protestants to public boards, I may add that a Protestant Unionist and a Quaker lady were (the latter for many years) elected guardians of the poor at Carrick-on-Suir. A Quaker Unionist has for many years been vice-chairman of the Board of Guardians at Clonmel, and I could give instances of Roman Catholics, including priests, writing to place Protestants in posts of profit and responsibility when they were suitable for such appointments.

"With reference to Miss Richardson's statement about Water ford, the Salvation Army ladies there told me yesterday that they hold their open-air meetings without molestation, sometimes wearing uniform. One or two police are at times present as spectators, and this good order has prevailed for a long time.

"The case of the Salvation Army officer who was injured on Waterford Quay about the year 1900 is an isolated occurrence, and if I remember rightly, tactfulness might have prevented friction. Within my own knowledge, two or more preachers, some in clerical costume, pray and preach at fairs in this district. They are listened to quietly, and are not molested; although they stand in the way of traffic, the country people drive their carts round them. It would be impossible to picture a better and more Christian reception. The fair folk are one hundred to one Roman Catholics.

"Three or four Protestants have, within the last few years, taken farms in this district previously occupied by Roman Catholics, and their relations with their Roman Catholic neighbours have been altogether harmonious.

"My father and mother and their family lived here through the disturbances in 1848 in William Smith O'Brien's time, and afterwards through the period of the Fenian troubles, but we never had any difficulty with our neighbours or any insult offered to us.

"I have, personally, no fear that whatever legislative changes may take place in the arrangements for the government of Ireland there will be anything to prevent Roman Catholics and Protestants from living harmoniously together in the land of their birth.—I am, sir, etc.,

"J. ERNEST GRUBB.

"Carrick-on-Suir, Ireland."

The *Cork Constitution*, the principal Unionist journal in those parts of Ireland, quoting Mr. Grubb's view that whatever legislative changes might take place, there would be nothing to prevent Protestants and Roman Catholics from living harmoniously together, adds (May 2nd, 1911):

"Few will be found ready to take serious exception to this statement, for it is not so much religious as political intolerance that is feared by the minority in Ireland."

Of this remarkable admission, Mr. Stephen Gwynn has justly said: "What the *Cork Constitution* means by political intolerance is, that Irish County Councils will elect as public officers persons in sympathy with their own political views. If this be persecution, then political persecution is universally practised in Great Britain."

I believe there have always been more Protestant Home Rulers in the Irish Parliamentary party than Roman Catholics in the rest of the House of Commons. "*For more than a hundred years the majority of leaders of the Irish people in the struggle for national free-*

*dom have been Protestants.*" Surely that should be enough to settle the question for Protestants in England. The majority of leaders have been Protestants.

## CHAPTER VI

### FENIAN, LAWYER, AND EARL

I DROVE one day in the south of Ireland a matter of twenty Irish miles to dine and sleep with a member of Parliament. My baggage was corded to the front of the car, and the jarvey on the right side and I on the left, behind a chestnut mare that tugged at the bit without a stop the whole length of the journey, scarcely exchanged a word. But for the exciting pace of the horse and the stimulating beauty of the country, this would have been the very dullest of my journeys.

"She is a fine mare," I said admiringly. "She is that, sorr," said the jarvey. After a considerable pause: "She doesn't seem to mind the hills." "She does not, sorr." Another pause. "This is beautiful country." "Och, it's well enough, sorr." Another and a longer pause. Then, very encouragingly: "Do you have excitement down here at election times?" "None at all, sorr."

A thoughtful hostess had given me a packet of gingerbreads for this cold drive, and I offered my jarvey the freedom of the bag. He helped himself with a momentary smile, and then became as grim as a mute, munching in a silence which could only have been broken with considerable danger. So we rattled along without speech, up hill and down dale, bumping and swinging through the cold air, till the twilight of a winter's afternoon settled upon the quiet earth.

My host, a solicitor, inhabits a handsome red-bricked house in a Georgian-looking terrace which would, I think, have pleased the eye of Thackeray. This terrace, with tall railings and steep steps to the doors, is only separated from a double-barrelled river by the road, a plot of grass, and a line of stately poplars. The island which divides the broad river is almost opposite the door. Standing before this tall and reeded door one hears the rush of water at a weir on the opposite side of the island, and nearer, the rustle of the dark poplars at the river's edge. On the further side of the river, dimly seen through the trees, are gentle hills planted with homesteads. A prettier prospect for the office windows of a solicitor I have never seen.

The door was opened by an elderly gentlewoman, who announced herself to be my host's housekeeper, and who conducted me, with a somewhat elaborate but most picturesque ritual of hospitality, to the floor above. In a large and lofty apartment, I found one end of a long table laid for dinner, while the other end was piled with books, which were not solely legal or Parliamentary. A huge coal-fire blazed in the grate. The windows were shuttered, the curtains drawn. Comfortable chairs stood on either side of the hearth. Cigarettes and matches were set ready on the mantelpiece.

My host, I was told, would soon be back, was indeed already overdue. He had gone to a meeting some few miles away, but he was driving a couple of horses and it could not now be long before he returned. The housekeeper expressed as much anxiety for my comfort and entertainment as solicitude for the dinner she was preparing in the kitchen.

I sat by the fire convinced that Ireland was the most silent country in the world. Then I fetched a book of Irish poems from the table, and read it nearly through. Occasionally the housekeeper mounted the stairs to express her growing anxiety and offer fresh apologies for the inconvenience I was suffering; then she would disappear, muttering, to look after her imperilled cooking. An hour of silence passed away. . . .

Presently the sound of trotting hoofs and rumbling wheels was heard in the night outside, and—yes, they stopped below the windows. I heard voices; the horses trotted away; a key was turned in the lock of the front door; the door closed with a handsome thud; voices ascended to me, and steps began to mount the stairs.

My host entered, quick, alert, pleasant, apologetic—a small, precise, trim-bearded, eye-glassed man, full of capacity and restrained force. He was followed by a slow-moving, heavy-shouldered, and solemn giant—a brother Member of Parliament.

Then came the explanation. There had been trouble at the meeting. When they arrived at the place, they found the people in a ferment and a body of police in occupation. The meeting had been proscribed! It was a gathering called to protest against the handling of certain grazing ground, and somebody in the neighbourhood had evidently telegraphed to Dublin Castle expressing alarm. That was enough. The result was a legion of warlike constables under the generalship of a County Inspector.

"And consider, sir, the fatuity as well as the scandalous insult of the proceeding," said the giant, appealing to my judgment. "The order forbade us to hold the meeting at a certain spot, but did not say that we were not to hold it at another. Could anything on God's earth be more foolish than that? 'Do I understand, Mr. Inspector,' I asked—I know the man well, and he's a very good fellow—'that your order forbids me to address these people, my constituents, Mr. Inspector, forbids me to address my constituents at this one spot, and not at that spot over there, ten yards away?' He ad mitted such was the case. But I was not to be fobbed off. Standing there, and addressing myself to the Inspector, I said all I wanted to say, and I said it with the greater force inspired by this disgraceful provocation. In fact, I made a speech ! The people crowded about us, and they were willing enough to resent the insult offered to me and to my honourable friend here ; but we held them in check. I told the Inspector that but for us, but for our restraining influence on the side of law and order, his presence there, and the presence of his constables, might have led to bloodshed. ' Take note,' I said, ' that we have ordered the people to keep the peace, and helped *you* to do your duty.' Then we walked across the road and held our meeting ! "

There was no hysterical excitement about these two heroes of a proscribed meeting. The giant was scornful, satirical, indignant. The lawyer was amused, and laughed as he gave his version of the adventure. We sat down to roast chickens in the best of good-humours. Silence was dissipated. Ireland had found her tongue.

I said that it would be an amusing day for Ireland when Lord Londonderry and Sir Edward Carson were run in for ferocious and inciting language—a brace of Pistols more dangerous, I was sure, than my present friends. The giant raised his huge hands, opened his eyes wide, and shook his head with reproach. " Leave them alone, sir, leave them alone. You know what the Irish constable said to the excitable gentleman at a meeting. ' Look here,' says he, ' if you don't behave yourself,' he says, ' I won't run you in ! ' Oh no, leave them alone. But, I understand. You're joking ; of course, of course."

I discovered that this giant, a most respected man, and a former mayor of the town, had been a Fenian. Conversation worked round to the old days of Irish agitation, and the giant held the field with stately eloquence. His iron-grey hair made an excellent foil to the purple of his skin ; the large eyes, now kindly with age, had once been fierce and challenging ; he wore a moustache, and looked like some old heavy-shouldered Prussian general who had soldiered with Moltke.

It was interesting to notice how the subject of old days worked up the Fenian slumbering in his soul ; amusing to observe how in the midst of a peroration which never quite perorated to a close, the precise little man of law vainly, but with perfect good-temper over the failure, endeavoured to begin a more modern speech of his own.

" I have seen men whipped at the cart's tail," said the old Fenian. " I have seen the blood streaming from their backs, and I have seen them hanged like dogs in the street ; and I say those men were murdered, I say they were martyrs, I say their blood was given for

God and country ; and although, glory be to God, the times have changed, and England is now ready to listen to Ireland's cry, and the justification for violence can no longer be pleaded, I say that the Fenians did a righteous work, and that Ireland will owe her eventual freedom, her liberty, and her life to the blood they shed for their country."

"There is a point I should like to——" began our host.

"But I say to England," broke in the old Fenian, "that if she denies us now the gift of self-government, if she draws back and plays the coward and the traitor, Ireland will no longer be at peace, the old spirit will manifest itself, and violence will confront her at every turn in her way."

"I think, perhaps, we ought to point out——"

"Let there be no mistake about it," cried the Fenian, with a bang of his great fist on the table, "Ireland is peaceful now because she anticipates justice, because she recognizes, gratefully and generously recognizes, that England is endeavouring to make reparation for the past, and God grant that reparation may be made soon, aye, and in full. But let England deceive Ireland once again——"

"Oh, but she won't," said the smiling lawyer, fixing his polished eye-glasses on the bridge of his nose. "We needn't fear that. I was going to point out——"

"I say, let England deceive Ireland once again," roared the big Fenian, "let Ireland once again be thrown back upon the bitter memories of her tragic history, and you will have a more angry and a more violent spirit at work than anything you have known in the past. But I confidently believe, and I thank God for it, that the day of estrangement is over, the long night of misunderstanding is at an end ; we shall live together, sir, in peace and honourable friendship ; and Ireland will be a source of strength to England, more loyal than Canada, more powerful for help than any other integral part of the British Empire ; and I believe that England will live to love Ireland and to thank her for showing her the path of duty."

"I don't think people quite realize——" began the lawyer.

"That is my belief, sir," continued the Fenian, now thoroughly urbane, flourishing a napkin and bowing in my direction ; "and I thank God, sir, I say I thank God, that I am likely to live to see the day when our two nations, burying the past and forgetting old offences, will stand together in the inseparable bonds of friendship and respect, firm for righteousness, strong for progress, and unconquerable against the fury of their enemies."

"Quite so, and——"

"But, as I said before, let England disappoint Ireland once again——" etc. etc.

It was a most excellent dinner, and I thoroughly enjoyed the unending peroration of the handsome old Fenian, knowing that I should have opportunity later on of hearing the more modern wisdom of my host.

"Ah, if I could tell you all I have seen and known in this very neighbourhood," cried the Fenian. "I remember old men being flogged and hanged, I remember the most respectable men in this town being thrown into prison for a speech to their fellow-countrymen on the glory of liberty and patriotism. Those things made a very great impression on my mind, but they did not assume a political significance; they simply made me hate the police and loathe the law of the land. But one day, when I was still a boy, I went with my father for a drive, and I saw a sight that made me from that moment a politician. It was a wet day, and as we drove up to the house of a land-agent, we saw the tenants, who had called to pay their rents, taking off their boots outside the house before they entered. I asked my father why they did so. He laughed bitterly and said that it was always done—it was a part of a tenant's duty to his landlord. At that moment there came to me not only a feeling of patriotism, but a feeling of manhood." He flung back his head, squared his great shoulders, opened wide his eyes, and, half smiling and half threatening, exclaimed, "I felt myself to be no serf! I would have felled that man to the earth—whoever he was—who ordered me to take my boots off at his door! And from that day I dreamed of giving my life for Ireland, dreamed of rescuing my land from the humiliation and debasement of a foreign tyranny; there was nothing I would not then have done to win my country's freedom. And there's not an Englishman worth the name who in like conditions would not have the same passions smouldering in his breast. I assure you that spirit of Nationality was like an agony gnawing at our hearts. I met an old poor man the other day, a little farmer not many miles from here, who recognized me, greeted me by name, and shook my hand; then he said to me in a whisper, smiling with a hundred memories in his eyes, *I've still got her.* That was enough. It was like a Freemason's sign between us. He meant that he still kept his old Fenian's musket!

"I can tell you a story which shows how men became Fenians in those days, and how Fenianism—let Englishmen despise and condemn it as they will—won Ireland the first steps on her road to freedom. There were two farmers in this country, one an old soldier with a wooden leg who let his land go as it would, the other a most industrious, hard-working man who did his duty by the land and grubbed every halfpenny out of its soil. The timber-legged gentleman was generously and indulgently treated by the landlord's agent; the other was rack-rented and persecuted by the police till his life was almost unendurable. Directly he improved his land, the rent was raised, directly he repaired his buildings or bought himself a decent coat, the rent was raised; and the other man lived on at the same rent, unmolested by the police and treated with respect by his landlord.

"One day these two men met at a wedding. A priest who knew them well, both the meek and patient man and timber-toes, asked the latter, 'How is it the police don't persecute you, as they persecute your neighbour here?' The old soldier laughed between his teeth, proudly, defiantly. 'Because, Father,' said he, 'they know I'd shoot!'

"Do you wonder, then, that men with the real stuff of manhood in them, regarded meekness, and patience, and docility, and subserviency as virtues too fine for this rough world? Do you wonder that these men armed themselves, and sought by any means in their power, lawful or unlawful, to defend their manhood and their honour? But, thanks be to God, that is all over and done with. The old rancour is past. The old bitterness and hatred are forgotten. Once, I do assure you"—his eyes blazed and he clenched his fists—"we would have plunged England to the bottom of the sea, aye, and, if we could, we would have ripped up the bottom and sunk her to another place below, down, down, down, as far as we could get her! But now, thanks be to God"—his face softened, his eyes smiled, and his voice cooed—"we have no other feeling in our hearts than a desire to forget the past and to live in friendship and goodwill with our friends across St. George's Channel."

When this interesting old man had departed, taking his leave with a really charming courtesy which reminded me of Sir William Harcourt, my host the lawyer drew his chair a little nearer to the fire, handed me the cigarettes, and began to speak of Ireland's future. The contrast was complete. Ireland's past is full of sound and fury, of poetry and heroism, of fighting and speech-making; her future is concerned with butter and eggs, a sensible adjustment of trading relations with England, and a development of industries.

The lawyer never once raised his voice, never once began an interminable peroration, never threatened or forgave. In the even tones and the direct language of a modern business man he discussed the future of Ireland with a sagacity that seemed to me of good augury for the Irish Parliament.

He said that all idea of separation from England is now regarded as absurd. No sensible man in Ireland dreams of such a thing. If Ireland is necessary to England, so much more is England necessary to Ireland. In a word, England is Ireland's market. No sensible business man will imperil his best market. "To quarrel with you," he said, "would be to quarrel with our bread and butter. We are not likely to do that. For selfish reasons alone, we shall try to inspire English confidence in Irish undertakings and English affection for the Irish people. We have our living to get."

The future of Ireland, he declared, lies in agricultural development. The possibilities in this direction are very great. With modern methods and improved machinery applied by so clever and industrious a nation, there is here immense room for evolution. Ireland must always be first and foremost an agricultural nation. It is quite possible, he thinks, for Ireland to become the market-garden of England. Another field in which the possibilities are considerable is the milk trade. At present it is hardly organized at all, and the methods are old-fashioned.

He spoke about the absurdity of sending milk in broad-bottomed cans which taper to the top like a sugar-loaf. Not only, he pointed out, is it difficult to clean those cans properly, but they waste enormous space in transit, and so add to the cost of carriage. This very obvious criticism had not occurred to me before. I had accepted the commercial milk-can with gravitation, decimals, and income-tax. But my host was a revolutionist. In future, he said, Ireland will send her milk to England in flat, trunk-like cans which may be piled in train or steamer one on top of the other, wasting no space whatever, and which can be thoroughly and easily cleaned. Stirring times! The Higher Criticism has no reverence even for immemorial milk-cans.

But my host is not a light-hearted Anarchist. He declared emphatically that Socialism is a quite impossible creed for Ireland. Of all European countries, Ireland is the most Conservative. He said that the grouping of parties in the Irish Parliament would testify to this Conservative instinct of the Irish nation. Mr. Redmond, he thinks, will be at the head of an overwhelming Conservative party. Mr. Joseph Devlin, with Belfast at his back, will lead a very intelligent and active Democratic party. Mr. Devlin will work for the revival of Irish industries, and for various social reforms on the model of Liberal legislation in England; Mr. Redmond will grudgingly and only under the greatest pressure yield to the mildest of these demands. "We shall develop village industries," he said; "but our social reforms will attempt nothing heroic. We are farmers and gardeners. And what is more, we don't want to be anything else."

For himself, he is devoted to the land question, of which he has made a particular study, and his conviction is that the tendency of Irish legislation for many years to come will be all in this direction. "Our battles," he said, "will be pastoral!"

I went from this pleasant terraced house overlooking a beautiful river flowing through a market-town full of activity and business, to the little exquisite Eden of Adare, where Lord Dunraven spends the greater part of his time in Ireland. The domain is so beautiful, with its river and lakes, its woodlands and its lawns, its ruins and its gardens, that one forgets the depression and ugliness of the surrounding country and forgives the rather pretentious and forbidding character of the mansion's architecture. It is a place for a poet, even more lovely than Penshurst, and to linger in those grounds is to forget the fierce struggle for existence, the defilements of competitive industrialism.

For Lord Dunraven himself one can only have admiration and real liking. He has done the bravest thing an Irish landlord can do —he has made friends with Nationalist members of Parliament. Moreover, he has spoken and written with convincing logic, and a wholly unquestionable honesty, on the subject of Devolution, and has publicly on many occasions associated himself with the national aspirations of Irishmen. This, and his lavish generosity as landlord and farmer, has secured for him a place in Irish life which is as honourable and patriotic as it is admirable in the eyes of many Nationalists, and detestable in the eyes of every Orangeman.

He grows old invisibly, and his laughter and cheerfulness are as middle-aged as the quiet vigour with which he expresses his opinions. It is difficult to realize that he was born when Queen Victoria was yet a girl, and has lived a life full of excitement and adventure.

I do not think that he is quite abreast of modern thought, that he is fully conscious of democratic idealism, or that he has so completely lost, as Sir Edward Grey, for instance, the rather hindering affection for the idea of social caste. But he is intellectual, he is practical, and he has the wisdom of common sense. If he does not march in the front rank of humanity, he at any rate marches in step with the general army. He adapts himself, or at any rate endeavours to adapt himself, to the changing world, with cheerfulness and good-humour. Mr. Lloyd George has hit him hard financially; Lord Dunraven does not minimize this effect of Liberal finance on his exchequer; but he agrees that such taxation is necessary, and accepts the burden without complaint.

I asked him how it was that he came to take an interest in the Irish question, how he found time in the midst of a sporting and fashionable life, with all the capitals of Europe for his playground, to study the somewhat dreary business of Irish politics. I asked this question because one meets in Ireland many men less wealthy and less involved in the bewitchments of society than Lord Dunraven who profess the most lofty contempt for Irish politics and only yawn at the mention of Irish Nationality.

My host smiled at the question. "I'm afraid," said he, "that I thought precious little about the matter in my youth. I was as bad as any other young fellow of my age in that respect. I was far keener on sport, on social life; and my literary and scientific interests carried me still further afield from Ireland. But I think I must have inherited from my father a tendency that sooner or later was bound to draw my attention to Ireland. He was an archæologist, and as an archæologist loved Ireland. He did not interest himself in Irish politics, but he was consumedly interested in the Irish people and in Irish customs and beliefs. My own first step towards sympathy with Ireland came in middle-life, and began with my perception that the root trouble of Irish discontent lay in the Land question. As an Irish landlord I was affected by Land Agitation, and this led me to study the matter. I began my study merely as an Irish landlord, and with no prepossessions in favour of Irish politicians—in fact, I suppose I rather despised those gentry. But my investigations brought me into contact with the Nationalists, and I very soon discovered that many of them were able, honourable, and very pleasant fellows. That was my first illumination! As I proceeded in my work I lost all antipathies in this respect, and came to see that a settlement of the Land question and a measure of Devolution were not only essential for Irish prosperity, but would transform Ireland into a powerful and loyal member of the British Empire. You can imagine that such a perception made me enthusiastic, both as an Irishman and as an Imperialist. But the work was extremely difficult and disheartening. The Conservatives flirted with the idea from time to time, but lacked courage and conviction to make it the centre of their Irish policy. And with the exception of a few very noble men, the Nationalists hung back, clung to their isolation, persisted in their aloofness, and would not concentrate with the rest of us on the work of Conciliation. However, the idea has penetrated every political party, both in England and Ireland, and I think that some day men will acknowledge the justice and wisdom of our propaganda. I am not a Separatist, not a Home Ruler in the professional sense of that term, but I am an Imperialist and a Devolutionist. Whatever may be the fate of our theory, I am glad of the little humble part I have played in Irish politics, if only because it has broadened my knowledge, enlarged my sympathies, and made me—I hope I may say so—a better Irishman."

Three brief extracts from Lord Dunraven's book, *The Outlook in Ireland*, will convince any open-minded reader of the immense seriousness of this Irish question. So many people are content to think of the Irish struggle as a game played by political agitators for the sake of a wage; very few people realize that Ireland is now at this moment heading for absolute bankruptcy, an impoverished, a bleeding, and a dying nation. Lord Dunraven's conversion should persuade careless thinkers in England that there is at least some Reality in Ireland's struggle for existence, and a perusal of his book should make them fighters for the Irish Cause.

Consider these three short statements :—

> In 1841 Ireland had over three times as many inhabitants as Scotland could boast; half as many as England and Wales claimed. At that time nearly one-third of the whole population of the United Kingdom lived in Ireland. *In sixty years the population of Ireland had fallen by nearly* 4,000,000 (for in 1903 the number was estimated to be 4,391,565)—a record of national wastage which is unparalleled in the history of the world.
>
> Let readers ponder on the fact that Ireland has a larger proportion of aged than any other country in the King's dominions, because the young and energetic have fled to other lands in search of happiness and fortune. In Ireland, out of every thousand of the population, there are sixty-four men and sixty-three women of sixty-five years of age or upward; while in England and Wales the figures are forty-two and fifty-one respectively; and in Scotland, forty-one and fifty-six.
>
> And there is another terrible leakage from which Ireland is suffering, namely, lunacy. The figures of the Census of 1901 tell an amazing story of the mental gloom which year by year has been settling down upon those who have remained in the old country. . . . The mental ravages among the Irish people are set forth with shocking lucidity in the last Census Report: "The total number of lunatics and idiots returned in 1851 was equal to a ratio of 1 in 657 of the population; in 1861, to 1 in 411; in 1871, to 1 in 328; in 1881, to 1 in 281; in 1891, to 1 in 222; and on the present occasion, to 1 in 178."

Drained by emigration, gloomed by the absence of the young, let and hindered by the sense of an immemorial political wrong, Ireland, now brought to beggary by English legislation, makes another eager, pathetic, and passionate appeal to Great Britain for the one boon which can avert her ruin and make possible her ultimate salvation.

Whether it be by the eloquence of the old Fenian, the common sense of the precise lawyer, or the passionless conversion to her cause of the aristocratic landlord, let the reader be persuaded that Ireland, whatever he may think of the matter, considers that she has suffered grievous wrong, is now in a perilous and most calamitous condition, and by self-government may find a happy issue out of all her afflictions.

# CHAPTER VII

## MONUMENTUM AERE PERENNIUS

CORK is a city full of encouragements for languid people. If the Fat Boy of *Pickwick* had lived there I doubt if he would have wakened even to take his meals.

It is a city composed of all the quiet corners and sleepy places of other cities. You find there a terrace of white villas on a green and leafy hill that has been lifted bodily from the Riviera, a neglected square transplanted from the inner quiet of Antwerp, a Mall that has walked in its sleep from Bury St. Edmunds, a riverside that has floated from Blois, and a suburban quarter that people must vainly be looking for in Wimbledon.

But this slumbrous patchwork quilt of a city has one scarlet oasis of trumpeting Violence. It is a National Monument—a monument to the patriots of other days. Not beautiful, but aggressive, not elevating, but terrifying, this mass of tortured stone stands in the centre of the city's peace like Boreas executing an *apache* dance in the fields of lotus-land.

I was taken to see it one morning by a peaceful and law-abiding colonel, retired from the Indian Army—an elderly and amiable man, entirely loyal to the British Empire, solemnly gratified by Britain's glory, a thoughtful orthodox Presbyterian, a steady Home Ruler, and a Christian living in love and charity with his Catholic neighbours. You could scarcely imagine a more delectable guide for so war-whooping a monument.

On one side of this fearsome erection is the following inscription:—

1798

Erected through the efforts of the Young Ireland Society to perpetuate the memory of the gallant men of 1798, 1803, '48, and '67—who fought and died in the wars of Ireland to recover her sovereign independence and to inspire the youth of our country to follow in their patriotic footsteps and imitate their heroic example, "and righteous men will make our land a NATION ONCE AGAIN."

Unveiled St. Patrick's Day, 1906, by the Revd. P. F. Kavanagh, O.F.M., President, Cork Young Ireland Society.

On the other side are the following words :—

We must not fail, we must not fail,
However force or fraud assail;
By honour, pride, and policy,
By heaven itself, we must be free;
Be sure the great God never planned
For slumbering slaves, a home so grand.—DAVIS.

If I could grasp the fires of hell in my hands, I would hurl them in the face of my country's enemies.—JOHN MITCHELL.

I looked from these tremendous words to the gentle colonel at my side, who, holding eye-glasses to his nose, was spelling out the words for, I suppose, the fiftieth time in his life. I inquired if the Protestants of the neighbourhood did not resent the challenge, the rather bloodthirsty menace implied by this inscription. He put away his glasses, looked up with a smile, and answered, to my considerable surprise, that among the many names of patriots engraved on the stone was a plentiful number of fire-eating Protestants.

Of the four names at the four corners, at foot of the statues, two are Protestants—Thomas Davis, whose verse is quoted above, and the famous Wolfe Tone. Among the hundred or so patriots whose names are enumerated under the three memorable years, 1803, 1848, and 1867, twenty-three were certainly Protestants, and perhaps there were others, for it is by no means assured that every other name on the plinth stands for a Catholic. But twenty-three of the glorious host were undoubted Protestants.

John Mitchell, whose fiery words are cut into the stone, was a Protestant, and among the other Protestants I found such names as Lord Edward FitzGerald, General Holt, the Rev. John Mitchell, and Catherine Countess of Queensbury, the last a very gallant "man."

We are apt to imagine, because a political organization in the north of Ireland has shouted the false rendering so vociferously and so continually into our English ears, that Nationalism in Ireland is only and entirely a synonym for Jesuitical Catholicism. But here in Cork is a monument that corrects this false notion. It was a vitriolic Protestant who wanted to hurl the fires of hell in England's face, and a Rudyard Kipling of Irish Protestantism who exclaimed :—

> Be sure the great God never planned
> For slumbering slaves, a home so grand.

Protestantism, with all due deference to so eminent an authority as Sir Edward Carson—who, by the way, was once alarmed by fire in the city of Cork—is not destructive of nationality and patriotism.

As we walked away the colonel told me that such language as burns on the monument is now completely out of fashion. There is very little rhetoric in modern Irish politics, he told me ; business men have taken the matter out of the hands of priests and poets, and these hard-headed gentlemen discuss Home Rule from the standpoint of trade ; it is a matter of business.

He smiled at the idea of Catholic intolerance, and told me he had no better or more agreeable friends in the neighbourhood than these libelled Catholics. "All that sort of thing—you'll forgive me for saying so—is tommy-rot." My stay in Cork confirmed this judgment.

I met at the house where I was staying just outside the town—a house on a wooded hill whose windows and balconies look towards the sunset across a curving river and a wide stretch of meadow-land glimmering far away to fold upon fold of distant hills—a most amiable and cheerful company composed of Catholics and Protestants. The whole atmosphere of that house, with its babies and flowers, its pets and toys, its music and literature, its hospitality and its cheerful domesticity, was quite charming and convincing ; one could not mix with the family and its guests, could not share in that kind and hospitable life, believing for a moment the wicked calumny of Catholic intolerance. It would have been like suspecting an English hostess of stealing from one's dressing-case, or an English host of cheating at cards.

To know the Irish people one must stay in their houses and share in their domestic life. One must not merely discuss political opinions, but must pay visits to the nursery, perambulate the garden, go a-shopping with one's hostess, take pleasure in the pictures and furniture, if possible make toffee, or toast barm-brach, at the schoolroom fire. The home-life of Ireland, among the upper classes, the middle classes, and the peasantry, seems to me entirely beautiful and pure ; here and there one may be conscious of modern vulgarity, an encroachment of Smart ideas ; here and there one may be harassed by a note of provincialism, or troubled by an effort to obscure normal simplicity with a show of prodigality to impress the English visitor ; but on the whole, whithersoever I went, my reception was kind and warm-hearted ; I was made to feel myself a welcome guest, and I encountered in most genial, kindly homes men and women who were grateful to God for existence and devoted to domestic life.

At a dinner-party in this particular house there was a white-haired but young-looking professional man, whose low voice and modest demeanour, whose rather timid and self-effacing manner, for some reason or another, suggested to my mind the character of Tom Pinch. I discovered that he is devoted to children, but has never married ; he supports by his profession his mother and sisters, living a very quiet and retired life, except for politics in which he plays an occasional and somewhat leading part.

I became better acquainted with this agreeable person, and we went a trip together to the beautiful harbour of Queenstown. He took a great delight in pointing out to me the lovely views from our carriage window, speaking softly and endearingly, as one who has come to patriotism through the door of nature worship. He loves the great river winding down to the sea, the rolling hills, the deep woods, the fields that glow like emeralds in sunlight, and the little whitewashed villages that nestle at the river's edge. He loves them because they are lovable; and because they are lovable he loves Ireland, loves her as the gracious creation of the God he worships, and as the land of the people and the race whose religion and sentiments his soul has inherited with its body.

"I have just received," he said to me, "a letter from a very old emigrant in the United States." He drew the letter from his pocket. "I think you will be touched by the love it expresses for Ireland, and struck, too, by the change which time has effected in the anger and hard thoughts of ancient days. Would you like to hear it? Shall I read it to you?"

And he read the whole letter, and afterwards he copied out for me the passage which I here set down in print:—

> I see that Churchill is out strong for Home Rule. God speed their efforts. I saw that Redmond had an accident; I hope he is now better and that he will live to preside over a Parliament House in Dublin. It is about time that England should do right. Many is the prayer I prayed for Ireland for sixty years, and if some of these prayers were heard I would now be sorry for England. But now that I am getting old I am praying God to forgive my enemies. How often during our Civil War I thought, if it could be possible, how much better it would be if it was a war with England instead of a war between brothers, and how much more "ginger" we five brothers whom our mother gave to the Southern Confederacy could have put into the fight to settle old scores. Well, thanks be to God, our country is now at peace and offers a good living for all who are not too lazy to work for it.
>
> In my opinion there is no such country on earth, and with Home Rule for Ireland there is no reason why you should not do as well. God helps those who try to help themselves.

He spoke of the love for Ireland which haunts the emigrant in alien lands. Men go away, earn high wages, live a fuller and more exciting life, but their hearts are with Ireland. Even when the habit of America has hardened in their nature, and when to return and live in Ireland would be something of a torture, the emigrant is still conscious of a love and a reverence for his homeland which is almost religious in its character. This love is indestructible. It is the monument more lasting than brass or stone.

"I often think," he said, "of the letters which are continually crossing the great Atlantic from America, and which find their way into our smallest and remotest villages. How much love they contain! How much patriotism! I have seen many of those letters, and they quicken my love for Ireland more than all the speeches of politicians on our sufferings and wrongs. They are so wistful with longing, so profound with loyalty to the home. I suppose many emigrants of other lands send money to the old folks, but I wonder if so many send so much as our poor Irish scattered all over the world. Home Rule would not stop, but it would check emigration, and, what is so important, it would alter the character of that exodus. I think if we felt ourselves to be a free people and not a subject people, our young men would go more cheerfully to other lands, would hold themselves there with more pride, and would hasten their return to the motherland. I feel sure that all the love for Ireland which now exists wistfully and rather tragically in other countries would become more vital and glad and serviceable to Irish nationality, if Ireland were free."

It was plain from what he told me that the bitterness and hate of the older generation of emigrants is dying out. Irishmen recognize that modern England, innocent of past bloodshed, extortion, and cruelty, is striving her hardest to restore the broken fortunes of their motherland. They have a growing respect for this new England, but they cannot love her and they cannot come back proudly from across the seas until Ireland is as free as South Africa, Canada, and Australia.

Mr. G. K. Chesterton, in some ways surely one of the most original, penetrating, and wholesome of modern thinkers, has defined as England's failure in the government of Ireland her determination to ignore Ireland's sense of nationality. He says :—

" I am quite certain that Scotland is a nation ; I am quite certain that nationality is the key of Scotland ; I am quite certain that all our success with Scotland has been due to the fact that we have in spirit treated it as a nation. I am quite certain that Ireland is a nation. I am quite certain that nationality is the key of Ireland ; I am quite certain that all our failure in Ireland arose from the fact that we could not in spirit treat it as a nation. It would be difficult to find, even among the innumerable examples that exist, a stronger example of the immensely superior importance of sentiment, to what is called practicality, than this case of the two sister nations. It is not that we have encouraged a Scotchman to be rich ; it is not that we have encouraged a Scotchman to be active ; it is not that we have encouraged a Scotchman to be free. It is that we have quite definitely encouraged a Scotsman to be Scotch."

The reality of an Irishman's love for Ireland was brought home to my mind on many occasions, but by no one, perhaps, so simply and convincingly as by this man in Cork who spoke of Irish emigrants so tenderly, and expressed so earnestly his hope for a united and contented British Empire.

I learned from this quiet and thoughtful man to realize how great a blessing lies in store for England when the vast numbers of Irishmen in the United States feel themselves related to the British Empire. If any man loves England, and has known the hunger for England in a distant country, he will understand the heart of the Irish emigrant.

Over thirty-one thousand emigrants left Ireland last year.

## CHAPTER VIII

### PETTY LARCENIES

Soon after my return from Ireland I was talking one day to an English clergyman whose political judgment I imagined to be as just and tolerant as his culture appeared to be wide and liberal. What was my surprise, then, to find this amiable, broad-minded gentleman convinced, and unshakable in his conviction, that Catholic tyranny not only will become a fact under Home Rule, but is actually a fact at the present time !

I gave him overwhelming proof to the contrary, and pressed him to tell me how he has brought himself to believe so unworthy an imputation on Irish character.

" I cannot tell you," he replied, " from whom I get my information ; but I have in my possession, sent to me from authoritative men in Ireland, innumerable cases of Catholic tyranny towards Protestants. The documents are private and confidential or I would show them to you. They have made a profound impression upon me. Yes, they are printed documents."

Does this mean, one would like to know, that Protestants in Ireland are secretly circularizing the clergy of England, and in their zeal for the Union are blackening the character of their fellow-Christians in Ireland ? If this is the case, I can imagine nothing more unworthy in the long unworthy history of Protestantism in Ireland. Cromwell's bloody club was an honest human weapon. But these whispered, confidential, and backstair scandalizings of a miserable sectarianism can proceed only from the Father of Lies. To associate these petty larcenies of character, these contemptible and furtive slanders of clerical backbiters with anything consecrated by the Character of Jesus is an infamy, almost a blasphemy.

Let me give the reader, in this place, the written statement of a Presbyterian minister living in the south of Ireland who has never once wavered in his allegiance to Protestantism, and who is now at the present time as out of harmony with Catholic doctrine as when he began his ministry.

The following letter was written hurriedly in answer to certain questions I addressed to my correspondent, but it gives an honest man's verdict, clearly, simply, and convincingly.

" It is difficult," writes this Presbyterian minister, " to get behind the reserve that shuts out the priest from ordinary social life. But it has been my peculiar privilege to have done so in one or two instances, and to have gained confidences that I greatly prize. I have made close personal friends among the priests, and I am glad to be able to say, from what inside knowledge I have, that morally there is no finer type of man in Ireland.

"The priest is a good fellow; and as a rule has none of those bitter prejudices (perhaps I should say none of that bitter intolerance) that so often disfigures his Protestant confrère.

"There is in every corner of Munster a Protestantism—more or less numerous—but always watchful and suspicious of Romanism, and especially of the priest. And in my opinion there is no stronger testimony to the moral worth of the Priesthood than the fact that that Protestantism has no word of disapproval for the priest individually.

"At our last Presbytery meeting in Co. Kerry (September, 1911) the local lay representatives of the Presbyterian Church (gathered from all over Kerry) were asked by one of the ministers: 'Is there any interference with you on the part of the priests, or any hindrance to your work because you are Protestants?'—or words to that effect. And the answer, prompt and ready from each one, was, 'None.'

"Our Presbytery covers the counties of Cork and Kerry, and part of Waterford, and never for the last twenty years, while I have been a member, has there been a single complaint of priestly interference or intolerance of any kind.

"As to the priest's spiritual influence, my opinion is that it is greater to-day than ever, because it is more enlightened and spiritual.

"The priest does not exercise to-day the influence that he did formerly in social and political affairs.

"But those Catholics who disagree with the priests in their political views are at the same time loyal and true to them spiritually. The priest himself knows this and readily admits that they are 'good Catholics.'

"And while it is difficult for the priest to keep out of politics, as it is for the parson to keep out of politics, the knowledge of the spiritual loyalty of his opponents has caused him to moderate his opinions and to restrain his opposition. And under Home Rule this will become a great national asset and will either rend the Church or drive the priest out of politics altogether. It has had the latter result in Cork, where the division in the Irish party is most felt.

"In seeking to exercise his influence, therefore, the priest has been compelled to work along spiritual lines; and any speeches that I have read by the politically minded priests of the South would not go to show that they seek to exercise a greater influence over their people than our leading political parsons in Belfast and the North."

On the subject of morality he writes :—

"The priests and nuns are watchful and in close touch with the people. And the people themselves have great natural gifts for amusements. And that seems to me to protect them from grossness and sordidness. And besides, religion has a real restraining power in their lives."

He speaks of Protestants who have stayed as paying-guests in Roman Catholic Homes, and mentions the impression made upon them by young people who, after a night of dancing or card-playing, go off to Mass at six o'clock in the morning before beginning the day's duties.

"Indeed," he goes on, "some of the young men connected with my own congregation who came here from Glasgow and have become Roman Catholics have told me that it was the place given to religion and its influence on the lives of their Roman Catholic companions that induced them to change.

"Personally I am at the other extreme from Romanism. But this has been my experience. Many young men in the city have joined the Roman Catholic Church, and while I know that Protestantism has ascribed less worthy motives, yet I believe that in this case also there must have been some very sufficient cause to make them brave the anger of parents and relatives and friends. I have a very high opinion of the moral life of the Catholic young men of this city. They are a credit to their Church.

"Under Home Rule nothing will be different, nothing very much for a time ; but everything will become different.

"There will be no intolerance, unless what is provoked by the insensate hate of a few in Ulster. But I have very little fear of that even. . . .

"What I have said of the priests, the people, and their religion will show you that I have no fear whatever for Protestantism, except that it may become merged in the predominant Romanism, as it has so often done before.

"Of course there is a considerable outcry on the part of the old ascendancy party who are still imbued with the opinion that it is their right to rule, but they will find their rightful place by and by, and will become a great strength in the community.

"For, should prosperity follow the introduction of Home Rule, as we have every reason to believe it will, the Protestants will by reason of their superior business organizations and methods benefit more than the Catholics.

"Protestantism in the South at least has no fear of Home Rule, and would gladly welcome a settlement of that much-discussed question."

Thus writes an honest, just man. Throughout my own wanderings in Ireland I encountered no single case of Catholic intolerance, and even by those Protestants who are opposed to Home Rule with real energy, I never heard the Catholic priest maligned. I was told that he is often a mere rustic, an unmannerly bumpkin, an ignorant, common person swollen by a sense of Apostolic importance—this from people inclined to emphasize social superiority—but not once, face to face with the actual facts of Irish life, did I hear one word of attack concerning Catholic intolerance or the morality of the Catholic priest.

If the reader will allow me to do so, I should like to make what members of Parliament call a personal statement. I have written so often on religious questions that I really owe to those among my present readers who are acquainted with my former work something of an explanation as touching the position I take up on this question of Catholic and Protestant in Ireland.

Until I visited Ireland my impression was that Irish Catholic priests resembled Italian Catholic priests, Spanish Catholic priests, and the more ignorant of French Catholic priests. I went to the country under this impression, and with the further notion that all the backwardness, poverty, laziness, and discontent which I had been so often told existed in the south of Ireland was largely attributable to the influence of priests.

I have inherited, and experience of the world has deepened, an almost violent antipathy to the Roman Church. Occasionally I have encountered, in England and abroad, Catholics whom I liked very much, Catholics who seemed to me charming, delightful, and quite sensible people. But my aversion from Rome remained constant. The dogmas of that Church have ever seemed to me only one more degree preposterous and unholy than so great a part of her history has been villainous and detestable.

In Ireland I came face to face with this problem. In the South, where Catholic influence is supreme, the people are almost enchanting in their sweetness of disposition, entirely admirable in the beauty and contentment of their domestic life, wonderful beyond all other nations in the wholesomeness and sanctity of their chastity. In this place I make no comparison of the South with the North—that I reserve for a later chapter; my present purpose is to speak solely of the South. Instead of a lazy, thriftless, discontented, and squalid people—as I had imagined them to be—the Irish of the South won my sympathy and compelled my admiration by qualities the very opposite. It seemed to me that these hard-working, simple-living, family-loving, and most warm-hearted people have done what we in England have largely failed to do, even in our villages, to wit, solved the problem of life. The charm which every traveller feels in the south of Ireland is the character of the Irish people ; and my investigation forced me to the judgment that this character is the culture of Irish Catholicism. My problem lay, therefore, in squaring the admiration I felt for these gracious people with my detestation of the Church which has guarded Irish character from the dawn of its history.

I was compelled to admit that I had greatly misjudged the Catholic Church. My conscience would not let me fence with this conviction. I saw that I had blundered by unconsciously entertaining the foolish notion that because one branch of the Catholic Church is scandalous, or one era of Catholic history is abominable, therefore every branch is scandalous, and every era of Catholic history to the end of time must remain abominable.

I came to see vividly and clearly what most of us have always suspected, that it is the character of the man, and not the set of dogmas to which he pins his faith, that makes the Christian. What a man thinks, what a man believes in the region of dogma, seems to exercise almost no influence whatever upon the Christianity of his life. It does not matter, says Goethe, what you believe, but how you believe. It is the spirit in which a man gives his heart to God, not the intellectual attitude of his theology, which determines the character of his life. I met many Catholics all over Ireland, and in only one or two cases did I feel any sense of uneasiness or discontent in their company. Over and over again I was humbled and abased by finding how immeasurably mean was my experience of spiritual life in comparison with the lives of these humble and ignorant Catholics, who love God with the clinging trustfulness of little children.

But my aversion from Catholic creed remains. I have gone once more patiently, and with an honest effort to be just, into the question of Catholic dogma, and I find myself more puzzled than ever before in my life to account for the fact of any man gifted with even a little knowledge being able to accept, to accept so that they subdue his life, these amazing and humiliating superstitions of magic-worship.

Such, then, is my position. Intellectually I am as out of sympathy with Catholics as I should be out of sympathy with a man who believes the world to be flat. I can no easier get on intellectual good terms with a Catholic than with an orthodox Hindu. Intellectually I am much more in sympathy with Mussulmans than with Catholics. No willingness to be gracious and modest and conciliatory can save me, in the company of Catholic theologians, from a feeling if not of scorn, at any rate of amazement and, I fear, of pity.

Nevertheless, I should feel myself guilty of a crime if I wrote one single word with the object of weakening an Irishman's faith in his Church. So beautiful is the influence of that Church, so altogether sincere and attractive is the spiritual life of Catholic Ireland, that I for one, rather than lift a finger to disturb it, like the man in the parable would stand afar off, bow my head upon my breast, and utter the honest prayer, God be merciful to me a sinner.

Let the Protestant reader ask himself this question, Whether his admiration goes to the Catholic priest living with the peasants of Ireland, sharing their poverty, and devoting himself to the beauty and chastity of Ireland's spiritual life, or to the Irish clerical politician who secretly slanders in England these fellow-Christians, with no other object in mind than to preserve his own social ascendancy?

## CHAPTER IX

### A CASE OF PERSECUTION

AFTER spending many weeks in Ireland, after going here, there, and nearly everywhere, after meeting numerous people circumstanced to know the truth of Irish social life, I returned to England with not one single case of Catholic persecution in my notebook. Among all the good and earnest Protestants I met in Ireland, none could tell me a single story of Catholic bigotry. It is most important for the liberal-minded English Protestant who reads this chapter to remember that no Irish Protestant ever complained to me of Catholic persecution, or hinted at Catholic intolerance.

But now the case is different. A friend in England to whom I had expressed my conviction that Catholic persecution is a rather shabby Wolf, a rather frayed and tattered Bogy manufactured in Belfast with chemises, comfortable Atlantic liners, and pocket-handkerchiefs, has sent me certain printed matter which witnesses to the fact, so he holds, of Catholic persecution. My friend begs me to find time for the reading of his documents. He is sure that I shall be persuaded, being an honest man, that Catholic persecution is a very true and very awful fact of Irish social life.

Now, I rejoice in these documents with all my heart because they prove in a most remarkable manner the very opposite truth of which my friend is convinced. They prove that Irish Catholics are the most tolerant and polite people in the world, and that at least some Irish Protestants are the most impolitic people on the face of this kindly earth. I could wish nothing better for my thesis than space to print these extraordinary documents *in extenso.*

This case of Catholic persecution concerns the town of Limerick. The martyr in question is a Protestant medical man, Dr. Joseph Long. He has been stoned in the streets, eggs have been thrown at him, flour has been emptied upon him from top-storey windows, crowds have followed howling at his heels, and jarveys have refused to drive him on their cars. Since his arrival in Limerick, an event which occurred in 1897, down to the year 1903, this gentleman endured so merciless a persecution that it is a matter of miracle he is still alive—not merely alive, but apparently satisfied with his life's work. Since 1904, so I gather, he has lived in peace, his only cross the jarveys' absolute refusal to take him as a fare. His real martyrdom, therefore, is eight years old, a part rather of ancient history than contemporary politics. But do not let the reader minimize it on account of its age. The same thing might occur again. Under Home Rule it might become even worse. And the story of it is now being handed about in England.

The story is this: An English body of people known as the Society for Irish Church Missions, with offices at 11 Buckingham Street, Strand, London, seeks to make proselytes of Roman Catholics in Ireland. It believes, so I gather from its documents, that the Catholics of Ireland are outside the pale of Christian Salvation; and, being moved with a great compassion for these doomed millions, it sends forth missionaries to Ireland, just as other societies send missionaries to China and the West Coast of Africa. Irish Catholics are regarded by this English society as heathen, and as heathen they are accordingly treated. Whether it would be nearer to Christ's instruction for these good and wealthy people to spend their money in feeding the poor and hungry of London, we will not inquire. They are convinced that they should employ people to convert Irish Catholics to their own particular notion of English Protestantism.

Dr. Joseph Long, employed by this society, was sent to open a Medical Mission in Limerick. He took a house, exhibited a dispensary notice-board announcing the hours of "free attendance," and, in his own words, "opened our door and awaited results, in full confidence that God, who had guided and provided for us so far, would also bring us into contact with needy souls, and send us patients." He was not disappointed. "In the quietest possible manner," he relates, "the Mission commenced its double work of ministering to the sick and suffering, and of pointing them to Jesus the great and only Physician of the soul." This double work, according to Dr. Long, has been wonderfully blessed by God.

The method of the Mission may be gathered from these words written by the doctor: "The average attendance at the dispensary each day is about forty—some mornings we have over sixty patients to attend to. They are first interested and entertained by Mr. Hare in the waiting-room; then, in turn, I have the privilege of dealing with them individually in my consulting-room; then 'Sister Millie' takes charge of them, either dressing them in the surgery or making up their prescriptions in the dispensary, and as they leave, giving them a parting word of encouragement. They are followed to their own homes by our united prayer that God may bless the message they have heard and lead them to a lively faith in the Lord Jesus."

Certain priests in Limerick resented the doctor's methods. One rather violent priest—I restrict myself entirely to Dr. Long's account of his martyrdom—denounced the missioner from the pulpit and publicly rebuked him face to face. Catholics were forbidden to visit the dispensary. A parish priest wrote a letter to one of the newspapers, concerning Dr. Long: "As priest having charge of the district where he has established himself, I feel it my duty to state publicly that he is here for proselytizing purposes. Dr. Long is simply using the noble profession to which he belongs as the agent of a Society that has for its object the perversion of Irish Catholics, and the sooner our poor are warned against this insidious attempt on their Faith the better."

The result of this skirmishing was vulgar strife. Dr. Long was boo'd in the street, he was stoned, he was mocked, he was called "old souper." The little children marched to and fro singing, "We'll hang Dr. Long on a sour apple tree." The women scolded him. The men despised him. People who attended the dispensary were roughly handled. In one street-ruction the police made arrests, and the case was tried in court. The Resident Magistrate, a Protestant, is reported to have said on this occasion: "It had been proved, not by witnesses, but by Dr. Long himself, that he was the paid emissary or agent of a certain Society . . . a paid official coming there for the purpose of proselytism, and there was nothing that roused indignation more than that word." You must understand, by the way, why it is the word proselytism arouses such passionate indignation in Ireland. It is not only that the Irish are obstinate enough to consider themselves Christians, but because during the great Famine Protestants from England offered soup to the starving people on condition that they renounced the Catholic Church. Hence the bitterest term of contempt in the Irish Catholic's vocabulary—"old souper." And to-day Protestant ladies in Ireland able to pay good wages, employ Irish servant-girls in their houses, and as soon as the girls are accustomed to their rich and comfortable life, begin the work of sapping their Catholic allegiance.

Nearly all the " converts " from Rome are these poor servant-girls. That is why the Irishman regards proselytism with such bitter contempt and with such vehement detestation.

On another occasion the Lord Chief Justice of Ireland, in charging the Grand Jury at Limerick, made the following remarks :—

> I see that the people of this city have been somewhat excited by the presence of a Dr. Long. . . . He is an agent of what I believe is described as the Irish Church Mission to Roman Catholics. He has been mobbed by the people. Now, of course, any violence on the part of the people is wholly indefensible ; it is much to be deprecated. But if the people would take my advice . . . they would leave these agents of that Society entirely alone. . . . They would not make martyrs of them, because, gentlemen, if they make martyrs of them they only secure that the monetary stream comes in greater volume from England. . . . The Protestant community, the respectable Protestant community of this city and of this country do not in any way associate themselves with these attempts. . . . The Irish Church Missions are supported in England by people who are very well-meaning, who are very religious, but who have no conception of the worthlessness of the Irish Church Missions in this country.

Dr. Long entertains a different notion of his place in the cosmos. He quotes in his book, from one of " the leading Christian papers," the following lines about himself—not because he is proud of the tribute, but because they give all praise to Him who is " our Life, our Sweetness, and our Hope " :—

> I see a warrior of the Word,
> Calm 'mid the crowd's uproar ;
> A Perseus, with a better sword
> Than Perseus ever bore.
> I see him stand amid the storm—
> Of noble port and manly form—
> To play the manly part.
> That clear, calm light is in his eye,
> To dare, direct, defeat, defy ;
> Light from the fire that cannot die,
> God kindled in his heart.

Now, I ask the English Protestant reader to consider what his feelings would be if a society composed of men of science organized in his particular parish a dispensary, advertised free attendance for the poor, and proceeded to use that dispensary for teaching people not to believe their religion ? There are many honest men of science who regard Christianity as a gross superstition, and who thoroughly believe that clericalism is a considerable obstacle in the path of rational progress ; suppose these men adopted the profession of medicine, ministered as doctors to the poor of an English parish, and disseminated among their patients secular, rationalistic, and infidel notions. What would be the feeling in that parish?

There are certain Protestants—happily growing fewer every year, and never representative of the true Protestantism—who, in their enthusiasm for the truth of their own creeds, do not often enough pause to consider the feelings of people to whom other creeds appear equally true, equally precious. It is one thing to write critically or scornfully of these creeds, as scornfully as you please; but it is a different thing altogether for a missionary to employ an active propaganda among the Christians he is seeking to detach from one Church to another—if that can ever be a rightful employment of missionary zeal. Such a man, for instance, as Dr. Joseph Long, "of noble port and manly form," of whom his poet says—

> That clear, calm light is in his eye,
> To dare, direct, defeat, defy,

is evidently the very last person in the world who would exercise those qualities of spirit which are necessary to the "winning" of souls. He believes that God is yearning to save Catholics, he boldly confesses himself a missionary sent by God, and he goes forth "to dare, direct, defeat, defy." And what is the consequence of this martial spirit? Mr. George Wyndham said of him in the House of Commons: "It is to be regretted that Dr. Long, or rather the Society which employs him, should conscientiously think it right to afford gratuitous medical attendance, with the avowed object of making converts in the midst of a Roman Catholic population." Even Dr. Long says of himself: "Many acquaintances were shy about being seen in my company, and the prevailing impression on all sides was that I was not wanted there at all." Finally, if you would see the attitude of this persecuted man towards the Church he is set to overthrow, reflect upon these words written by his own hand in the book which contains the laudatory verses quoted above:—

> The Word of God and the Holy Spirit of God alone can successfully overcome the power of Rome as a system full of arrogance and hypocrisy, of superstition and idolatry, of tyranny and darkness, and deliver from her paralysing slavery human souls, leading them into the enjoyment of the light and liberty of the children of God.

Is it not manifest that a man who can write such words, who can issue such a book—his own portrait forming the frontispiece—is the very last person in the world to attract men and women to the beauty and gentleness, the humility and sweet reasonableness of the Christian life? Is it not manifest that for a man of this kind to go a-proselytizing among a Christian community whose Christianity has flowed into all the nations of Europe, a Christianity which has preserved their nationality through centuries of the grossest tyranny, and has so consecrated their kindness of heart, their docility, and their chastity that they are now things proverbial in the two hemispheres—is it not manifest that such a man and such proselytism—however unintentionally—are in the nature of insult and affront, far more likely to do incalculable harm, to create the most damaging impression, to stir up violent and angry feelings, than to spread the difficult but only saving gospel of sweetness and light?

Compare this gentleman's view of Catholicism with the opinion of those two heroic and well-known missionaries to the Congo, the Rev. John Harris and his wife. "Both Mr. and Mrs. Harris," says an interviewer in the *Daily Chronicle*, "bear testimony to the wonderful results of the Catholic missions in the French and German Congo. . . . 'With regard to industrial progress,' said Mr. Harris, 'the Catholic missions are far in advance of the Protestant missions.'" Catholics at least may claim to be treated as Christians.

Let English Protestants honestly say whether they would permit a double-working Roman Catholic propaganda, such as this, in their own parishes. Would they not hotly resent it if Irish Catholics came to England to proselytize their poor people by means of gratuitous medical attendance, to teach those poor people that Protestantism is "full of arrogance and hypocrisy, of superstition and idolatry, of tyranny and darkness"? Would they not feel justified in condemning the poor who used such a dispensary, and would there not be Kensitites enough in the district to work up brawls and riots in the streets?

This apparently famous, almost classical example of Catholic intolerance, proves, I think, the extraordinary meekness of the Irish people. A Roman Catholic playing Dr. Long's rôle in England would be driven from pillar to post, would be hounded out of the place, would be fortunate to escape without a broken limb or a cracked skull. But Dr. Long has been in Limerick since 1897, the eggs and stones ceased to hurtle in 1903, and he is there still, and as long as the Society which employs him is in existence, he is likely to remain in his double character of doctor and proselytizer. Moreover, he appears to be happy, satisfied, and comfortable. Time may possibly plump that "noble port and manly form," age perhaps may dim that many d'd light in his eye, but the good doctor, faithful to his precarious post, will still "deal with" patients in the dispensary, still make a dyspepsia the bridge for a heart to heart talk on the subject of the Scarlet Woman, and still address delighted parlour-meetings in the comfortable houses of Christian England which contain supporters of the Irish Church Missions. Hear his last words:—

I wish to thank with my whole heart all those dear friends

> everywhere who have supported the work in prayer to God. The work is God's, and we are all, whether directly or indirectly connected with it, co-workers together with Him. He has graciously answered the prayers of His children, and given us the Victory, and "To Him be the glory for ever." Amen.

I cannot think that any truly religious or fair-minded Protestant will pass a verdict on this story of persecution unfavourable to Irish Catholics. Dr. Long's quarrel with the dogmas of Rome cannot be greater than my own—I can believe that few men more heartily than myself dislike the Roman version of Christianity or more thoroughly regret the superstitions of its rites—but I have read this story of the Limerick Medical Mission with humiliation, with anger, and with shame, read it with something more than sorrow and compassion for misguided zeal.

Take, for instance—and then let us have done with this sad business—Dr. Long's reflection on the Limerick jarveys' refusal to drive him on their cars :—

> I have borne this petty and insulting persecution, trusting that God would overrule it for His glory, and use even this car-boycott to help in bringing many in this city to a conviction of sin, to faith in the Lord Jesus Christ.

I know perfectly well what Dr. Long means, but thus expressed is not this paragraph likely to seem to an ordinary man the sentiment of a sanctimoniousness which he has long been taught to suspect ?

Dr. Long is not insincere ; it is, indeed, his very sincerity that is so dangerous. He is no doubt a good man, an earnest man, an honest man ; but I think he is clearly misguided. An arrant hypocrite would do no harm, but a true and earnest man, misguided and zealous in a wrong direction, can do little but mischief. He must misrepresent, albeit unconsciously, the Character of Christ ; he must alienate, albeit unwillingly, the sympathy of men with whom all Christians should be desirous of working for the victory of the spiritual life.

The attraction of Christ is universal ; anything which tends to make it sectarian, anything which tends to make it unattractive, is to be deplored and condemned. I am convinced that every liberal-minded Protestant in England and Ireland will take this view of the matter and support my criticism of Dr. Long's pamphlet. It is of immense importance, when materialism is everywhere degrading and brutalizing life, for all who profess and call themselves Christians to make religion beautiful and attractive in the eyes of mankind.

With no fear of its effect upon my argument, rather the other way, I set this historical instance of Catholic intolerance—the only one I have found—in the midst of a book inspired both by admiration and affection for the Irish people,

# CHAPTER X

## THE FINE FLOWER

AMONG the very agreeable people in the south of Ireland who represent what one may designate as the English Character, it is but seldom that the traveller encounters a virulent or an irreconcilable attitude towards Home Rule. They have not a sip of Orange in their blue veins.

Their attitude to the question of Irish politics bears a family likeness to the attitude of our own well-off people in England towards labour questions. They regard Irish politicians rather contemptuously as agitators, they believe that at the back of the national movement there is a sinister plot to compass the downfall of the British Empire, they quote, not vehemently, but sorrowfully, the most bloodthirsty passages from an antique Fenian oratory, and they assure you with real honesty, and just a touch of impatience, that farmers and peasants would be perfectly "loyal" and contented with things as they are, if the politicians, the "paid agitators," would only leave them alone.

Thus, all over the world, does Mrs. Partington flourish a mop in the face of the Atlantic. It is impossible to make these people understand that agitators are created by world movements, and that the desire for higher wages, better houses, and easier conditions of labour is the natural and righteous aspiration of industrious men, whose wages are poor, whose houses are sunless and ugly, whose conditions of labour are dangerous and unhealthy.

We must not be cross or impatient with these nice people. When a man like Mr. Austen Chamberlain, who resides, one may say, on the very river-side of tendency, solemnly assures the House of Commons in a speech seriously praised by the London newspapers, that the recent strike of colliers—concurrent with similar strikes in America and Germany—was due to the rhetoric of Mr. Lloyd George, we must surely agree that there are certain minds incapable of perception, denied the gift of vision, and prevented by some extraordinary mental aberration from forming rational judgments. Certainly we must not expect in country-houses and villages, remote from a lemon, to discover over elegant teacups complete sympathy with modern thought.

Just as in England intelligent and honest people hate the Labour Member of Parliament, resist the movement for a living wage, and distrust the working-classes on whom they depend for their existence, so in Ireland the Protestant English garrison detest the Nationalist politician, oppose the movement for self-government, and distrust the Catholic democracy whose toil and goodwill are essential to their welfare. This distrust is almost incurable. It is the spirit of a frontier town continually in fear of invasion. We can do nothing but hope that a more tolerant and enlightened posterity will learn from experience that a democracy determined to improve its conditions need be no more inimical to virtue and culture, need be no more godless and bloody-minded, than a fortunate aristocracy determined to preserve its privileges.

In England there are people who think that the best way to resist the democratic movement is to encourage what they call "patriotism." One is continually meeting in the country some earnest soul who believes that by the singing of "God save the King" as often as possible, by teaching children to salute the Flag, and by organizing parades and pageants on the occasion of national anniversaries—never mind how many slums there may be, how much sweating, how much inequality and discontent—they will effectually slay the dragon of Socialism. One finds the same fatuity in Ireland. People make one almost hate the tune of the national anthem by the inappropriate occasions on which they rise to sing that rather un-Christian prayer, almost make one loathe the Flag by the affectionate cloying terms in which they speak of it, and almost make one wish that England had never won a battle or founded an empire, by the boastfulness and triumphant Cæsarism with which they drag these attainments into contemporary politics. They not only do nothing to hinder Socialism, but they tend to make of Patriotism something mean, provincial, second-rate, and offensive.

Now, although the English garrison in the south of Ireland are thus minded, one finds, on pressing them in polite conversation with rational arguments, that they are not in reality opposed to the idea of self-government. Like their fellows in England, who most willingly admit that civilization has some very dirty corners and some very ragged edges, and who are even enthusiastic for social reform so long as it does not proceed from the opposite side of the House of Commons, the English garrison in the south of Ireland frankly confess, when driven to it, that the present system of government is expensive, irritating, and unsuccessful. If the Conservative party proposed a measure of Home Rule, and if that measure assured the social dominance of the English garrison, those nice people would vote for it and work for it without a moment's misgiving. What they really dread is not the loss of English interference, but the loss of their own place and power as social overlords.

To stand upon a hill and overlook a slumbering market-town in the valley below, is to see the Irish question visibly spread upon the living map of Ireland. Just outside the clustering habitations of the town rises a huge and solid building, stronger, handsomer, more elaborate and impressive than any house in the town itself. This building represents English rule. It is the Workhouse. Wherever you go in Ireland you find in the neighbourhood of towns these immense, costly, and complex structures born of the indiscriminate application to poor Ireland of those laws for dealing with poverty which have been so singularly unsuccessful in rich England. Few things have been more disastrous to modern Ireland than her dose of England's Poor Laws. The great massive workhouses established all over the country have created tramps, beggars, unemployables, and villains of a horrid type ; they have embittered the honest poor who are taxed to support them ; and they have added an enormous charge to the debit side of Ireland's ledger. If you would realize how preposterous a thing it is to apply English legislation to Ireland, to make Ireland do whatever England does, to make of England's necessities the measure of Ireland's needs, visit one of these mighty buildings and ask any man of business in the town what effect it has produced on Irish life.

From the hill-top, looking to the hills on the further side of the valley, far away from the town, the traveller sees large and beautiful houses planted at spacious distances from each other and surrounded by fruitful land, by beautiful woods, and gardens shining in the sun. These houses represent the English garrison. They are occupied by the descendants of those obliging Protestants who went, for England's glory, to a starved and shattered Ireland, and made themselves masters of the land. The fertile fields, the rich woods, the convenient rivers, and the rent-paying villages scattered over their profitable acres, were not purchased by their ancestors ; they were taken by force ; some people would say they were stolen. The strong walls surrounding for many miles some of these fine properties cost their owners not a penny-piece. Some were actually paid for—quietly reflect upon this fact—by the money England subscribed for the relief of the great Famine ; others were not paid for at all—they were built by forced labour. The houses, the gardens, the walls, the land, the splendour and beauty of these places, represent England's conquest of Ireland. They stand for that aspect of the Irish question which we are now considering, the English garrison.

When the eye has taken its fill of these noble domains, it returns for a moment to that other aspect of English influence, the great pompous workhouse ; then, it studies the centre of the picture, the town itself. Great is the comparison. Against the central street—with its mayor's humble residence, its town-hall, its hotel, its shops, and its market-place—huddle and press a thousand mean, miserable small houses, packed and congested together in utmost confusion of smoke and squalor. These little cabins are like so many limpet-shells stuck to a rock, and, as the limpet-shell is packed with limpet-flesh, so are these human shells stuffed with humanity. Three and four generations may be found in those dark, ill-ventilated, and sunless tenements. The tiny streets and stifling courts are full of children. The struggle for existence seems to have crowded their houses and their occupiers together like a flock of sheep hurdled in a damp and trodden corner of a turnip-field. On every side there is land—green, sunlit, and fertile land—but these cabins are herded and squeezed and fenced together as if they were a London slum. They represent the Irish nation.

With the English garrison lording it over the pastures, and with the English Workhouse bleeding the virility of the nation before their very eyes, bleeding it and charging them with the leech's fee, the Irish nation, crammed in its rotten cabin, is conscious of something wrong and hindering in the union with Great Britain. It is conscious of being "squeezed."

Such in landscape is this Irish question. The Workhouse stands for the imposition of unsuitable and therefore disastrous laws enacted by another country; the domains stand for an alien landlordism; and the struggling town, toiling for existence, and almost powerless to express its will, stands for the Irish nation.

It is quite certain that, by a transformation of nationality, many people now loyal and satisfied in England would be disloyal and dissatisfied in Ireland. And I marvel that so many of the poor and struggling Irish are not infinitely more bitter and fierce in their quarrel with the Union.

'̇s for the English garrison, one finds among them all sorts and conditions of men. I met, for instance, a cavalry subaltern who stretched his long legs before the fire, assured me with a laugh that the whole agitation for Home Rule was merest blatherskite, and begged me to come and stay with him at the house of a jolly old cock who was training his horses, knew all about the Irish Nationality, and could tell me dozens of good stories. "You can hardly get upstairs to bed," he said, laughing, "for dogs fighting on the stairs, but it's not a bad little crib, and the old fellow himself is a topper. He knows Ireland. By gad, he does! better far than the Brothers Redmond." On the other hand, I met men like Lord Dunraven, landlords who have spent large sums of money in building cottages, improving land, introducing new crops—such as tobacco—and who are devoted with something like enthusiasm to the development of Ireland's resources. Such men, while they stand apart from Irish politics, candidly admit the justice of Ireland's claim for self-government. Then one meets people who are in the stage of our own squires at the beginning of the last century ; they farm a little land themselves, go regularly to the Bench and the parish church, take a rather kind but condescending interest in the lives of the peasants, and regard hunting, shooting, and fishing as the main occupations of a Christian's life. Again, one encounters little rural communities of culture, where the women are devoted to water-colours and music, where Mudie's library and the *Athenæum* are of weekly importance, and where visits are paid to cottages, entertainments organized in the village schoolroom, and garden-parties provided for the county in the summer.

It would, perhaps, be difficult to find a thoroughly bad landlord in modern Ireland ; but it is not easy to find men and women of the English garrison who perfectly or even partially comprehend the movement of democracy. And that is the tragedy of all aristocracies. To be suspicious, distrustful, and afraid of democracy, to believe that every movement of the many towards more sunshine and purer air, to consider that their own happiness, their own ease, their own refinement and virtue are of essential value to the poor—this is the blunder of all privileged classes in all countries of the world.

In Ireland it is almost pitiful to see how these little groups of nice people in nearly every part of the country form themselves into superior oases of mortality, stand entirely aloof from the national life, and narrow the noblest qualities of the human spirit in a proud exclusiveness to which neither their parts nor value entitle them.

It is the belief of many Nationalists that Home Rule will draw the whole nation together, and that the English garrison will step down from its pedestal and bear an honourable part in the daily work of the commonwealth.

Many of these pleasant English people—for so one must really call them—are admirably gifted for the labour of government, some of them are capable of exercising a valuable influence on political thought. It is certain that they can be of service to the State.

But they must first learn—I speak, of course, only of the ruck—to trust democracy, to know that anything in the nature of snobbishness is now quite vulgarly out of fashion, and to realize that every man in the modern State has duties which cannot be devolved and responsibilities which cannot be shirked. They must, above everything else, apprehend the inwardness of those great tidal movements of democracy which are now altering the configuration of history and shaping the destinies of the human race. They must rid their minds of petty intolerance, trivial bigotry, and irrational prejudice ; they must put themselves into line with modern science and modern politics ; and they must open their doors and invite to their firesides all those who are working for the future righteousness with clean hands and honest hearts.

## CHAPTER XI

### BECAUSE IT IS ALWAYS DUBLIN

THERE is something about Dublin that wears the look and breathes the character of an old French town. It might be a quarter of Paris or a neighbour of Tours. One thinks that Balzac would have well liked to rummage in its unconventional dark streets, that Turgeniev might have lived his quiet, gentle, expatriated life in one of its formal squares, that Daudet, leaning from a high window overlooking the river, would have seen the very theatre of his dreams.

Cork, when you get to know it, has also something of the French spirit—a beautiful city, full of surprises, and compassed about by a wonderful prettiness of landscape. But Dublin is this, with the added grandeur, the more sombre tone, of a settled antiquity and a sad illustrious history. One is conscious in this old city, with its wide streets, its churches, its bridges, and its statues, of a once splendid renown, a once glowing enthusiasm for nationality, and a once brilliant devotion to the excitements of social life—all of which have grown prouder and more exclusive with the shabbiness of declining prosperity. It is like some venerable lady living in a bath-chair at Tunbridge Wells who once tapped Palmerston's arm with a playful fan and suggested to pretty little Queen Victoria a new arrangement of her ribbons. You seem to be aware in these grim and ancient streets of the rumble of coaches over the cobbles, of the swaggering, dicing, and mohawking excesses of gilded youth along the narrow pavements, and at night of open doors showing bright interiors in the now gloomy and deserted squares, music and the sound of dancing coming with a decorous joy from the long French windows on the upper floor. There is scarcely a tree in the gardens that does not whisper of an amorous past.

And also one is conscious at night, in the dark and empty streets of this tired city, of a rolling of drums, a turning of gun-wheels, and the tramp of a gaunt army marching with torn banners and bandaged brows through weeping and wailing multitudes. Great battles have been fought, sublime causes have struggled with adversity, incomparable transports of delirious joy and overwhelming breakers of tribulation and despair have swept like a flood through these ancient sombre streets crowded with ghosts, where now the policeman walks listless and unemployed, where the gaudy electric tram scrapes a string music from the overhead wire, and where the clerk and typist going home in the twilight stop to smile at a window full of comic picture post-cards.

But Dublin is still the Mecca of every Irishman conscious of social gifts. There is no other city in Ireland where Beau Brummell could take the air or Sheridan invite a party of wits to dinner. Dublin is the unchallenged capital of Ireland's poetry and fashion and philosophy. One may call it the Salon of the Lady Next Door.

There are streets as brilliant with luminous shops as the Narrows of our own Bond Street. There are statues of national heroes at every corner. Huge and solemn architecture congregates at a single dramatic point with the impressive authority of a capital city. Beautiful gardens with winding walks and glowing waters receive on a fine morning the perambulators of the city. Gentlemen and ladies go riding in the park. Merchants arrive at their offices in motor-cars and phaetons. Cavalry orderlies trot bumping through the central streets with blue envelopes carefully held in the fingers of their white gauntlets. Protestant clergymen in gaiters and Catholic priests in shovel-hats rub shoulders and avert their eyes in the sauntering crowd. Professors from the rival Universities meet and avoid each other in bookshops. Students lounge at college entries. Apostles of great causes and secretaries of vital movements, oddly and romantically dressed, haste through the streets with transfigured faces and long hair. Exquisite girls, their complexions unequalled on this side of Paradise, go shopping under the striped awnings of the fashionable quarter. Thick-clothed, heavy-booted workmen, as in every city of the world, loll gloomy, torpid, and savage against the shiny walls of street corners. Little impudent-faced boys run across the roadways with bundles of newspapers under their arms, a placard blowing about their bare legs, the end of a cigarette smouldering at the dirty corners of their elderly mouths. Women, with babies rolled sausage-like in melancholy grey shawls, sell gorgeous flowers to chaffering middle-class ladies. In the gutters crawl ruminating red-nosed sandwich-men announcing incongruous music, theatricals, bazaars, bargain sales. The butcher's pony rattles by at a sharp trot. The jarvey lifts his whip to attract your attention. His Excellency's limousine glides up to the pavement's edge. . . .

You get the impression from these interesting streets, particularly on a bright morning in spring, or a very cold, rosy morning in winter, that the city has little to do but enjoy itself. You are disposed to guess at the golf-handicap of the men rather than to surmise their profession, and as for the beautiful women you wonder what romance nestles at their heart even when the red, green, and chocolate-coloured pile of tradesmen's books in their hands argue a considered and prosaic housekeeping.

The city is just of a size. Men can be really famous in Dublin, importance can feel itself important, beauty can know itself known by name, even a knighthood is aware of inspiring awe. As for Bullion, it may go about the world of Dublin, conscious of a most satisfying envy, for people there are not distressingly pecunious. If any man is truly witty, everyone knows him; if any man is a mighty scholar, everybody tells you so; if any lady gives delightful parties, she is a Queen with Dublin for her court. Why anybody who is anybody in Dublin should wish to drown himself in the Atlantic Ocean of London is a matter that would be painful to explore.

It is worth noticing that with all its gaiety and disposition to be fashionable, Dublin is almost entirely free of the common vice which disfigures other cities. There is nothing in the whole town that suggests for a moment anything approaching to the central and unblushing shame of London. Indeed, a man might live all his life in Dublin and never see a single tragedy of this kind. Girls fall, perhaps willingly take to that way of getting money, but they do not remain in Dublin. Dublin does not pay. A father devoted to his children might take them at all hours about the streets of Dublin and never have to lie away an awkward question.

But Dublin has its shame. There are slums, hidden away in the dark places of this city, which are so atrocious that I think they must long ago have destroyed all virtue in their inhabitants but for the constant vigilance of a ruling priesthood. In these foul, inhuman dens—one dreadful closet for a double row of houses—you come across little interiors decorated with pictures of St. Mary, and discover so kindly and virtuous a family life that you are disposed to believe the dictum of Dean Inge, "It is the pig that makes the sty, and not the sty that makes the pig." But the poverty is frightful. The struggle to keep head above water is very nearly intolerable. People do go to the devil, because for them all sense of heavenly reality is obliterated in these noisome alleys of earthly wretchedness. I cannot conceive of any man with one smouldering glimmer of an expiring conscience taking rent for these burrows. To be pickpocket or murderer would be more downright honest.

Yet in these slums of Dublin there is an atmosphere which clothes them with some different guise from the slums of Belfast. To begin with, they have the excuse of age. They do not say to the visitor, "Here we are; the handiwork of Industrialism; the expression of Capital's attitude to Labour; the last word in red brick and slates." They existed before factories darkened the skies. They seem older than the city that surrounds them with dwarfing magnificence. They speak of a simpler age, a more primitive people, and of fields that were once green to their very doors. In a certain way they are picturesque. At any rate they are only anachronisms, not contemporary iniquities.

I paid a visit to these slums with a notable saint. Had he lived in the Middle Ages this good man would have been "all heart," as we say; living in the twentieth century he is nearly "all head." Let me present the reader to this excellent good man—the Reverend Father Aloysius, a Franciscan, a temperance reformer, and a student of municipal reform.

He is a tall, bony, angular, small-headed gentleman, of an age between thirty and forty. He wears spectacles which keep slipping to the end of his nose. As he talks, the thin long beard projecting from his chin wags like a flag-signal. His large mouth is seldom closed—through the wide and genial gateway of his lips you see an incredible number of teeth all jumbled together but living apparently in the greatest amity. His eyes are round, vivacious, feverish. His brown hair is brushed forward over his forehead. The face is that colour of heat which hints of a digestion addled by too ceaseless an activity of the brain.

Father Aloysius, in his thick brown-girdled habit, his little skull-cap at the back of his head, and his long feet sliding about in loose sandals, seems always to be in a hurry—as if he had just jumped up from a table strewn with facts and statistics and was afraid of being late for an appointment at the other end of the world. He walks on his toes, with a little hop in his steps; he carries books and papers under his arms, and talks at a pace which stretches the drum of one's ears to keep up with it. As he hurries you along he will wheel suddenly round to show something important in the street just past; or, pushing his spectacles into place and catching you by the sleeve, he will plunge across the traffic of the roadway, and stop dead on the other side, craning his thin neck and looking to right and left for a particular house that he thinks is worthy of your inspection.

And you feel that four hundred years ago this electric person would have spent the whole day kneeling in his hermit's cell or poring over a sacred book of mysticism. The times change and the saints with them. Love of God has become devotion to humanity.

One trivial thing in my walk with this good man made a considerable impression on my mind. Every man we passed doffed his hat to the monk, and children came charging towards him with the cry, as they collided with his legs and raised their smiling dirty faces to his eyes, "God bless you, Father." Labourers mending the road, carters driving vans and waggons, postmen going by with empty bags limp across their shoulders, jarveys driving their cars along, working-men lounging at street corners, gentlemen of the commercial traveller persuasion, and dangerous-looking roughs at the beginning of a slum manhood—all these men, certainly hundreds of them, and so far as I saw with no single exception, looked respectfully towards the monk, and lifted hats and caps.

Father Aloysius seemed to see none of these salutations. He acknowledged only those that came as it were face to face with him, and that with briefest inclination of his head. But again and again he slackened his pace, bent down laughing and delighted, and touched with his hand the head of some child calling upward from his knees, " God bless you, Father ; God bless you, Father." " God bless you, child," he would say, gently and sweetly, and then guide them affectionately out of his way.

Perhaps it is fear on the part of ignorant people. Perhaps it is admiration for a life of self-sacrifice. But whatever the cause of this respect, I was struck by its universal accord in a neighbourhood so terrible and soul-destroying that I should not have been in the least surprised to hear scoffing and mocking words aimed at the servant of God. Think of such reverence for a monk, or anybody else, in a slum of Liverpool, Manchester, or Portsmouth.

" Everybody seems to know you," I said.

" Our Order has worked here for a long time," he replied. " They are genuinely fond of us, and they respect the habit. You would be really interested, I think, to discover how these poor people cling to religion, and how kind they are to each other. That is what gives us such great pleasure. Their kindness to each other, particularly in distress, is amazing. It is quite, quite beautiful."

He turned to me, smiling, the eyes shining.

" On the whole are they fairly virtuous ? "

" Their one vice is drink. People say they are lazy, but I am sure it is untrue. They grow indolent because looking for a job or standing about for work disheartens them. They are not properly nourished, and their houses are insanitary ; one cannot expect them to be efficient. If they had regular work they would be brisker. But all the same, drink is a real vice. We are making a great fight for temperance with our Father Matthew Guild, and the difference is already extraordinary. You will see our Father Matthew Hall where we get crowds of working-men every night. You see, they have been neglected. Little has been done to amuse and strengthen them in their leisure. And drink in Ireland has always been regarded rather indulgently. I don't think the poor of Dublin are worse drinkers than the poor of London or Glasgow. But there is too much drinking. It is our worst enemy. In everything else the people are wonderfully good, and as soon as a man gives up drink he becomes happy."

" You think the slums are responsible ? "

" We find that very soon after a man signs the pledge, he grows prosperous, and leaves the neighbourhood. He can afford a better house. And as the good people go out, the bad people flow in, so that we have always got a population of miserables. If the slums were swept away and decent houses erected, the character of the people would improve, our work would be infinitely more easy. These slums are the sink of the city to which all the unhappiness and failure and poverty and drunkenness gravitate in a steady flow. People can live here on next to nothing."

We entered some of the dens in the worst slums, and in every case the Father's visit was evidently regarded as a supreme honour. With the deference paid to him, there was also admiration and affection. I detected nothing of that moroseness which so often characterizes the spirit of poor people in London slums. These depressed Irish have a certain grace—a charm of manner and a tone of voice—which poverty seems to spare.

Father Aloysius carried me off to see the Father Matthew Memorial Hall—a vast building excellently planned for the entertainment and instruction of working-men. He showed me these premises with the pride and enthusiasm of a collector exhibiting his spoils. His conversation showed him to be well acquainted with many movements of social reform in England; I discovered that he is something of an expert in public questions; he is a convinced and keen-spirited optimist, believing that it is good to be alive and fighting for the progress of mankind. He would make an excellent member of Parliament, invaluable on Committees and Commissions; his letter to *The Times* would receive the most respectful treatment.

As we parted he jerked the bundle of books and papers from under his arm, and began to go through them with his accustomed speed in everything. "I have here," he said, "some printed matter which I think may interest you." And I drove away with most of his books and nearly all his papers in my unworthy hands.

The phrase "printed matter" is one of the most common in Dublin parlance. If you are a sentimental traveller, and go about this city asking questions and seeking information, you will find that nearly every one you meet has "printed matter," which he begs you to take away with you and read at your leisure. An extra portmanteau is advisable.

I did not realize until this visit to Dublin how vast a boon to the printer are those multitudinous and conflicting "movements" which characterize our period. In Dublin there is any number of such movements, their name indeed, like certain of their relatives, is legion; and everybody connected with a movement has an inexhaustible supply of "printed matter" dealing with that particular cult. It seems to me that like those thrifty and inventive people who live by taking in each other's washing, the inhabitants of Dublin must spend their days in becoming proselytes of each other's proselytism. There must be a perpetual game of Family Coach among the various stacks of "printed matter." Sooner or later, I think, every thought in the brain of Ireland wings to Dublin and there materializes in pamphlet form, becoming "printed matter."

Belfast, as we shall see presently, is differently engaged. But this passion for "printed matter" is characteristic of the Irish capital. It shows, I think, that Dublin is a city of ideas, it shows that the Irish nation is awake and alert, it shows that interest in the art and science of human existence is as pregnant in Ireland as it is in London. Dublin, if it is not exactly a seething cauldron, is at least a kettle singing pleasantly on the hob.

I am quite sure that Futurist poets and Futurist painters would receive homage in Dublin. I recommend, indeed, all ladies and gentlemen with cranky ideas to make the Irish capital their habitation. Provided with money enough to indulge themselves in a little "printed matter," they are sure of interest and may confidently reckon on disciples.

And this it is which makes Dublin so interesting and beguiling a city. You are not depressed by the inky shadows of a mechanical commerce, you are not bored by a formal sameness in humanity, you are not teased by the trifling littleness and the sated cynicism of a conventional society. Every other man you meet has a patent medicine for the ills of the human race, or is working heart and soul for millennium, or is looking about him for a fad and a crotchet to which he can devote the passion of his life. Everybody wants to be enthusiastic about something. Men there are in love with existence. You feel that a nation is thinking about life. You encounter Mr. Pickwick and Don Quixote at the same dinner-party, and adventure is the spirit of every table talk. One man strikes an idea to light his pipe, and sets fire to the box of Dublin dreams. I met two professors in one evening ; the Professor of English Literature was enthusiastic about political economy ; and the Professor of Commerce was enthusiastic about poetry.

I long for Home Rule, that I may go to Dublin before I die and see the city shining in the glory of a national Parliament. It will be a living capital.

Much virtue, believe me, in "printed matter."

## CHAPTER XII

### THE DAME

SOMEWHERE in the wilds of County Derry—I think it must have been in the neighbourhood of Magherafelt—I made acquaintance with a mild and beautiful old woman who was very amusing and interesting, and who seemed to me in one particular typical of the Irish Mother.

She lives alone in a diminutive dwelling, like a little whitewashed fowl-house, at the gates of a great house occupied by a doctor. To enter the old lady's cabin you descend two steps, stooping your head to avoid a blow from the lintel. The interior is bright and cosy. A tall bed, spread with an elaborate quilt of patchwork, is the principal article of furniture. The walls on every side are pasted with most incongruous pictures and advertisements cut from magazines and newspapers—advertisements, among others, of corsets, gartered stockings, and high-heeled shoes. There are three little deep-set windows, with flower-pots on the ledges. A door in the back admits to a garden. A peat-fire burns in the grate. On the mantelpiece are china ornaments and brass candlesticks.

The dame is white-haired, and wears a black cap with a frill of white muslin in the front. Her face in repose has the austerity of a church dignitary. The eyes are pale blue and severe. The colour of the skin is like ivory. Her cheeks are hollow. Nose and lips are pinched and refined.

She said to me, in a low voice, speaking quickly and impressively: "I am alone in the world, after a long and heavy life; but it's the Will of God; and who am I to complain? Tut, who am I? But, ah, the weary time, the weary time! I bore seven sons to my husband, and I reared five of them, tall men and strong, and they all left me and went away, tut, tut; and now they're dead—dead and buried in foreign lands. Not one of them lies in an Irish grave. Two of my boys are buried in America, one in Australia, one in a place they call Glasgow over in Scotland, and one of them in Canada. Ah me, ah me! Three of them were married, and their children, I suppose, are alive now; but I've never seen them, I never hear a word from them; I don't even know their names. But it's the Will of God; and people here are very kind to me; the good doctor comes to see me, a rare gentleman he is, and he sends me milk from his cows; and I've got the Old Age Pension; and when I die I shall be buried beside my husband, who was always a good man to me, and a true father to his sons. Dear, dear! But how I'm cracking to you!" Her face lit suddenly with a smile. "You'll think me bold to be talking so freely."

Something of the romance of our race seemed to shine over the old dame as she was speaking. Withered and pale, solitary and pensioned, this venerable cottager, sitting beside her peat-fire in a derelict corner of Ulster, has given of the fruit of her womb to the uttermost parts of the earth. Seed of her seed are now planting and reaping in lands across the sea, and she does not know how they fare, does not even know their names. Over her fire alone in the world, but not friendless, she dreams of the past; and none of her children's children will come to close her eyes and follow her to the grave. Something of her temperament, something of her heart, something of her soul may be interwoven in the destinies of America, Canada, and Australia—perhaps indestructibly.

She said to me: "It's wonderful how many people live as if they'd got nothing to do but look for their own pleasure. To think of that! I'm always telling people here that our real life is to come, that we ought to seek God and think about Him—for isn't it true that after death we shall live for ever and ever? Tut, of course it's true. I think it is dreadful, oh dreadful, that people don't think more about God. And what a glorious thought it is. A Father in heaven! God is Love! Our Father! Could a body have anything more beautiful to think about? But, you know, there are some people who never say their prayers! Tut. Imagine it! Never say their prayers! Now, isn't that a dreadful thing? Oh, I can't think what's coming to the world. But, there, there! You'll be laughing at me soon. I haven't had a crack like this for a long time. Oh dear, aren't I talking a lot!"

I encouraged her to continue.

"I've seen something of the world, and I've crossed the sea," she said presently. "I once paid a visit to that place they call Glasgow, over in Scotland across the water—oh, a terrible, terrible place! Tut, I don't know how people can live in such dirty places, not fit for the animals, I'm sure. I went there to see my poor boy; he was an engineer; and there he lies, dead in the cemetery. Ah, he was a beautiful boy! Tall, oh, yes! and strong and fine-looking—a great man every way. Oh, you should have seen his father—a *grand man!* But he's dead; yes, he's dead. And now I'll tell you something interesting. When I went across the sea I heaved. For the first time in my life. Never before and never since I did it, but I heaved then. Up it came! Oh, dreadful! *Whish!*—you never saw such a thing in your life. And when I got to Glasgow there was only a narrow board from the ship to the land; and do you think I was afraid to walk down it? Tut, why, I ran! Yes, my son said he never saw such a thing in his life. Everybody thought I should fall and wanted to hold me; and I ran! But the truth is I was so glad to be rid of the ship. Yes, I ran down the plank. Oh, I've seen something of the world."

Always she returned to the subject of religion.

"Don't you think it is awful, the way people set themselves up against God? They make themselves to know more than the God Who made them. Just think of that, now. I heard a story in my young days which shows how God punishes people like that. There was a poor man in Ireland who married, and every year his wife bore him a child. When there were five of them, he said to her, 'I cannot afford to live with you ; your children will soon eat up all I've got.' And he went away, and left her, so that he should have no more children. Yes, he went over to Scotland, where the wages are high, and every week he sent money to his wife in Ireland, just enough for herself and the five bairnies. And at the end of three years he came back ; and what do you think happened ? The very next time she was brought to bed, she had three at a birth—triplets ! Yes, one for every year he had deserted her. So he might just as well have stayed at home. And that's how God punishes people who set up their dirty ignorance against His laws. Sure, doesn't He know what is good for us better than we know it ourselves ? "

Towards the end of our colloquy she grew more whispering and confidential. A look of cunning stole into her pale blue eyes. I noticed that she studied my appearance and the details of my clothing with a hungry curiosity, almost a murderous greed.

She leaned quite close to me, put her hand on my knee, and in a very low voice, moistening her lips with excitement, and speaking as if she was imparting a tremendous secret for my everlasting benefit, she whispered :

" Now, I'll tell you what you should do. You listen to me now. Hush ! I'll tell you something ; yes, something good. You must think about God. You must always be looking for Him, and listening to what He says. Sure, He's always near, always quite close to us. Always telling us what to do. For instance "—drawing her chair even nearer, sinking her voice even lower, and speaking with extraordinary rapidity as her hand passed excitedly up and down over my knee—" for instance, suppose you should come across a poor old woman, living all alone, and with only just enough money to keep body and soul together ; and suppose, being a fine rich gentleman, you feel inclined to put your hand in your pocket, and you think to yourself that you'll give the old body a shilling, or say half a crown—well, do you think it's your own thought at all ? Faith, it's not so—not at all ! Tut, it isn't you that's thinking you'll give the money. But, my dear, you do it ! You do it ! Hush ! Take my advice now. Do it, do it ! And I'll tell you why. *It's God telling you.* It's not you thinking ; it's God. Yes, that's how God acts. He tells us to do these things. You give the poor old woman half a crown, or if that's too much, give her a shilling ; and in the next world you'll get it back—God Himself will give it back to you. Isn't that wonderful, now ?—but isn't it beautiful ?—and, mind you—hush !—*it's true.* I know it. That's how God acts. Now, my dear, be sure you always do what God tells you."

This beautiful old woman, a Mother in Ireland, had dropped suddenly into cunning senility. She addressed me as a little child and spoke herself as a child. It was like an animal to watch the licking of her thin lips, the covetous peering of her eyes, the twitchings of her hands.

I thanked her with becoming gratitude for her revelation, and before taking my leave begged her to accept a terrestrial half-crown, given, however, with no thought of a celestial crown.

She threw up her hands, her eyes lit with laughter, her lips broke into smiles, her pale face became suffused with the warm colour of delight, and she exclaimed, taking the money:

"But I had no thought you'd be thinking of me! There! but I hope you don't think I've been asking for it? Tut. The thought never entered my mind! You'll believe me, won't you, now? Sure, you must believe me. The thought never entered my mind."

And, cancelling all merit from my charity, perhaps imperilling my soul, I said that I perfectly believed her.

She followed me to the door, a most sweet and beautiful figure, praying God to prosper me and give me joy all the days of my life. Her benediction chased pity from my heart. After all, it was only a reflex action of her brain, a return to the hard and bitter struggle for existence. I dare to say that she was hardly conscious of guile.

A blithe and jovial but a very Turveydrop of a guard on one of the smallest Ulster railways said to me, "If your honour had the time, I could tell you things, och, many things, that would be worth half a crown to go in a book or a newspaper."

I was unable to discover how he guessed that I had any connection with books or newspapers, and had to content myself with ruminations on the evident ubiquity of English half-crowns in Ulster.

At a little station, just before the junction where one changes for the main line, this smiling guard came to my window, lifted his cap, and inquired deferentially, "Will your honour allow me just to take a nip?" I began to fumble in my trouser pocket—for he had been singularly obliging; but he stopped me with a jovial laugh. "Oh, no, your honour," he implored, producing a ticket-punch, "not a nip out of the bottle, but only a nip out of your honour's ticket! Now, is that worth half a crown? Oh, no! not at all." And giving me back my ticket and raising his cap again, he departed wreathed in smiles.

At the junction I saved one shilling and sixpence.

## CHAPTER XIII

### A CORNER OF ULSTER

PORT-NA-BLAH, meaning Buttermilk Harbour, is the name given to a few scattered cottages clinging to the rocks about Sheep Haven.

These two names, so gentle and pastoral, better suggest the occupation of humanity in those parts than the actual earth and actual ocean to which mankind has attached them. For while man folds his sheep on the mountain side and drives his cows from wind-swept bogland to the shelter of the homestead, the terrific force of the Atlantic thunders against a bleak coast of incomparable grandeur, sending the tide of its power flowing far inland over strewn and shattered rocks which are like the ruins of a great city. In winter a more desolate, a more terrible, a more ferocious coast than these broken sea-walls of Donegal can hardly be found in the sister islands, and the great sea, contemptuous of its name, far from wearing a sheepish look or chanting an Arcadian song, comes leaping to the heaped chaos of the shore with a howl that seems to set the firmament in fear.

The savage nature of the landscape and the hateful menace of the sea bestow extraordinary charm upon the little cottages. They are so child-like and helpless, so meek and lowly, so trustful and complacent, that, contemplating their little white-washed walls and trivial roofs from such a distance as the height of Horn Head, one seems to see in them an expression of man's truest attitude to the universe which enfolds him. The wind roars against the shattered cliffs, the waves hurl themselves upon the streaming rocks, the wild tumultuous air is filled with a clangour full of sovran scorn or furious malevolence, and in the little ramshackle byre built of planks and gorse a girl is milking a cow,at the peat fire in the kitchen of the farm-house a woman is baking bread, and down from the mountain side, carrying a lamb in his arms,comes a man whose face is kind and tender.

I cannot decide whether it is more difficult to express in words the grandeur of this tremendous landscape or the gentleness, the sweetness, and the pleasant grace of the simple people who live in its midst. Perhaps a remark made to me by an old woman may better help the reader to feel the nature of the scenery than a catalogue of its qualities.

One morning, after a night of snow, I started to walk from the farm-house where I was lodging in Port-na-blah to the distant and lofty scar of Horn Head. It was one of those clear and ringing days when the sun burns like scarlet blood, the snow throbs and vibrates with metallic light, and the wind against the face has the cutting sharpness of a razor's edge. Seaward, where the air was filled with powdered mist, the moving ocean glittered like an agate ; inland, where the lochs lay at the feet of the hills, there was a dull grey shimmer, as of hammered steel. For the rest it was an utterly, a dazzlingly white world—the only true white known to man, a white which makes white linen and white paper look dingy and ashamed

The lonely roads were smooth with this thick whiteness from hedge to hedge; the fields blinded the eyes with the same unbroken flash of white, rolling, heaving, and sinking into immeasurable distance; the great mountains, sprinkled and patched with white on their rock-strewn sides, lifted summits to the troubled sky which were as smooth and thick with snow as the level field beside the loch. The cry of sea-birds wheeling through the cold air had the wail of starvation. Rooks, with puffed feathers and dishevelled heads, loaded the leafless trees with a sense of mourning and death. No cattle were visible throughout that frozen world. No human creature was working in the fields. And the wind pierced and cut, so that even little birds were forced to run like mice through the hedges.

I passed through the empty streets of Dunfanaghy, a small town with I know not how many rival churches, and getting on to the fields made a short cut of the long laborious ascent to Horn Head. These fields, pricked with the feet of birds and spurred by the feet of rabbits, brought me once more to the road, and soon I was in the very teeth of the wind, marching with bent head up a steep invisible track with cottages here and there on one side and a line of moaning telegraph wires on the other.

At the extreme end of this long straight road was a cottage, and when I first saw it a woman—barely distinguishable as a woman—was moving from the door to some sheds at the side. As she came back, walking slowly and carrying a bucket in her hand, she caught sight of me in the distance, and stopped, shading her eyes and watching my approach. After some moments, she lowered her hand and shuffled into the house. Again she appeared, and standing by the door again shaded her eyes and looked in my direction. Thus she remained, as I climbed the stiff hill and came well within sight of her.

She was apparently very old. The face was forbidding, almost repulsive. She wore a dull red handkerchief tied over her head; the thick grey skirt reached only to the tops of her boots, which were like a man's; a black shawl was crossed over her breast.

I felt I should like to speak to this lonely old woman, and went to the gate of the cottage and inquired the best way to Horn Head. She came towards me, after a moment's inspection, slowly and surlily, shuffling rather than walking. The dark eyes were like dots in the big yellowish face; the skin was infinitely wrinkled and pitted; the upper lip was long, severe, implacable. One thought that such a woman had never laughed, had never thanked God for the gift of life.

In a gruff man's voice she told me where I must leave the road and make across the fields to the Head. Then, looking me up and down, she asked sulkily and enviously, "You come from far, from over the water; there's plenty of money from where you come?" My answer did not satisfy her. " Ah ! " she exclaimed in the rich Scot's accent common to the Irish of the North, " it's fine to travel and see the world, and have plenty of money."

" It's better, perhaps," I answered, " to bide here patiently, working out one's duty, and waiting quietly for what's to come."

She shook her head. " I'm told it's grand in other countries," she answered ; " grand, grand, they say. Plenty of money over there."

I laughed. " Why do you talk of money ? " I asked mockingly. " Isn't all this "—pointing to the landscape and the sea beyond—" a great deal better than money ? Just look at it all. What a picture for human eyes ! "

She regarded me with a penetrating interest. Then, slowly nodding her old head, and rolling her " r's " with a wonderful emphasis, slowly she uttered these words, " 'Tis the hardships of the world up here, and cold."

So we parted, and her words haunted me on my way. I got to Horn Head, and, as well as the wind would let me, stood breathless and buffeted and almost stifled gazing at the vastness of ocean and the sombre line of tragic coast on either hand. Tory Island was visible far away on my left, looking like a naughty boy who has paddled dangerously out to sea, while the three smaller islands between it and the shore seemed like less daring brothers linking hands and calling him back to safety. On my right was a tortured and broken coast, with ocean flowing far inland behind me, and the confusion of writhing hills about Port-na-blah blazing white and glittering against the sky.

The words of the old woman came to me with a touch of Lear in their grief. I looked about me and felt that for those who had to wring existence out of these rocks, and who had to face the long winter on these mountains, her judgment was a true one, and just. Nature herself seemed to say, " 'Tis the hardships of the world up here, and cold." Desolation stretched away on every hand, interminable, wasteful, heartless and indifferent. Nowhere was visible the kindness of God's hand ; nowhere the lingering impress of caressing power. This veritable upheaval of a world, disfigured and racked and riven by persecuting storm, looked like materials of creation on which had fallen once and for ever the shadow of God's back as He turned His face inland to the shaping of the valley.

And as I stood there, first hail, and then snow, blown by winds that shrieked in my ear, filled the whole sky with storm and blotted out the hills.

The hardships of the world, and cold ! Yes, true enough. But surely there is poetry in that grumble, surely the very words proclaim a spiritual influence from the haggard earth that inspired them. Lear himself might have cried out, The hardships of the world, and cold! What Cockney would so express his complaint against creation? . . .

I turned my back on the snow, and repeating the words in my mind, came to the thought that even a desolate existence on a wind-swept mountain disdained of God and abandoned by civilization confers something of grandeur on the soul which the urbanity of cities fails to give.

And when I got back to my peat fire and my dinner, and the lamp was lit and the shutters closed, and Maggie stood talking beside my table in her adorable Scots music—vowing and protesting she is Irish to the last drop of blood in her body and no taint of Scotland in her nature at all, at all—I felt that the hardships of the world and cold have their great rewards in domestic contrasts.

Maggie is the eldest daughter of the house. Her father is dead, her mother is now too old for incessant work, her brothers labour the fields and tend the cattle. It is Maggie's duty to care for the lodgers, cooking their snipe to a turn, grilling their mutton chops which are like porterhouse steaks, baking bread and cakes for them, and seeing that the fire in the parlour is always bright and roasting, the lamp always well trimmed and unoozing, the beds always smooth and warm.

To speak socially she is Miss Mullen, but when I so addressed her, she blushed a timid scarlet, smiled as though I had been derisive, hung her head for a moment, and pleaded to be called Maggie. "You are Miss Mullen?" I had inquired. "I'm Maggie," was her answer.

She does everything well. There is not one London cook in seventy who can equal her performance; she bakes such bread as might entice the gods from ambrosia, and from the way in which your bed is made to the manner in which your lamp is trimmed you recognize in everything of Maggie's doing the genius of a careful soul. But with all this efficiency, Maggie is hundreds of years behind humanity. She believes in the wee folk, there are lochs she would not care to pass at night, she cannot understand infidelity concerning ghosts, and she is sure the saints have only to be asked properly to do for us whatsoever we desire.

I forget her age, but I am sure it is the youthful side of thirty. She is of medium height, with dark hair, a pale skin, and long-lashed eyes in which violets and hyacinths have mingled their colour to a most harmonious blue. The corners of her mouth are unsteady with smiles, and when these smiles get quite out of control the lips part and the teeth shine with the eyes in cheerful laughter. But she never laughs as you hear a factory girl laugh in the street—her laughter is soft, low, and beautiful like her voice. The upper lip is dusky with an almost invisible down.

It was delightful to listen to her thoughts as she stood at the door, a dish or tray in her hand, half going from the room and half inclined to stay, the head hanging, the eyes bright with amazement at her own audacity in discussion. Seldom did she raise those eyes to look at me direct, mostly they regarded the dish in her hand, or looked towards the shutters, or explored the carpet. And of course the body was never still, but swayed with her words.

She believes in God as perhaps no little child does ever quite believe. But her faith is childlike—it is not theological. She is more sure of God than of her own thoughts about Him, she speaks of heaven as if she had spent her childhood looking through its gates, she prays for her Dead as if they were kinsmen across the sea. One word expresses her religion ; it is Love. Never does cross or angry word escape her lips, never does indignation harden the timid beauty of her eyes, never does she express herself with the emphasis and challenge of self. Always she is tolerant, kindly, self-depreciating, anxious to be of service to others. I never heard her say one strident word or saw her do a single thing noisily, awkwardly, ungraciously. She seemed to breathe the blessing of a gentle kindness on the burdens of her daily life.

The sternest words she said to me concerned a landlord who was shot in that part of Ireland some years ago. " He was very cruel," said Maggie, in her solemn voice, " and he ill-treated the poor people very sorely, so that many were starved and homeless ; but they would have borne all if he had not done worse things than that."

I pressed her to tell me those worse things. After some hesitation, she raised her eyes frankly to mine, regarded me with a solemn look, and said : " He would give some of the tenants nice cottages inside the domain, and then take their daughters into his house and bring them to shame."

" And they thought that a worse thing than being starved ? " I asked, to get her mind.

" Oh, but surely ! " she exclaimed. " Oh, but yes, of course ! " She regarded me with something like reproach in her eyes. " They killed him for that. It was wrong to take his life, wrong to do violence ; but they could not bear that he should do that. He was a bad man, a very wicked man, I fear, and it was no life at all while he was alive."

Maggie's views of life are extremely simple. She is untouched by the rather muddied movements of great cities. She would be regarded as a savage by advanced women in London. But I do not think you will find a sweeter or a gentler creature under heaven, and if sweetness and gentleness are admirable qualities of human spirit, London should go to Port-na-blah, not Port-na-blah to London.

This farm-house, which has lately added to itself wings for summer lodgers, is in many ways representative of Irish home-life. It is set, as I have said, in a wild country. The potatoes, boiled in their brown jackets, have had their leaves blown by westerly gales, their flowers drenched by Atlantic spray ; the milk has come to the pail from cows that get a living from little fields rescued by years of toil from bog and moor ; the sheep can be seen silhouetted against grey skies on the top of rocks that would try the stamina of a brave boy ; turnips and wheat are grown in land that wellnigh rattles with stones ; only the cocks and hens in the shelter of the homestead are removed from a frightful struggle for existence. But the life of the people is more beautiful and gracious than the life of Italian peasants.

Many a morning, when I woke early and shivered in a room whose fireplace was filled with the thick brown ashes of last night's fire, I looked from my frozen window upon the work of the farm and felt cheered and warmed by the spectacle of such courage and good-humour. One of Maggie's brothers, followed by a couple of barking dogs, flapping his arms together and stamping with his thick boots as he came slowly along, would be seen driving the cows over the crown of the snow-swept hill ; another of these brothers would cross the frozen yard wheeling gingerly a barrow of piled and balanced turnips to be sliced in the barn ; Maggie's sister would run from the house, her head bent against the wind, and fetch corn for the fowls that streamed after her in hungry excitement ; and Maggie herself would come to the door with something domestic, whose dust required to be shaken in the wind, and she would call cheerful words to her brothers through the flakes of snow, and they would look up with smiles and answer her with the breath smoking at their lips.

And when the earth was so iron with frost and so buried under snow that work was impossible, these brothers would take their seats in the family kitchen, light their pipes, stretch their legs, and laugh at the weather. Every now and then one of them would jump up to lift a heavy weight for his sister or to get something that the mother required from across the room ; and these actions were done with an unconscious courtesy that gave them singular charm. Delightful it was to sit in the warm kitchen and listen to the talk of a family so united in love, so contented with the toil of simple life, so untroubled by our problems.

Port-na-blah is so many miles from a town and so long a drive from even the smallest railway station, that charity there is not organized, and humanity is not "inspected" and rate-divided into the rigid compartments of local government. If a man falls out of work, everybody knows it and many will come personally to his aid; if a woman is to give birth to a child, the knitting-needles of the neighbours are busy long beforehand and someone is there to do all she can for mother and child in the hours of labour; if there is sickness, sorrow, accident, or death, the people are as one family, as one household, united in brotherhood and kindly affection.

Maggie very often bakes her beautiful bread or brews a wonderful soup for a poor neighbour, and the brothers often walk across the moors to see how some old man is getting along—whether he has potatoes and meal enough for his needs. As for Mrs. Mullen, she is like a mother to that community and can tell you the most moving stories of the courage and the virtue and the faith of her poorer neighbours.

One of the brothers took me to call on a fisherman, and I was much struck by this man's noble face and dignified speech. Just before I left the neighbourhood I heard that he had sat up the previous night with a dying man, because it would be morning before the priest could reach Port-na-blah.

"But I thought he was a Presbyterian," I said, of the fisherman.

"So he is," replied Maggie; "but why wouldn't he be kind to the Catholics? Oh yes! He often goes to sit with invalid Catholics, and we all respect him greatly, for he is a verra good man."

"Then there is no quarrel between Catholics and Protestants?" I asked.

She smiled, shaking her head. "We are all good friends," she replied. "And I cannot see why people should fall out about their religion. Why is it, I wonder? It seems so funny. One is born a Catholic, and another is born a Presbyterian, and each must get the best he can out of his religion. That is surely right. But why wouldn't they live neighbourly? Their religion ought to make them do that."

I visited some of the surrounding villages and met in every case the most pleasing courtesy and the most delightful people. Perhaps they are not so intellectually alert as townsmen, but they have calm and peace and repose. Nor did I once hear from these great-limbed men a grumble about the struggle for existence. They said nothing about the absence of light railways, the distance from a market, or the cost of transit. They spoke about the fish in the loch, of a famous salmon landed by Mr. Stephen Gwynn—"Musther Gwunn is a great gentleman"—and of the beauty of the mountains in the summer. They smoked their pipes over the peat fire, chatted of snipe and woodcock, told stories of fashionable visitors in summer, recalled mighty storms that had swept the coast, and laughed indulgently over the perturbation in Belfast at Mr. Winston Churchill's meeting.

I do not know in what way these people of the North differ from those of the South, save in a rather more vivid cheerfulness and in the rich Scot's accent of their speech. One would never take them for Irishmen. The very words, as well as the intonation, are Scottish. But in tenderness, in sweet courtesy, in dignity and warm humanity they are like the peasants of the South. You feel that the scenery has changed without altering a thread in the fibre of Irish character. No words can express the difference between the green pastures of Kerry and the rock-strewn moorland of Donegal, but the people in both counties are the same.

"You ought to meet Hannah," said Maggie to me one day; "she's a rare one for tales; and she is verra old and has lived a strange life, and she has seen the wee folk, oh mony's the time! Mr. Law has been kind to Hannah—that's the landlord here; he's a member of Parliament; a verra good gentleman. Mr. Law has built her a wee house, all for herself; and when it was finished and Hannah was going in, didn't all the children in the place come with gifts for her? It was verra funny. One brought a frying-pan, and one a broom, and one a cup and saucer, and one a plate, and one a knife and fork, and one a teapot, and one a kettle, all out of their own pennies—oh, you never saw such a thing!—and Hannah was quite provided for, just by the children. Yes, it was verra pretty, verra pretty indeed. But everybody's fond of Hannah. She's had a terrible life of it, poor thing. You ought to see her, yes, you really ought. Oh, she's a rare one for tales, Hannah is."

Could anything sound more inviting?

"Where does she live?" I asked. "Certainly I must go and see her."

Maggie went to the window and, pointing out of sight, began such a rigmarole of directions, that I stopped her with the plea that she herself should take me.

Maggie's eyes opened wide, and her lips fluttered with smiles. "Would you like me to?—really?"

"Oh, but yes, of course I should."

Maggie was delighted. "I will gladly go with you," she said, and her eyes sparkled, her cheeks burned, and she looked like one at whose door a great adventure has arrived.

Such is the quiet uneventful calm of Port-na-blah, such the sweet and humble nature of Miss Margaret Mullen.

## CHAPTER XIV

### HANNAH

On our way to Hannah's cabin I realized how beautiful a place Port-na-blah must be in summer time and autumn. Maggie told me what wild-flowers grow in the fields, and told me how the hills blaze with heather and gorse, and how the sea lies in a lulling calm, dark blue against the tasselled rocks and cerulean blue, where it spreads itself like a lake far, far inland, in the midst of a green country.

But it was hard going for us just then. We crossed the iron snow-powdered furrows of a ploughed field, skirted the ice-cracking sides of treacherous bog, scaled precipitous hill-sides, clambered over stone walls, made a way through a wilderness of furze, and at last arrived before Hannah's door rather blown and stiff-legged, but warm with our exercise in spite of bitter cold.

Hannah's chimney was smoking, and the old lady in consequence was out of humour. The neat cabin—with its bed in the corner, a bright dresser against the wall, a little table in the centre, and a low chair before the fire—was hazy with peat-smoke. Even as we entered a great puff from the chimney sent a cloud of this thick and choking smoke across the room, and set Hannah grumbling afresh, and set Maggie and me dissembling our coughs.

But when we had sufficiently ingratiated ourselves, Hannah became pleasant, and we sat down together for a friendly talk. On one side of the offending fire sat the little old woman and the beautiful young woman, close together on a backless form, Hannah's hand in Maggie's lap and Maggie's fingers caressing that old brown wrinkled hand with strokings that were full of endearment. On the other side of the fire, and nearer to the welcome fresh air of the open door, sat the reader's humble servant, listening to Maggie's questions and Hannah's answers, and watching the face of the old woman.

Hannah wore a dark blue bulging skirt, a shawl of fading orange, and a bright red-patterned handkerchief over her head. Although she is nearer eighty than seventy, her hair is a coal-black without one tinge of grey. The tint of her skin is yellow, like a Parsi's, a deep dull yellow which suggests vitality and enduring strength, not biliousness. Her eyes are brown as chestnut skins, the features are small and regular. The total expression of the face is one of passive acquiescence in the hard experience of human life.

She sat crouched up on the backless form, attending every now and then to the peat fire, which was raised a few inches above the hearth.

Maggie, very skilfully, asked questions about ghosts, and spirits, and the wee folk. Wearily and rather grumblingly, like one who is near the end of life's journey and desires to be let alone, the old woman told us of two visions she had seen herself, and of many stories she had heard from other people concerning fairies and dwarfs. When she was a girl in her father's house, she came down-stairs one morning to find a superb gentleman seated on an even grander horse at the cottage door. He was dressed in blue, she told us, and had gold spurs at his heels. He smiled, made a sign that she should mount behind him, and bent towards her. Amazed by the sight she ran to her father with the news, and the father asked if the stranger had beckoned her to go away with him. Hannah said that he had certainly done so. " Then," said the father, with conviction, " he is a Spirit." They both went hastily but fearfully to the door, and the stranger was nowhere to be seen.

" And you are sure it was a ghost, Hannah ? " asked Maggie, smiling.

" Whista, but of course it was. By God, Maggie dear, but he was terrible nice. A great gentleman, och sure ! I never saw finer man before or since. And he was gone in a minute ! Divil a sign of him at all ! "

On another occasion, as she was coming over the mountain she saw a woman kneeling at the loch-side, washing linen. The loch was known to be haunted, and Hannah had an eerie feeling about this woman. It was twilight. The hedges were whispering with the antics of the wee folk. A cold wind was stirring in the trees. Sure enough, when Hannah got to the side of the loch the woman was nowhere to be seen.

These stories, as the reader may surmise, did not impress me, in spite of Hannah's eloquence in their narration. I prompted Maggie to ask other questions.

" You remember the bad times, Hannah ? You know how the people suffered in those days ? You were through the Famine yourself, weren't you ? "

" Thim times, Maggie dear, were divilish bad. Dear God, I shall never forgit thim if I live to be a hundred. We had nothing to eat, Maggie dear, but turnips, boiled, bruised, and sprinkled with a wee pinch of salt. No praties at all, at all. Och, those were terrible times ! And people who could not pay the rints were turned out of their cabins. Ochone, 'twas a most awful time ! But some of the landlords were good to us poor folk. There was broth kitchens, Maggie dear, and terrible good broth too. Och, but the nearest to us was six miles away, and the children sent to fetch the broth was so starving that they could not walk back without eating the broth on the way. Och, many's the child who came home with an empty tin and near dead with the walk. So the people were driven into the great workhouse, and my father and mother and all of us children were among them. But that was the worst of all, Maggie dear ! By God, it was terrible bad. Och, but you've no idea ! Do you know what they did to us ? They served out some male that killed poor people like flies, a kind of gypsy-male they said it was.* Och, but you niver saw people go

* I understand that the meal was some inferior Indian corn.

so quick in your life. They was standin' in the mornin' an' stiff in the evenin'. And I saw things you'll niver believe. I saw the Matron take the corpses by the heels, pull thim out of bed that way, and go bump, bump, bump down the stone stairs wid thim. True as God! They was buried, those poor people, Maggie dear, without washing or dressing—divil a bit! Ochone, Maggie dear, but thim was terrible times."

Partly from Hannah and partly from Maggie I got the story of the old woman's life. I do not know a living person who has made me so conscious of the immense gulf which separates the beginning of the nineteenth century from the beginning of the twentieth.

Hannah's father, a field labourer, fell out of work in the bad times, and when the family came from the workhouse it was impossible for him to support his family. Hannah went out as servant to a Presbyterian farmer.

Her work was not confined to the house. She cooked, washed, swept, scrubbed, and made beds; but very much harder labour fell to her lot. She fed and milked cows, she pulled turnips, she hoed and dug potatoes, she went with a creel made of sally-rods (sallows) down to the rocks to get rack (seaweed) for the farm. When you hear people lament the good old times I beg you to think of this farm-servant.

"Och," she exclaimed, with flashing eyes and snarling lips, "that was a job that broke the heart of me, fetching the rack from the rocks. It scourged my legs, for I niver had boots in thim days. I was barefoot and bare-legged on the rocks. Ah, Maggie dear, 'tis terrible bad to have your feet and hands aching at the wan time. I could not wash me feet at night. The skin was scourged clean off of thim. If God had made a hole in thim rocks and offered to put me in head down, I'd have gone, I'd have been glad to hang head down—just to get off my feet. Ah, sure! It was devilish bad in the rain and the wind up in the turnip fields, but, by God, it was worse on thim rocks. You'll never know the like of that, Maggie dear; and as true as God's above us I'd rather die to-morrow, or next day, than live my life over again—och sure, I would!"

Now, what wages do you think this farm-servant received? In those brave days no blasphemer had arrived to say that human flesh and bones must receive a living wage. It was believed by all mankind, as it is believed in Belfast to this hour, that wages are not to be measured by the work done or by the cost of living or by the laws of God and Brotherhood, but only by the numbers of hungry people asking for work. Many hands, small wages; few hands, high wages. The proposition was so simple and emphatic, however damnable, that no man questioned it. Even to-day, in St. Paul's

Cathedral, at the very heart of Christian civilization, a sermon was preached on Easter Sunday of the present year, expressing alarm and misgiving at the manful, law-abiding demands of colliers for a wage by which a man may rear his family just out of the shadow of privation.

Well, Hannah's wage was not five shillings a day, as you may well suppose. But will you believe that it was ten shillings a half-year?

"They paid me ten shillings a half-year, and my keep; but I had to find my own duds. The food was stirabout and praties; och, there was not too much of it! Meat?—divil a bit! I niver tasted it." She laughed bitterly at the idea.

This place was too hard for the young girl. She fell ill and was turned away. Apparently the Presbyterian farmer and his wife did not care a rap what became of the friendless and orphan girl; they were too busy, I suspect, in deciphering the Word of God. After a spell of idleness she became nurse and general servant in another farm-house, at the same wage. There was in the neighbourhood at that time a hedge preacher whom the people called Old Livingstone. Some boys on one occasion were sent to prison for pushing him as he walked through the road where they were playing; the case was cited as one of Catholic Intolerance! Old Livingstone, with his Bible and staff, came to the Presbyterian farm-house where Hannah was employed. His penetrating eyes, which tore the Judgments of God out of Holy Writ, detected a rash on Hannah's red arms. He warned the mistress of the house against having such a woman with her children. So Hannah was turned away, and having no home to go to, no friend in the world to take pity on her, she went to the workhouse.

Maggie told me the next part of Hannah's story as we walked home across the moor. "Poor Hannah, she was terrible bad in the workhouse, and they told her there that if she didn't go into the hospital she would surely die. The hospital was at Strabane, forty long Irish miles away, but Hannah set out, all by herself, and walked the whole distance. Oh, that must have been terrible, terrible for Hannah. I often think of her, ill and weary, walking that long way, all by herself!"

Then Maggie's face, which had been sad and sorrowful, suddenly brightened. "But it was a happy time when she reached the hospital. Oh, it was so different! And didn't the doctor's wife, who was the Matron, take a fancy to Hannah because she was so clean, and didn't she take her into her own house to look after her children, and wasn't Hannah treated like one of the family, and all so happy and kind? I do not know how long she was there, but it was some time, and she was verra grateful; but gradually her health got worse and worse, and at last she was too weak to do the work, and so she had to leave. And then poor Hannah drifted to the workhouse again."

From this point in her life down to quite modern times Hannah lived by "collecting." Maggie made me feel the difference between begging and collecting. "Hannah," said she, "started collecting—she was not a beggar-woman, you understand, but she went from village to village, and she called at farm-houses, and they gave her food and shelter, and sometimes a sixpence to help her on her road."

Thus lived Hannah for half a century, a homeless wanderer on the face of the earth, but with many a kitchen where she might lie down and sleep for the night, and many a friend who was glad to give her a meal of potatoes and a cup of cold water. She was always clean, always polite, always grateful for a kind word.

She asked for "bits" in the name of God, and paid for it by telling the news she had gathered on her way or by doing service in the house.

Her old head nods, and her eyes have a far-off melancholy look as she speaks of those days. "People was terrible kind to me," she says; "I don't suppose anybody ever had more friends than I have had; but, Maggie dear, it was lonely, it was terrible lonely. Ah, to live fifty years without a home, all alone, all alone, going to and fro, to and fro—by God, Maggie dear, but that's hard on a woman!"

People for miles round had a great respect for the wandering gipsy-like Hannah. They attributed to the old woman some mysterious relationship with the saints. They believed that she was different from the common herd of mortality. A sailor lad once gave her half a crown, because she prayed for him, and because her prayers had brought him luck. People would gladly give the old woman a sixpence in the hope of receiving a cake from heaven. But Hannah seldom spent this money on herself. She would give nearly all of it to Sisters of Charity or to the priest of the village church at which she went to Mass. Once, when she was very hard-driven, someone gave her a florin; she bestowed the whole of the money on a fund for building a village chapel.

"Och, but I knew I should niver want for it," she exclaimed; "and sure enough that very night I made up one shillin' and nine-pence!"

"Hannah always gives with the heart," said Maggie.

"Oh, God, would you give with anything else, Maggie dear? Isn't it the duty of all of us to love and to give? Is it any use to us, saving and putting by, whin there's heaven waiting for us in the next world? Sure, I'd give myself away if it would help a poor body."

"And God has been good to you, hasn't He, Hannah? You've got plenty of friends and now you've got this nice little house. . . ."

"But the chimney's a terrible worry, Maggie dear. Ochone! what can I do to keep the place clean, wid smoke pouring out and spoiling everything? By God, I wish Mr. Law would do something to the chimney."

If the reader would like to meet Hannah and to discover if the chimney has been put right by her indulgent host, let him write for a room to Mrs. Mullen, at Port-na-blah, Dunfanaghy, By Letterkenny, Co. Donegal. But if he must have a French cook to prepare his meals, electric light for his reading, fashionable people to amuse him, and a lift to carry him up to a prince's bedroom, let him write to Lord Leitrim's now famous Rosapenna Hotel, at Carrigart, which is within a motor drive of Port-na-blah.

I can promise any man who loves great hills, a wild coast, a splendid sea, lochs like inland oceans, and a kindly aristocracy of peasants, the very Paradise of his desire at Rosapenna or at Port-na-blah.

I hang upon this page, dreaming of my walks and drives and meetings on that wonderful coast, not only because the memories are so sweet and gracious to my thoughts, but because in turning the page I turn my back on all that is most beautiful, affectionate, and comforting in Ireland, and come face to face with that which is sinister and harsh.

Kind, gentle Maggie, I hope that you may never go to cities; poor, grumbling Hannah, I hope you may never exchange the smoke of your peat-fire for the smoke of factory chimneys. Winter may be long, and loud may be the storms that beat upon your tortured coast, but the summer comes with flowers for your fields, with sweetness for your pure air, and with sunsets flooding the smooth waters of Sheep Haven with glory and with calm.

## CHAPTER XV

### AT THE GATE OF DEMOCRACY

We have now arrived before a door which I shrink from opening. Behind us are green fields, green-bordered roads, the wayside cottages of a happy peasantry, the beauty of primitive existence, the humble contentments of natural life, the scent of flowers, the shadows of trees, the music of cool waters, the silence and repose of the hills, the quiet going of the day, the quiet coming of the night. And beyond the door there is the factory, the slum, the struggle for wages, the problems, questions, and confusions of unnatural life, a murmur of many voices, a thrusting of many hands, the unrest of many hearts.

Poverty can be beautiful; and toil, even for a bare subsistence can be gracious. Such poverty as I saw in the villages of Ireland did not distress me, did not ever shock or pain me ; and the labour of the fields, however hard and disheartening, did not depress my feelings. On the contrary, I was often conscious of a certain envy in my commerce with the peasants of Ireland ; for if their poverty is afflicting, it does not embitter them ; it seems to purify and sweeten them ; and if their toil is hard, it is at least never out of partnership with hope.

A peasant has always the weather to make every day an adventure. The mere sitting of a broody hen lends curiosity and expectation to three whole weeks of human life. The farrowing of a sow is like a great ship coming into harbour. Can a man be ever broken to settled melancholy who has a garden to dig, a field to plant, and a byre to bed down with bracken for a heifer or a kid ? Is life ever an unbroken spell of dullness when the frost of one night may darken the young leaves of a potato crop, and a shower of rain may bring a shining greenness to a field of drooping wheat ? And consider the excitation of the weekly market in the town across the moor. It is something better than a boom on the Stock Exchange.

Few things in rural Ireland are prettier than the blithe co-operation of the children in the life of their parents. You see very jolly pudding-faced boys driving home the cows through glens and over moors ; you see them at sunset coming back from hunting the hedges, holding by the four corners red handkerchiefs swollen out with hen's eggs ; you see them with buckets and boxes collecting stones from a tillage field ; you see them scaring rooks from the young corn ; you see them on a perilous cliff of black bog learning to cut peat for the winter's stack ; and you see them hoeing between the lines of potatoes or stumbling proudly beside their fathers at the plough's tail. And you see the girls feeding the fowls, scalding the cream over a peat fire, helping their mothers to bake bread, mending the family linen, and driving along the country roads in donkey-carts little bigger than a wheelbarrow, rope reins in the left hand, a hazel wand in the right, a baby brother's fat scared face peeping over the side of the jolting cart.

Such life is natural and happy ; it is like the playing of a game. Even the boys picking stones from tillage probably imagine themselves victorious soldiers collecting loot ; while in scaring rooks from the wheat, without doubt they are unconquerable knights defying ogres and giants. But imagine the feelings of the pretty maids who sit on the edge of a tiny cart, and drive a diminutive but trotting donkey into the market-town ! Cinderella, we may be sure, never journeyed in more gorgeous coach. Children always make a game of everything they do ; and the only life that God provided for the children of men is full of opportunities for play.

How many children in cities, even well-off suburban children, would think it heaven to possess a little donkey in a tumble-down shed, whose coat they must brush and whose manger they must fill? —a serious and real donkey, of course: a donkey to be harnessed and backed and buckled into shafts for important journeys, who must carry chickens, butter, eggs, and cream to the market and return proudly with shillings and half-crowns, with wonderful jars and bottles and tins and packets from the grocer's shop, to be greeted by an excited family at the cottage door—not a mere seaside donkey, thwacked up and down the sands, kicking but depressed, with hysterical and purple-faced spinsterhood bumping on its back.

Catch a child young enough, keep his mind uncorrupted by the contagion of noisy cities, see that he has a sufficiency of raspberry jam with his bread and butter, and this is the life he will enjoy, this is the employment which will best develop the most vigorous of his virtues. Such a child will not miss, because he has never known, the heating excitement and the feverish raptures of picture palace and skating rink, the whistling obsession of a music-hall song degrading love, or the satisfaction of a cynical catch-phrase that cheapens earthly life. He will grow in communion with the elemental powers of nature, will take a colour from sunrise and sunset, will respond to the great rhythmic movements of the labouring year, will acquire the calm, the serenity, the confidence of his travelling companions the beasts of the field, and, if he has poetry in his mind, love in his heart, and faith in his soul, he will go down the hill of life, even into the shadow of the grave, without fear and without regret. There will be a certain dignity in his face, a wonderful sweetness in his soul.

"Have you ever seen one of our peasants die?" I was asked by a Roman Catholic theologian. "I have not seen very many," he continued, "but as long as I live I shall never forget the experience. I confess that I myself am afraid of death. It seems terrible to me. But these people see the angels, they smile with transfigured faces, they reach out their arms, they expire with a sigh of rapture and content. Nothing could be more beautiful. Nothing, nothing. Oh, most beautiful! And all over Ireland it is the same; our parish priests tell us that at the death-beds of the peasants they seem to feel the presence of the angels, almost to see the invisible world."

This life of which I am speaking, man's natural life—the life, be it remembered, to which the poet and the painter go for beauty and tenderness—has religion for its determining power. A peasant, one knows very well, may be a brute, a degenerate, or a mere dense, solid, and unreachable clod; and if he is starved in childhood, left ignorant throughout boyhood, and in manhood is housed like a hog and paid a dog's wage for incessant work by a master who despises him, one of these three he must almost certainly become. But if love —consecrated by religion—nurses him on her breast and watches over him in his cradle; if kindness—inspired by religion—teaches him in childhood not only to read and write, but to observe and reflect; if in manhood he has land of his own to cultivate, a house of his own to roof and paint and care for, children of his own laughing at his knee, a wife of his own saving and contriving for him and sharing all his hopes and fears, a soul of his own to address its quite simple and articulate longings to the God he naturally loves and instinctively worships—then there will be such a beauty in his life as the dweller in cities can never reach and an almost perpetual gladness in his heart which they but seldom even glimpse.

It is a matter of religion. The greatest illusion of modern life is the illusion bred by crowded and distracting cities, where men herd together out of all touch with mortality's natural environment—the illusion that religion is a school of thought, a code of morals, a disputed field in the hazardous territory of philosophy. To the savage, above everything else, religion is fear. To the Christian, it is love.

Religion, first and foremost, is worship, adoration, love. Religion is poetry. The theologian's effort to make it mathematics has been disastrous, both for religion and for his own authority over mankind. No; religion is poetry.

A peasant walking home from his fields under the stars, shadowed by the mystery of night, conscious of an indestructible self in the midst of a universe's silence, and moved by the majesty of the firmament to lift his thoughts to the many resting-places of immortality, knows as certainly as he knows his work in the fields that religion is worship, adoration, love. You might make havoc of his theology, you might prove to him that he had never thought out his definitions; but you could not shake him an inch from the ground of his spiritual life—that the soul of religion is worship, adoration, love. He can conceive of no other relation for his soul towards his Creator.

"Love God," said St. Augustine, "and do what you like." Catholic teaching lays all its emphasis on Love; and because Protestantism is given to insisting on errors and manifest follies in Catholic theology, we are apt to miss the central reason of its persistence and its power—the emphasis of Love. More perhaps in Ireland than any other country of the world does the Catholic priest teach his people before everything else to love God, to love, worship, and adore the Infinite Father. And because the Irish are by nature loving and imaginative and tender, they respond to this teaching, develop it in their daily life, and die with a smile of love upon their lips. Religion to them is as real as life.

To the man bred and born in a city, and accustomed to get his religious notions from books, it seems a difficult thing to love God. He uses the phrase, but he doubts the idea. Religion, for him, is not safe without elaborate safeguards. He cannot move without a dogma; one blow from science on a single article of his belief and the whole edifice of his religious life shivers with apprehension. But a child whose world is nature, taught to feel reverence and love for the Creator of all visible things, brought gradually to conceive the beautiful idea of Fatherhood in the universe, does not find worship difficult, is unconscious of the need for dogma. It is almost impossible not to love God in a life that is full of blessing.

I do not know, but I imagine, I am almost certain, that no religion can really penetrate and transfuse with divinity the whole nature of man that is without the exaltation of worship and the sweetness of love. "Love God, and do what you like"—this seems to me the only theology that can endure, the only exposition of religion that can satisfy the heart. It is the highest teaching, the simplest, the most natural. Love God, and everything else follows.

But, this all lies behind us in the green fields. The door must be opened, poetry and imagination must be put into quarantine, our baggage must be examined for superstitions and sentiment at the custom-house, and we ourselves must cross the frontier and enter the courts of Materialism like good sensible commercial travellers, or at any rate like rational positivists.

Ere this be done, however, I would ask the reader to keep in his mind, as we pass over the threshold to the other side, the character of the Irish peasant and the nature of his simple life. I would ask him, before we enter the other Ireland, to question civilization's pity for primitive field-labourers, and to ask himself whether the life of the humblest peasant, in the ultimate analysis, may not be full of the truest beauty and the purest grandeur.

After all, how far is the Irish peasant—"the minister in that vast temple which only the sky is vast enough to embrace"—how far is he worse off in all that makes for happiness and beauty, for dignity and grandeur, than the shop-assistant in Clapham, the retired captain in Kensington, the palmist in Bond Street, the club waiter in Pall Mall, the commissionaire at the door of a draper's shop in Regent Street? He sees fewer people; but his relations with those that he does see are close and intimate enough for real affection or decided aversion. He has neither theatre nor music-hall to relieve the fatigue of his evening; but he goes early to bed and sleeps deeply, gloriously, without the jingle of a vulgar song running through his dreams. He has no bus or tram roaring past his door, and no underground railway vibrating beneath his kitchen floor; but his walk to his work is over sweet-smelling fields with larks singing in the sky above his head. He earns less money ; but his needs are simpler. He knows nothing of the victories of Progress ; but he escapes its vulgarities. There is no movement in his life ; but he goes where he would. His contact with civilization is less vital ; but his contact with nature is continual. He is behind the times ; but he has time for his home. He is ignorant of art, literature, music ; but his life *is* art, literature, and music. He is boorish ; but he is real. He has no vision; but what need?—he believes that God is at his side.

## CHAPTER XVI

### MANUFACTURED MORTALITY

ALL the problems of civilization belong to congested cities. And the great concernment of modern existence in these massed and knotted thickenings of the human race is a matter of Money. For it is not only the dim millions of the labour world who struggle for higher wages. The greed of all men is for greater wealth. The manufacturer and the merchant, the tradesman and the company promoter, strive every day to augment their annual profits. The landlord increases his rent, the professional man his fees. The salesman already rich advertises to get more customers. The newspaper, already boasting an immense circulation, has a staff at work perpetually engaged in poaching the circulation of a rival. No one sets a limit to his desires in respect of money. Money is the great reward. More money, and ever more money, is the object of existence. Humanity begins to think that there is nothing else.

One may say fairly that every crowded centre of industrialism is a Capital of Mammon. It represents humanity's definite rejection of Christ's fundamental teaching, the definite determination of society to organize itself without God. And yet not quite without God ; religion is there as policeman, and conscience is bribed by charities towards others to leave its own soul in quiet. But you can have immense religious activity without God. From time to time a rumble of discontent from the underworld of labour frightens and terrifies civilization ; or a struggle, a pressure, and an actual upheaval from those who are below, stops the running of the huge complex machinery of social life and brings national existence to the edge of confusion. But the difficulty is adjusted ; the engines throb again, the wheels turn, and society pursues its accustomed way—in quest of money.

Cities breed the forger, the swindling financier, the burglar, the pickpocket, the hooligan, the pimp, the bully, and the harlot—all monstrous deformities of human nature, and all engaged, like the more reputable members of the community, in a hunger and thirst after money

And the joys and sorrows of a great city are tinged by this supreme and overshadowing question of money. The utmost blessing is to make a fortune ; the utmost disaster is to lose one. A man's happiness is measured by the amount of his income. A man's lack of money is the standard of his wretchedness. Everybody struggles to dress as if he were richer than he really is. Everybody is anxious to seem prosperous and fashionable and successful. Men and women even deny themselves the highest and most rapturous blessings of existence in order to deceive the general world as to their social position. Women will avoid having children in order that they may have furs ; men will do without a garden in order that they may go in coloured socks. And the lack of higher things is not felt ; the sacrifice of all that is beautiful and noble is made quite willingly, even cheerfully ; in their judgment they have chosen the better part, they are perfectly content, they are happy. A chorus girl in a comic opera despises the peasant woman smiling at a baby on her breast, and is not conscious of her own abysmal inferiority.

The degrading meanness of this life, the destructive triviality of this vulgar burlesque of human existence, is only possible where contact with natural conditions is either slight or broken, or where religion and imagination are inoperative. But such a life has a most extraordinary infection, a most bewildering contagion. Certain writers, for instance, have always been fond of pointing to the suburbs of London as the exclusive region of what we call snobbishness ; but to anyone who truly knows the world precisely the same spirit of snobbishness which characterizes the suburbs characterizes also the very centre of metropolitan existence and the very slums of deprivation and misery. Among aristocracy there is a money rivalry, a competition of fashion, a childish and unworthy delight in ostentation and mere show ; indeed, although the people themselves are more agreeable and charming, I think the spirit of snobbishness is worse among aristocracy than among the middle-classes. It is only the " scenical differences " that hide the truth. As for the workman and the artisan, you will find, at any rate among their wives, more vulgar pride, more foolish conceit, more contemptible efforts at show and vainglory than exists in the most polished corners of West Kensington. " Tenpenny Dick," said Mr. John Burns, " will not speak to Sixpenny Jack."

But the strangest contagion of this mean life is to be found among the thinkers of a great city, the writers and philosophers, the preachers and the politicians, who probably began life with far other notions. Men otherwise free from all snobbishness, able and brilliant men genuinely in search of truth, are so infected by the general vulgarity that they too exalt this question of Wages to the supreme place in modern problems. They actually believe, apparently, that could wages be handsomely raised all round society would be safe, civilization would be secure, and civilization could pursue in peace its progress towards—What ? That is the question. Do they ever think that without its natural purpose and its natural objective, the soul of man can never be at rest ?

Every political party is engaged over this question of Wages. The Conservatives declare that Tariff Reform would raise wages ; the Liberals declare that Free Trade alone can keep the cost of living within the limits of the average wage ; the Labour Party and the Socialists exist to force expenditure and to increase wages for the working-classes. Every serious man is now thinking of life in terms of political economy. It is the illusion of cities, the obsession of unnztural and artificial existence.

But Life is more than Wages. There is something which money cannot buy, something indeed that the very possession of money may destroy, something at any rate the value of which a covetous pursuit of money must obscure and obliterate. The oldest platitudes are the simplest truths. The shirtless man may be happier than the king. Not what a man possesses but what he enjoys is the blessing of his life. Let a man gain the whole world and lose his soul alive, and the bargain is a bad one.

Until mankind comes back to the ancient wisdom of human experience, the problem of civilization will be the problem of cities, and the problem of cities will be the problem of Wages. And that problem is insoluble. Raise wages, and if you do nothing more, you increase your difficulties a thousandfold. Corrupt human nature by concentrating its thoughts on money, turn it from the divine goal of its existence by encouraging this search for happiness in wages, and you will bring into the world a race of beings with whom no Act of Parliament can deal, no communism of a democratic State can satisfy. You will have then not a race of men made in the image of God, but a race of gods made in the image of animals.

Among the peasants of Ireland—whose joys and sorrows are commingled with the great business of Birth and Death, whose lives are lived in unbroken communion with nature, whose human centre is the family, and whose divine objective is God—men and women talked to me of Life. Among the people of Belfast men and women talked to me of Wages. Every conversation with the peasants came round, sooner or later, adequately or inadequately, to the great issues of human existence. Every conversation with the workmen of Belfast came round, almost at once, and with tremendous earnestness, to the question of Wages.

This is the difference between the land we have left behind and the kingdom into which we have now entered. We are done with Life. We are confronted by Economics. We have left the Ireland for which Home Rule is a part of life's poetry, a part of the religion of the national soul, a part of the self-respect of a country conscious of a destiny ; and we have come to the Ireland which is so obsessed by the problems of social democracy, so absorbed in the business of money-getting, that it can think of nothing but Wages.

" God made the country, and man made the town." There are still signs of a divine creation in the humanity of the one, the marks of a manufacturer growing obviously clearer in the humanity of the other.

## CHAPTER XVII

### THE ORANGE CAPITAL

BELFAST is like Tottenham Court Road, filled with the population of Oldham. Its principal streets are thronged by women with shawls over their heads, by workmen in grimy clothes, and by barefoot children. You never escape the feeling of factory, warehouse, and shop. It is a place of business and nothing but a place of business. It has no beautiful corners like the cities of Touraine, no sudden and restful charms like London. One is ridiculed for suggesting that it should have attractions of this kind. It is not so much a place where people live as a place where people toil.

It can justly boast an immense and solemn city hall, a remarkable technical college, factories which, I suppose, are without their equal in the world, a few streets of really splendid shops, a pleasant suburban circumference, and fine scenery outside, easily to be reached by excellent electric trams. But at the heart, this packed and crowded city is the most depressing, dismal, and alarming exhibition of what competitive industrialism can make of human existence that I have yet explored.

York Street is typical. It is composed of chapels, factories, shops, pawnshops, public-houses, and small hotels. Till eleven o'clock at night you may see ragged and unwashed children of six or seven years of age going with their pennies to buy supper in sweetshops. I have seen swarms of tiny girls, barefoot in the rain, carrying a baby wrapped in their shawls at ten o'clock of a wet and bitter night. I have seen at least a dozen tiny children wandering forlorn and miserable in this single street between one and two o'clock in the morning. Drunken men, half-drunken men, and melancholy sober men ; little, stunted, white-faced women, and fat, bloated, coarse-featured, and red-faced women, pulling their shawls over their heads, come from the public-houses and pass along the pavement in a pageant of shabby gloom. The faces of these people are terrible. They are either fierce, hard, cruel, and embittered, or they are sad, wretched, hopeless, and despairing. Factory girls, without hats, pass in hordes, sometimes singing, sometimes laughing discordantly, sometimes larking with boys. Among these young people it is rare to see a big, well-built, and healthy specimen of humanity. They are wonderfully small, pale, and flat-chested. It is a population of bloodless dwarfs.

But York Street is like heaven to hell in comparison with the slums of West Belfast. In only one quarter of London do I know of more terrible dog-holes.

Some of the houses are like the ancient cabins which once disgraced rural Ireland, and are now only to be seen occasionally. But here in these courts and alleys of Belfast they are joined together, they are grimy with the dirt of a manufacturing city, and they smell with the acrid bitterness of beggary and want. I was so stifled in some of these dens that I could scarcely breathe. The damp, the foul smells, the ragged beds, the dirty clothes of the poor wretches huddled together in these dark interiors assailed me with a sense of such substantial loathing that I felt physically sick. The faces of the children literally hurt my eyes.

I find that Miss Margaret Irwin, secretary to the Scottish Council for Women's Trades, experienced this same feeling of repugnance and nausea. She declares that the Belfast worker is worse housed than the Scotch. "In one particular instance," she says, "I encountered such filthy conditions that for the first time in many years of experience in this work I found myself unable to enter the house, and had to conduct the interview from the doorway. The house was quite unfit for human habitation."

Even where the houses are of more modern design, the wretchedness of the interiors cannot be exaggerated. I visited a house where the one water-supply was a tap in the wall of the kitchen, which was the only living room. The tap dripped on the floor. One of the ragged and dishevelled women, nodding her head to the tap, said to the friend who accompanied me, "Yes, that's our scullery."

In these streets you see dirty fowls picking chaff as it falls from the nose-bag of the carter's horse, costermongers' barrows laden with bulging sacks stand against the kerb, boys kick about the road a sodden and punctured football or a wad of paper, slatternly women, whose faces look as if they have never been washed, and whose hair looks as if it has never been combed, stand scowling in the doorways. A reek of human mildew comes from the houses. Melancholy cats crawl in the gutters. Existence is felt to be a curse.

The only thing which gave a sense of real vigour to these dispirited and despairing streets was a splendid black and silver hearse, the handsome black horses, with their silver harness, trotting smartly and eagerly as though to get away from such animals as the women in the doors. That empty hearse flashed through the torpor of the streets with a sense of sunlight and joy. It advertised the superiority of Death.

I visited a lodging-house with one who knows the neighbourhood well. In the back kitchen four or five miserable men were cooking their meal; the landlady sat in the front kitchen, which was bright and cheerful; one of her children swaggered to the door of the back kitchen, and surveyed the broken lodgers in that gloomy interior with a look half of ownership and half of scorn, humming and eating bread and jam. We went upstairs. The bedclothes were thin and quite filthy; I have never seen sheets so iron-grey, one had to look twice to realize that they had once been white. We inquired the price of these beds, which were packed pretty close to one another. "Eightpence," said the landlady. "What!" we cried; "eightpence a night? How can these men afford to pay eightpence?" "Oh, they only pay fourpence," she replied; "two go to a bed, fourpence each, making eightpence; that's the charge."

In one house we came upon a little old crop-headed man, like a plucked sparrow, sitting huddled up on a low stool close to the kitchen fire. He never spoke a word the whole time we were there; never smiled, never showed a sign of intelligence. With wide staring eyes he looked into the fire, his bony fingers closing and unclosing on a little stump of a stick held in his right hand. He was the hero of the house—an old age pensioner whose life was exceedingly precious to his affectionate relations. His daughter-in-law told us that her husband was out of work, but that her two daughters and the old man by the fire kept things going. The two daughters appeared before we left. One was fourteen, and dreadfully anæmic; she wore neither boots nor stockings. She told us that she earned about six or seven shillings a week as a spinner. She said it was hard work, and complained that the yarn of late had been very bad. She discussed a recent strike, wages, and questions of trade—this child of fourteen. She said that bronchitis was bad. The factories are kept heated, the girls stand barefoot all day on sopping wet tiles, and they catch cold going home. She coughed as she spoke. She was about as tall as an ordinary girl of ten or eleven; her face was quite yellow; her poor little thin hair was plaited and pinned up on top of her head; she had large, dull, vacant eyes, and seemed lost in her black shawl. I don't think she has ever been really happy.

Think what this interior reveals! An old, inarticulate man nodding his head over the grave, and little girls who should be playing in the fields, support a family. I exclaimed to my friend as we left this slum house: "I have children of that age in England. They have leather reins and a whip; they play at horses and drive round the garden; they are big, strong, and overflowing with the joy of life. But that little worn-out girl we have just left talked about labour questions, discussed factory conditions, told us the history of a strike!"

We went to see a young man who is ill with bronchitis. We entered a small house, passed through the occupier's kitchen, and ascended to the lodger who rents the floor above. He lay gasping in bed, yellow and distressed. The room was like a loft. The atmosphere was suffocating. His young wife and three children crowded the space unoccupied by the one bed. He pays the woman below two shillings a week; the rent of the entire house is two shillings and sixpence. This young man is handsome in a rather theatrical fashion. It was sad to see him wasting and breathing stertorously on the dingy bed. He left his trade to sell toothpaste and lecture about teeth at street corners. He could once make five pounds a week. "Ah, but I'm stale now," he sighed; "a man can't keep up that sort of thing for long. I wish I had never left my trade."

Let the reader consider what these figures mean: In the March quarter of last year the percentage of infant mortality in West Belfast was 28·1; in the whole of the other urban districts it was 18·8. In the June quarter 29·7, as against 17·0 for the other districts. In the September quarter 38·6 against 30·8. In the December quarter 24·1 against 18·3. During last year 1521 infants under one year of age died in the city of Belfast.

It was curious to observe in nearly all these slum houses occupied by Catholics coloured pictures of Christ, the Pope, and Robert Emmet on the dingy walls. Men in the lodging-houses go to early Mass. Immorality is scarcely known among the Catholics. But drink is a frightful cause of misery and destitution.

"Drink," said my friend, "is not by any means the beginning of wretchedness. Mr. Lloyd George is quite right. First, sickness; second, unemployment; third, drink."

It must be said that here and there among these slums one found homes specklessly clean, radiant with brass candlesticks and china figures, the inmates decent and self-respecting. But the houses are really abominable; the only two things in their favour are the lowness of the rents and the fact that some of them are condemned. My friend, most anxious for me to think well of Belfast, said repeatedly, "All these houses are condemned."

Someone else said to me, "Yes, but they have been condemned a long time!"

So long as they stand, so long as they are inhabited, particularly by children, the City Corporation deserves to be condemned, and the landlords deserve to be hanged. I have not told one-half the horror of West Belfast. It covers a large space of the loyal city, and it is packed, thick packed, with misery, depravity, ugliness, and bitter suffering. And West Belfast is only one of the squalid quarters of the city where the poor are herded in a dense and swarming mass, with less room, less light, and less cleanliness than the criminal can claim in penal servitude. In every part of the city almost any side-turning from civic splendour and private wealth will bring you face to face with destitution and ugliness.

And it is not only the slum quarter, by any means, which depresses the visitor to Belfast. The slum sickens and disgusts, but the everlasting streets of little red-brick villas, the respectable streets of the well-off working-classes, fill one with depression. The monotony is almost worse than squalor. The contentment of the inhabitants is inexplicable. Thousands of people are massed together in these hideous villas, which have been built, as it were, by the gross, which have economized everything essential to a house and omitted everything necessary to a home, which are crowded together in a dense monotone of gloom, rows of cramped dwellings separated by niggard roads, with no sign of a tree anywhere, no garden of any kind, nothing but red bricks, grey slates, and smoking chimneys.

An able and sympathetic clergyman of the Irish Church told me that the courage and the virtues of the people who pack these incessant streets are wonderful and amazing. He was enthusiastic about their moral qualities. But is it possible that posterity, bred in such ugliness and environed by such unnatural conditions, should be conscious of gratitude for existence, should feel, however high their wages may rise, that life is a great and wonderful experience? The scowl on the faces of the men, the worn look on the faces of the women, the almost total absence of beauty and joy among the children, force one to believe that humanity cannot prosper in conditions so entirely divorced from the motherhood of nature.

## CHAPTER XVIII

### BABIES

WHERE home-life is beautiful, the coming of a baby is an event of unparalleled excitement and the most delightful joy. All the pets which have hitherto engrossed the thoughts of the children lose the sharpness of interest; dolls and toys are regarded only as presents to be hoarded for the new-comer; picture-books and paint-boxes are employed merely to get rid of the almost unbearable suspense in waiting for the great miracle to occur; the corner of the garden for which they are responsible begins to show a crop of weeds,

And the baby of such a home—I mean the baby of a kind man and a good woman—is almost always beautiful. Indeed, I doubt whether there is anything in the world of so exquisite a beauty, so adorable a perfection, so enchanting a fascination. The large eyes, which see nothing, the little ears, which hear nothing, the tiny and most perfect rose-coloured fingers and toes, the heavenly sweetness of the breath, the unearthly softness and purity of the skin, the absolute innocence and the profound mystery of new-born life, the evolution of the brain-cells into a settled and distinct Personality—are not these things a rapture and a benediction?

I saw one such baby in Belfast. In the home of well-off people living in the suburbs of the town I had the delight and amusement of worshipping a baby that was lovely and wonderful. I watched the older brother and sister playing with this infant, saw the mother take it on her knee and press its little face against her breast, agreed with the happy father that the child was amazing at all points of the compass.

But I saw in Belfast hundreds of other babies, every day and every night I saw hundreds of other babies; and they were not beautiful, they were not lovable—they were the most pathetic, sorry, and ugly little creatures imaginable. They were what people call "brats."

The look in the eyes of these chalk-faced, rag-dressed, unwashed, uncared-for, slum infants is almost the most awful sight I have seen. It is an expression of apathy and acquiescence in misery. They have cried in their pain, they have rebelled against starvation, they have roared and kicked with instinctive but unconscious indignation against their maltreatment; but the fierce hands of the mothers have shaken and stricken them into silence, the ferocious voice of their mothers has shouted down their cries—and now they are afraid to utter sound, afraid to protest; they submit, they surrender, they acquiesce.

Have you ever heard the voice of a slum mother shouting at her child? Have you ever seen one of these slatternly mothers seize up her crying baby from a grocer's filthy box on the floor, shake it with frenzied violence, thump it brutally on the spine, and then thrust it impatiently back into the box-cradle which had far better be its coffin? And have you listened for a moment to the frightful silence which followed?

But have you not noticed that the whole spirit of a poor neighbourhood is one of brutality? Consider for a moment, and think whether you have ever heard in a shabby quarter of any large town in the world a single word addressed to children that was gentle and tender. I have often been struck in these dreadful quarters by the angry fierceness with which even children speak to their younger

brothers and sisters. They shout at the child that tarries behind; they run back at last, snatch up its hand, shake the arm violently, and then drag the lingerer forward at a pace which the little feet tumble over each other to maintain. The elder sister, even when she is caressing the baby in her arms, will shout angrily into its ears if it utter a whimper or kick to be set down in the road. A party of boys, playing at a game in the street, will rush up to each other in a moment of dispute, yell in each other's faces, roll up their sleeves in threat of battle, push forward, stamp their feet on the ground, and to express the full righteousness of their indignation will contort their faces into demoniac hideousness and passion.

The good father in these crowded quarters of great cities thinks it right and natural to address his children harshly and with threats. He is ashamed of tenderness. He has no faith whatever in gentleness. His method is the loud word and the sharp blow. Even where religion or humanity saves him from actual tyranny, his conversations with his children, certainly his corrections and commands, are always in a brutal key.

Perhaps most of us who are shocked by this barbarous defamation of parental love would be no different ourselves if we lived in a slum. The cry of a baby is utterly maddening in a dark hot room where the mother is busy at sweated labour, and where the other children are ceaselessly asking questions as to the hour of the next meal. And the baby of such a mother is not beautiful and worshipful, but is ugly and unlovable, is pale, pinched, peevish, and nasty. It is difficult, I think, for the most loving-hearted person to feel anything but pity for these unnatural infants. They are so ugly and unreal. They are so nearly abortions.

Let us remember, too, the utter ignorance of the parents. Civilization has bred a race of mothers who know nothing of maternity. A doctor in Belfast told me that he very often finds a mother feeding her infant on tinned meat, bread, and tea. He says to one mother, "You must give the child milk, or it will die." And the mother answers, "Only milk, doctor?—is it to have no food, then, at all?" And he asks another mother, who complains that her child will eat nothing, "Have you tried milk?" The mother declares that the child will not touch it. "Let me see," he says; and they have to send out for milk, "a hap'orth of milk"—for there is not a drop in the house. "I assure you," he told me, "that I have difficulty in preventing the poor mites from eating the teaspoon, so greedy are they for the milk directly they taste it."

Let a man reflect on this state of things, and he will surely agree that civilization has got dangerously astray from nature's road. For myself, I can say that the mere spectacle of babies in the streets of

Belfast had more meaning and more warning for my mind than all the disputation and controversy that I held with politicians and reformers. I would take supper with a clergyman and discuss the religious difficulty, sit smoking with a Socialist and discuss the political difficulty, or dine with a doctor and discuss questions of science; and then, sauntering back to my hotel through the back streets of the town, I seemed to feel that everything said to me an hour before was vain and meaningless, that its interest for me had been delusion, that here in these dismal streets, wrapped in the dirty shawls of their mothers or carried in the arms of little sisters, here in these grey-faced, dull-eyed, listless and bloodless babies, was the Fact, the Reality, the Absolute Truth of Industrialism.

What a scene it would be—strive to imagine it—if one day when the House of Commons was solemnly engaged in debating whether, in a dawdling clause of some fatuous bill, the word "may" should be altered to the more drastic "shall," or when a brilliant and pungent master of irony was delighting the House by recalling the former utterances of a Cabinet Minister on the question of closure by compartments—what a scene, I say, if the doors were to open slowly, quietly, and a swarm of haggard children from the slums of industrial cities, carrying anæmic and wasting posterity in their scraggy arms, advanced a little way up the floor of the House, and stood waiting there, waiting for life in a silence of death.

Honourable and right honourable gentlemen, gallant and learned members, noble lords and grinning coxcombs, practised liars and specious humbugs, honest men and faithful Christians—what would they say to this interruption by Reality, how would they deal with this invasion of their dialectical territory by living Fact?

If the children of the slums, now cheated of joy, beauty, and natural health, were to raise their voices in one agonized scream of rebellion, one bitter cry of revolt against the laws of God and man, we should spring to our feet and plunge into the blackness and morass of our social misery to rescue and to save. But I think the silence, and the lethargy, and the acquiescence of these little children is, of all facts and realities, the most awful. It seemed to me in Belfast that I could have better borne the gaze of those atrophying babies of the slums if they had accused me, if they had pleaded to me, if they had mocked me. But the glazed, dull, lifeless, and indifferent look in their eyes filled me with desolating horror. I felt, first of all, that I could understand the woman who murders her child—for these babies are unlovely, one may even say, God help us, that they are revolting. Then I felt that nature did well to mow down these sickly and artificial deformities of human kind with her wide-sweeping, merciless, and never idle scythe of destruction. Then

I felt that we do wrong to send doctors, and nurses, and sanitary inspectors into the slums of great cities to preserve a generation that can only be miserable in itself and that must inevitably be the cause of even greater misery in the generation to follow. And, finally, I felt afraid.

When you think how beautiful a thing is a natural baby, how its health and its joy create an atmosphere of delight about it infecting the most solemn or the most careworn, and how it rules like an absolute monarch a home consecrated by love, when you keep this thought in your mind, it is with a sudden clutch of fear that you see the frightful peril of industrialism beholding these hordes of poor, ugly, misshapen, and actually repugnant infants. We have made the most beautiful thing in nature the most hideous, the most lovable work of creation the most repellent.

Civilization is breeding these deformities of humanity by hundreds of thousands. Not all the inspection of the State, not all the reforms in education, not all the self-sacrifice and devotion of religious philanthropy can make them whole. Till they drop into their graves they must crawl in the unlifting shadow of a curse which can never be annulled by Act of Parliament—Nature's curse on defiance of her laws. They are things that have never been mothered.

When next you smile into the cradle of a happy, natural baby, or lift the cover on that wonderful basket where powder-box, hair brush, safety-pins, needle and cotton, blunt-pointed scissors and white linen are set in the neatness of good order, or examine the soft and beautiful garments which a mother's fingers loved to make before the hour of her travail had arrived, remind yourself, and see the awful significance of it, that this is one of the commonest requests made by tiny children over the counter of pawnshops in our crowded cities :

" A penn'orth of rags for baby."

## CHAPTER XIX

### MAIDS OF THE MILL

As you pass through the back streets of Belfast, which have an extraordinary monotony, an extraordinary ugliness—as if a city without trees and without green spaces and without gardens has some particular power to oppress the poorer quarters with an added force of unnatural melancholy—you may see little children, grubby of face and ragged in garments, sitting on the doorsteps with their backs to the home, their faces to the street, playing at a self-invented game.

It is delightful to watch the sparkle in their eyes, to follow the sudden movements of their little hands, to hear the laughter and discussion of their baby lips. Behind them you may see the shadowy figure of a woman working at embroidery or attending to a fire ; in the broken road of the street boys kick without much energy a sodden football ; at the corners there are little groups of unemployed casuals ; the grimy slates, the dull windows, the broken shutters, and the lifeless red bricks of the continuous houses seem to be dark with ruin, pauperism, and brooding death.

The little girls on the doorstep are happy. Their happiness continues till they go to school, and until they are old enough to become half-timers. Then for the rest of the thirty-eight years which make the average life-time of a woman mill-worker existence for them is a progress of suffering. It strikes like a blow at the heart, observing these infants of the slums, to reflect that their trivial happiness, their innocent and baby happiness, is passing away from them, swiftly, even while they play; that it is the only happiness they will ever know.

To send a little schoolgirl into a linen mill is really inhuman. The only excuse for this barbarity is the matter of wages. They can earn —these poor babies—half a crown or two-and-ninepence a week. People say to you, " They help to support the family " ; or, " It is better for them to be employed than idle in the streets." But they go from these unhealthy slums, and from a most imperfect educational system, and at just the very period when they should be living in the open air and getting the very best of nourishment, into an atmosphere that destroys the vigour of adults, and to work which tears the nervous system into shreds. Like a shuttle these little, sleepy, ill-nourished innocents are driven backwards and forwards from school to factory, from factory to home, and from home to school. Their brains are confused, their limbs ache, the blood runs sluggishly in their veins. They contract whooping-cough, bronchial pneumonia, and consumption. They die in what should be their prime, worn out, rattled, and husky—dry as the dust on the road, empty as an old shuck.

At half-past five every morning the smoky air above the roofs of Belfast vibrates with the scream of sirens. Thousands of little girls, roused by these continuous and piercing yells, spring frightened out of slum beds and drag on dirty garments. At ten minutes to six, as if each siren were striving to outscream the others, there begins a pandemonium of this furious screeching, which lasts unbroken for ten minutes. While it is proceeding the back streets are filled with women and girls hurrying to the numerous factories. They have eaten nothing. With shawls pulled over their heads, they pace through the streets in a great army, shivering with cold and dull with bodily want. Some of them chew starch or ginger, or cloves and even camphor ; some of the mothers have dosed their babies with a drop or two of laudanum before leaving home.

They enter the great factories and pass to the various departments. Some of the women and girls go to dry spinning, and some to wet spinning. In the wet spinning-rooms the heat is so great that a person unused to it would faint in five minutes. The atmosphere is thick with steam. The floors are kept sloppy with water. The girls fling off their shawls, and, wearing nothing but a thin skirt and a shift which leaves the neck and chest exposed, begin their work at the machines. In the dry spinning-rooms the air is dusty with a choking fluff called pouce, which gets into the throat and clings to the air channels. When a girl begins to break down in her lungs, the others say, hearing her cough, " She's pouced." It is possibly the beginning of consumption. Some of the factories have been improved by recent legislation, but no contrivance can altogether remove the dangers of unnatural heat and flying fluff.

When the girls go to breakfast, they proceed, most of them barefoot, from these frightful rooms straight to the cold and wet of the streets. The shock to the system is terrible, and it is amazing that they live so long. When our children have been in warm rooms we wrap them up before they go into a colder atmosphere. These girls pass barefoot and thinly clad from the tropical heat of the spinning-room to the weather of the outer world. It is as if a man went from a Turkish bath, barefoot and thinly clad, to the muddy pavements and wintry wind of London streets. And when they get home their breakfast is a cup of tea and a piece of bread.

So the day passes, with an interval for dinner, till nightfall is at hand ; and then fagged, gloomy, and coughing, the army of womanhood shuffles back into the slums for more tea and more bread. At the end of the week the little maids have earned six or seven shillings.

Thousands of these girls support their families. The father is very often a casual labourer, and has become, by unemployment and self-contempt, a loafing drunkard, a sponge upon his wife and children. Three little daughters in the mill can earn enough to pay the rent of his slum home, to provide the family with bread and tea, and to keep him in stout and tobacco. Why should he stand in a shivering wedge of broken humanity at the docks, waiting for hard work to be thrown at him for a mean wage ? Has he not brought children into the world ? Has he not bestowed the immense boon of human existence on these little ones ? Surely, he may live upon them.

A few of these girls with spirit in their blood, pull their shawls over their heads at night and go walking in gangs before the barrack gates, ready for any adventure that may befall them. The competition of little short-skirted shop girls, with rakish hats, is generally too much for them, and they watch with real envy and with genuine pain the gorgeous red coat of the British soldier moving away beside these fashionable rivals. Then, as the hours wear away, they begin to mock and laugh, to join arms and move singing through the streets, till perhaps they join forces with a gang of factory boys and finish the night in some trifling horseplay. These children are always to the front in a street riot, they are often the cause of a fight between Catholics and Protestants, they have battle-cries which rouse a neighbourhood.

But most of the girls bide in their homes, except on summer nights, while many of them actually work for another firm in the little family kitchen which is their home, until it is time for bed. The great concern of Belfast is Wages.

You will see stout matrons of forty and fifty in the linen mills, but the average life of the stunted, anæmic, skinny little creatures who compose the immense army of mill workers is thirty-eight years of age. They become sallow and dull. Their teeth decay and fall out, their lungs break down, and they wind up their experience of terrestrial life with a dignified funeral.

A gentleman in Ireland devoted to the development of Irish industries was one day asking for support from a rich man in Belfast. At the end of their conversation the Ulsterman said, " Well, I wish you luck. Go on developing Irish industries as hard as you like, but, for God's sake, don't set up another Belfast. If you knew what goes on behind the scenes you'd lose a good deal of your enthusiasm for industrialism." It is said that the business prosperity of Belfast—one single firm made a profit of £80,000 last year—is built upon credit. A serious rise in the bank rate, it is said, would bring the commercial glory of Belfast tumbling to the dust of bankruptcy. In some cases at least this advertised prosperity is certainly built upon the slavery of women and girls. No man can say that the life of these girls is good. No man can pretend that it is desirable. No doctor could do anything but denounce it. At fourteen years of age they may earn seven shillings a week, and in their decrepitude at thirty-eight they may earn ten or twelve shillings a week ; but even if the seven shillings had grown to a hundred, who can say that to die broken and tired at eight-and-thirty, with no experience of joy, with no enthusiasm for beauty, with not the faintest knowledge of the boundless universe that enfolds the mystery of human life, is a reasonable existence, is a just destiny ? From such loins what posterity can spring ?

And if life in the mill is dreadful and wicked, it is scarcely less inhuman in the home of the out-worker, even the country out-worker. " A gentleman," says Miss Margaret Irwin, " who has given special attention to this question, speaking of the evil conditions of the work, and the serious results it was having on the health of the girls, said, 'The girls carry in heavy burdens of shirts, say on the market day, which is Tuesday. They may get a lift on the road; if they do not it means a three miles' walk for them each way, which they have to undertake over-weighted and underfed. Consequently they arrive home at night in a perfectly exhausted condition, and without any wholesome appetite. Their day is something like this. They get up badly rested and unrefreshed after a night spent in an insanitary, ill-ventilated house, and make a "boil of tea," say, at six o'clock, for breakfast. Then they do a little housework. A second breakfast, also of tea, may follow an hour later. Sewing may begin at ten, and six or seven of them may club together in one house to do this, as, of course, they get through more work that way. If there is a man in the house, something in the way of dinner may be made between twelve and one; if not, it is tea and bread again. Tea again at five, and once more tea at nine. They work on this food sometimes up to eleven or twelve at night when they have a big order on; go to bed after midnight, it may be; rise unrefreshed in the morning, and begin again da capo.'"

Miss Irwin herself gives a striking account of a visit she paid to a young woman, "probably the most highly skilled worker I met with in my inquiry":—

> "When visited she was embroidering a silk parasol with coloured silks. The work was exquisite, and demanded a high degree of skill. She was to receive 2s. for the parasol, and it would take her three days' steady work. She showed me a blouse piece, finely embroidered, which would take two days' steady work, from eight in the morning till ten at night—for this she was paid 2s. For an embroidered robe piece, which took over three days, she got 3s. She had done one of these previously, which took more than a week of steady labour with late hours every night, and the price paid her was 8s. A sister gave corroborative evidence. They occupied a very clean and well-kept house. The witness was an anæmic, delicate-looking girl, about twenty-two years of age, intelligent, and with gentle and refined manners. Her mother, engaged at the wash-tub in the kitchen, kept up a running commentary during the whole of my visit. 'Sure, tell the lady now; it's time that someone heard about it. It's a black shame and a disgrace, and it's blood-money they are paying you.' As I was going out the mother came forward, seized my hand, and said, 'Ye *will* tell about it now? Promise me ye will? My little girl sews and sews until she has nearly killed herself.'"

Whether it be in the mill or in the home, the life of these girls is destitute of joy. Some of them possess the consolations of religion, and the week of toil is endured without complaint, cheered by the anticipation of a service on Sunday in church or chapel. The little drama of the street—its births, deaths and marriages, its drunkenness and quarrels, its departures and arrivals—these things supply the narrative of their gossip. For the rest, life is bread and tea, sewing and toiling, from morning to night—a life without one glorious impulse, without one spring of gratitude. And life, says George Sand, to be fruitful must be felt as a blessing !

What strikes me as the most terrible fact about Belfast is this—it is a city without childhood. The scowl which settles darkly on the face of adults is present as a cloud upon the brow of children. The radiant face of infancy may be seen here and there, but the joyous shining eyes of childhood never greet one in the crowded streets. Except for lads kicking a football or a wad of paper about the roads, except for foul-mouthed, barefoot newspaper boys smoking cigarettes and tossing for halfpennies in the gutters of Royal Avenue, and except for little stunted factory girls larking in the streets at night, I have not seen a single child playing in Belfast.

When the mother and the elder sisters are employed in factories, you cannot have home-life, you cannot have childhood. The little children shift for themselves. Fed upon bread and tea, turned into the factories while they are still at school, settled as regular mil, hands at the age of fourteen, these girls become neurasthenicl anæmic, and consumptive before they are out of their teens. The noise of the factories, the incessant clangour of the machines, the stretched attention of their immature brains, and the unwholesome atmosphere of the rooms where they work, crush and exterminate their childhood.

I would rather see my own children dead than working in the very best of the Belfast linen mills.

## CHAPTER XX

### WEALTH

Two principal delusions exist about this great and loyal city of Belfast. One that it is religious, the other that it is rich. I do not think I exaggerate when I say that a man would have to travel far before he found a city where the foundational principles of the Christian religion are more perfectly ignored, and where the labour of the poorest people is more inadequately rewarded.

In this chapter I confine myself to the question of wealth. There are men in Belfast who are very rich ; there are skilled workmen in the shipyards and factories who earn high wages ; but the vast multitude of the city is horribly, wickedly, and disastrously poor. Because Belfast is doing what men call " a roaring trade," it is supposed that the entire population is prosperous and contented ;

because a few isolated cases of high wages are trumpeted here and there, it is supposed that only a few are poor, only a remnant is sweated. But multitudes of men and women in Belfast are dreadfully poor, and numbers of women and girls are outrageously sweated. Before this chapter is concluded I think the reader will perceive clearly one of the strange truths of civilization, to wit, that the prosperity of a town may co-exist with the misery of its inhabitants.

Among the great host of ordinary workers in the linen mills wages may be said to range from 12s. to 16s. a week for men, 10s. a week for women. This is a fair average. Some men are employed on night work in these linen mills, married men, and they earn 13s. 4d. a week. Home-life, of course, is rendered difficult in such cases; family life is disorganized; and the price is 13s. 4d. Among the young people in the mills, boys earn from 9s. to 10s., and girls from 6s. to 7s. When there is an agitation for higher, for juster wages, the almost invariable remedy is a threat to put the workers on half-time. Nothing so frightens these poor people as the prospect of half wages—6s. or 8s. for men, 5s. for women, 3s. or 3s. 6d. for girls. School children employed as half-timers in these flourishing mills earn 2s. 9d. or 3s. a week.

Now, it is not possible for a man earning 12s. to 16s. a week in Belfast to support a family in decency and make provision for times of unemployment. Therefore in most cases the children are pushed early into these unhealthy mills, with their heated air and damp floors, and even the wife contributes to the family income by working at home. Life is not very agreeable in these working-class quarters. After a long and wearisome day's work the man is inclined to take his ease in one public-house, and the wife in another. Drink is expensive. And therefore even in cases where man, wife, and three or four children are all earning money it is possible to find degrading poverty.

But what of the home-workers?

There is an inquiry now proceeding in Belfast on this subject, an inquiry which is secret. But in spite of that secrecy I hope a report may be issued, with all the evidence presented before the committee. It should astound the conscience of mankind. This sweating of the home-worker in Belfast is so scandalous that it staggers the mind to imagine how civilized men can reap the profits of it, and when one knows that many of these men are enormously rich and ostentatiously religious, it stirs an angry indignation in the soul. I give a few typical cases, which have been most carefully investigated by an expert in this particular dodge of the capitalist to grind the faces of the poor—an expert in the tragedy of the home-worker.

One firm gives out to its home-workers linen tablecloths stamped with a blue design for these wretched women to embroider. The cloth is about forty-five inches square; the design is floral and complicated, the embroidery has to be heavy and fine. To embroider one cloth it takes three days, working eight hours a day. The remuneration is 8s. for a dozen cloths; in other words, 8d. a cloth—less than 3d. a day. Divide 3d. by eight and you get the rate of pay per hour.

Another firm gives out an immense amount of work called "top-sewing"—that is, tucking in the tiny ragged corners of fine cambric handkerchiefs and stitching them neatly down. It is work that puts enormous strain upon the eyes and demands the very nicest care with the needle. The cleverest worker can top-sew two dozen handkerchiefs in an hour. And the wage is ½d. a dozen! In one hour the woman earns a penny. A day's incessant work of eight hours brings eight coppers into her purse. But she must go to and from the warehouse, wait her turn with a crowd of other miserables, and buy her own needles and threads. I saw the wage-book of a poor young widow who does this work, with the help of her three little boys, who separate the handkerchiefs and thread the fine needles. These were the weekly earnings, varying with the amount of work she could obtain: 3s. 2d., 6s. 11d., 6s. 0½d., 4s. 5½d. The wage-book of another cambric worker showed that between the 4th and 16th of March she had earned 11s. 2d. These books would not look well either in an employer's library or on the table of a director's board-room. They are documents that are fitted for the Congo.

To sew lace upon handkerchiefs demands exceeding skill; the lace is often valuable and no risk of spoiling it must be incurred. A firm would not give such work to blunderers or disreputables. Their workers must be skilled, honest, and clean. The pay is 9d. a dozen handkerchiefs. It takes three-quarters of an hour to finish a single handkerchief. The rate of wages works out at a penny an hour. There is a case in Belfast of a widow supporting three young children and an invalid sister by this difficult work which gives her a penny an hour.

An army of women go to the warehouses for bundles of print skirts. They take these bundles into their shabby homes and stitch them with a machine, buying their own thread. They are paid 1s. 6d a dozen skirts. It occupies two days to stitch a dozen. The rate of pay is 9d. a day. They carry the skirts back, and are responsible for the running of their machines. One woman, with six children, whose case has been carefully investigated, supports herself in this manner.

Here are a few instances, briefly given, of other wages in this great sweating industry of Belfast:—

Ladies' blouses, 1s. 4d. a dozen; one hour to a blouse; cost of thread 1½d. a dozen blouses. Chemises, 9d. a dozen; ten hours for one dozen; cost of thread 1½d. a dozen garments. Men's heavy cotton shirts, double sewing, 1s. 4d. per dozen, less 2½d. for thread thirteen hours for one dozen; rate of pay 1d. an hour.

Thread-clipping parasol covers, removing stitches from machine embroidery and the paper used for stiffening the back of patterns, 3d. a dozen; nine hours for one dozen; rate of pay ⅓d. an hour.

These appalling figures may be in the nature of "revelations" to English people, but apparently it is general knowledge in Belfast that the foundation of the city's prosperity is oppression of this kind. In a Belfast newspaper I have just read the evidence of a district nurse to the effect that ill-health is due, among other causes, to the "low wages paid to the labouring classes." She added that the quality of milk sold in the slums was not worth the money expended upon it. "In slum areas it was very poor, and it was anything but clean." In another Belfast newspaper I read that the rector of St. Aidan's Church declares that part of his parish is "plunged in dense and hopeless poverty that could not be equalled within the boundaries of Belfast." Think of those words—dense and hopeless poverty!

At the present moment Belfast is suffering from an abnormally high death-rate. The medical officer declares that this excessive mortality is almost entirely due to pneumonia and chest affections. Whooping-cough is visiting the city. "During the week 15 deaths were caused by this disease, 73 by pneumonia, and 67 by disease of the respiratory organs . . . during the past week 146 children under the age of five years had died, which was equal to a rate of 19·4 per 1000 of the whole population."

Fully to realize the condition of Belfast it is necessary to visit the slum quarters, to enter the kennels of the poor, to examine the wage-books of the home-workers, and to make a study of the ragged, barefoot children in the streets. No honest man who has conducted such an investigation can doubt that the condition of Belfast is a disgrace to civilization and a frightful menace to the health and morals of the next generation. The heavy scowling faces of the poor, the stunted and anæmic bodies of the children, haunt the soul of an observer with a sense of horror and alarm. One feels, regarding those swarms of children in the streets, that nature has made them grudgingly.

That Belfast is rich except in poverty is a delusion; it remains to consider whether the city is religious.

## CHAPTER XXI

### THE GOSPEL OF MAMMON

If Belfast did not advertise itself as the most religious city in Ireland, I should refrain from making this charge against it. If the clerical politicians of Belfast did not vaingloriously and most odiously trumpet from pulpit and platform the commercial prosperity of Protestantism, I should not make war upon them. And as it is, I confess at the outset that many of these men are honest, many of them are sincere and energetic, and some of them make sacrifices for their religion. But my charge is that the religion of Belfast, as a whole, is not the religion founded by Christ.

The reader has seen that the slums of the city are utterly unfit for human habitation, that the ill-health of the poor is attributed to "the low wages paid to the labouring classes," that sweating exists in a most atrocious degree, and that part of the city is "plunged in dense and hopeless poverty." Such things might be said of London, but London is vast beyond comparison with Belfast, a great army of Christian workers is there in constant service on the poor, and many of the clergy of London either protest against the condition of the masses or publicly deplore the failure of Christianity in this respect. They do not boast. On the other hand, Belfast is small and compact, the city may be explored in a day or two, the poverty is conspicuous at every point, and instead of challenging the unholy prosperity of the rich, the ministers of religion, paid by these rich sweaters, spend their time in denouncing Roman Catholics, in exalting the political principles of Lord Londonderry, and in boasting of their city's prosperity.

There is excessive religion in Belfast, excessive religious activity, but I declare that it bears but little resemblance to the religion of Christ. It is in some cases at least a religion of organized self-righteousness from which the ministering spirit of Christianity is lacking. It is a religion of large and comfortable churches, prosperous and well-dressed congregations, cheerful and well-satisfied tea-parties, Bible-classes for the saved, meetings for the elect, and gatherings for the oiled and bland. There is not a manifest devotion to the poor and suffering, not an active and vital crusade against Mammon; but too much opportunism, too much self-satisfaction.

Penetrate to the individual soul, and you find that the religion is hard, repellent, and Pharisaical. It breeds bigotry, self-esteem, and a violent intolerance. The large and liberal spirit of charity is wanting. Meekness and humility are excluded. Only here and there do you meet a gentle and sweet-minded man who has escaped uninjured from the iron vice of this hideous theology. The majority do not attract, do not win, do not prepossess. They disgust and repel.

Now, the Founder of Christianity foretold that on the Last Day those most sure of heaven, those who in His Name had done great things, would be turned away, and that those welcomed to the Kingdom would be surprised and amazed, conscious of no merit, ignorant even that they had rendered service to Him. Moreover, in another account of the Great Judgment, He showed that no theological tests would be employed, that no questions would be asked as to what creed a man professed, or in what particular church he had membership, but only what he had done to help the poor and suffering. Since this is the Founder's own description of the great, eternal, and ultimate judgment of terrestrial life, we must conclude—there is no escape from the conclusion—that the life of love and service is the Christian life, and that theology can have no value or weight of any kind whatsoever, save, of course, in so far as it influences men to live the devoted and loving life commanded by the Founder.

By this test the religion of Belfast is weighed and found wanting. Under the very eyes of the rich and respectable as they go to church are swarms of half-starved, ill-clothed, and barefoot children playing in the gutters of the streets. All about the worshippers as they give thanks in their well-warmed churches for health and prosperity are hideous and congested slums of " dense and hopeless poverty." To right and to left of them in their daily lives is an appalling sum of sickness and suffering caused by " the low wages paid to the labouring classes." Throughout the city, from one end to the other, and spreading even from the city to the villages beyond, such sweating of women and children is practised as must wring the soul of heaven. And all these terrible and iniquitous things are not lost in a multitudinous world like London, but are obvious, staring, and emphatic in a small city which boasts of its Christianity.

What strikes one as the worst feature in the religion of Belfast is the self-satisfaction of religious people when you speak about these dreadful things. They tell you, for instance, that children go barefoot for choice. They smile at your sentimental ignorance. Press them, and ask if it is right for children of five and six years of age to be out in the wet streets at ten o'clock of night—whether they like it or not !—and they reply that one must expect that sort of thing in a crowded city. They seem to be callous and untouched by this wholesale exposure of childhood. It seems to them a small thing that thousands of parents in Belfast use their children as no other animal uses its young. The natural duties of parentage are denied on every side of them, and they do nothing. Fathers and mothers pack the public-houses till late at night, while their supperless and half-naked children wander shoeless in the mud outside, or stare through shop windows at picture post cards which degrade love, mock maternity, and at least suggest indecency. And these religious people raise no protest. They say we must expect these things. They never loose their imaginations to contemplate what they must expect in the next generation from the children of this. They never ask themselves whether Christ, if He came to Belfast, would attend Protestant churches and listen to violent denunciations of Popery, or whether He would go into the tragic streets seeking the lost, comforting the unprosperous, and blessing the neglected children. They seem to think that Christ would even like Belfast.

Would you not think in a relatively small city, with such misery and heart-breaking cruelty to children on every hand, that the churches would unite for mercy and enlightenment? Would you not expect a religious crusade? Consider. Would any of those religious people leave their children to wander barefoot in York Street on a winter's night? Would they drink in a public-house while their children hungered outside? They know these things are evil. They say you must expect them in cities, they chide you for making too much of them, and they grow indignant when you ask if they could bear to think for a moment of their own children in a like condition. And they have only to think for a moment, only to reflect for an instant, to assure themselves of terrible responsibility. But they not only resent criticism; they are satisfied. Belfast is rich. The churches are prosperous.

And this seems to me the great pivotal cause of Belfast's misrepresentation of the Christian religion. Everything is money. Speak of drunkenness and cruelty to children, and they tell you complacently that it is the fault of the workers, for "they are earning good wages." So long as they can add up to a respectable total the shillings and pence going into a home by the labours of father, mother, and children, they feel their conscience to be absolved. They seem unable to realize that if a man gain the whole world and lose his soul, the transaction is bad even from an economic point of view. They do not apprehend, so fatally does money rule the life of Belfast, that the very fact of both father and mother earning money is certain evidence that home-life is impossible. The mother's duty is to feed, clothe, and rear her children; to labour so that the home may be happy and restful; to make those little rooms attractive to her husband and sacred to her children. She cannot do one of these things if she is working all day in a factory, or toiling all day as a sweated home-worker.

The factories are extending to villages outside the city. People rub their hands, and say that it will increase the wages of the peasants. They destroy the contentment, the simplicity, the natural existence and the home-life of the peasant, and they say that Industrialism is a blessing. It increases wages.

I have never before visited a city where the beauty of life is so completely destroyed as in Belfast. I believe this ugliness is due more than anything else to the false religion which has preached the gospel of money to every class in the community. Everything in

Belfast, even the success of church life, is tested by pounds, shillings, and pence. Nothing is worth while that does not pay. Presbyterian ministers with liberal minds dare not preach sweetness and light, dare not declare themselves Home Rulers, because it does not pay. And drunkenness, child neglect, squalor, and slums are laid to the charge of the poor because they are earning good wages, and therefore ought to know better! Everything is money. So far as I am aware, among all the preachers and ministers in Belfast who preach political sermons and organize the dull ranks of respectability, there is not one who has ever moved a finger to save the children from the streets, to bring the slum landlords to account, or to check the headlong advance of the mammon-worshippers. Certainly there is no one, if my informants are correct, who has ever warned the rich patrons of religion in Belfast that a man cannot serve God and Mammon.

I would beg the reader to bear in mind that which was said at the beginning of this chapter. Belfast is in some ways uglier and more depressing than any other city I have yet visited; but I do not mean to imply for a moment that it occupies a worse position morally and religiously than other centres where money-making is the paramount concern of humanity. It is specially detestable and particularly shameful only because it makes so loud a boast of its Christianity, lording itself over the rest of Ireland, and appealing to the conscience of England on the ground of religion.

That there is something twisted and abnormal in the religion of Belfast may be gathered, I think, from a letter which has just appeared in the *Dundee Advertiser* from an old and representative Presbyterian minister of Belfast, rebutting my charges against the false Christianity of his city. This gentleman had received a newspaper containing one of my articles "sent"—this is how he writes—"by an anonymous cad, with a most offensive pencil scrawl on the margin." In the midst of a very violent and entirely ill-mannered denial of my charges, this Presbyterian minister, so jealous for the Christianity of Belfast, reverts to his correspondent, the aforesaid "anonymous cad," and says: "My correspondent has gallantly prevented me from getting at him, either with evidence or with a horsewhip." I do not wish to labour so small a matter, but is there not something very extraordinary and rather amusing in this Christian's idea of vindicating the religiousness of his city with a horsewhip? Imagine what Tolstoy would have thought of such a Christian. The letter is worth quoting because of its naturalness, its spontaneity, its self-satisfaction, and its absolute innocence of being antithetical to the religion of Christ. But I really believe this letter to be characteristic of Belfast Presbyterianism. It is a religion, unconsciously, I am sure, that ignores the centre of Christ's Heart.

I should wish the reader to know that many men and women in Belfast expressed to me their horror of the human conditions and their contempt for the political pulpits. One woman told me—not a sensitive and neurotic woman of fashion, but a very sensible, hard-headed woman of business—that she cannot bear to face a crowd of workers coming from the shipyards and the factories. "They frighten one," she said; "their faces are so hard; they seem to scowl at one with hatred." Others spoke with extreme sorrow of the little ragged children who are to be seen in York Street at night, ragged and barefoot even in winter-time.

And here—that the reader may not think I have exaggerated—is an extract from an article in the *Ulster Guardian*, concerning the indignation of its contemporaries at some of my observations. With this frank and honest confession of a local critic I am glad to leave a matter which only gave me pain to investigate and which I have exposed with more scorn and anger than is altogether good for peace of mind:—

> But who is responsible for the daily descent of English specialists upon our shores? Surely the very party which is continually parading on English platforms the sores of three-fourths of Ireland and enlarging upon the sound mind in the sound body of the remaining fourth. This Pharisaical "Lord, I thank Thee I am not as other men are, even as this poor Nationalist" attitude simply invites inspection. We have never noticed the journals who condemn Mr. Begbie for what he says about Belfast protesting against the descriptions that appear constantly in English Tory papers from special correspondents of "the frightful state of the South and West of Ireland." What right have they to complain if English Liberal papers succumb to the temptation to discover how much ground there is for Ulster's self-righteousness and how far justified is her claim to prosperity and happiness and the rest of it? Mr. Begbie has weighed us in our own balance and has found us wanting. We may be no worse in our conditions of life than similar big towns across the water, but we have been bragging as if there were "none such," and now we are asked to start whining because we are not accepted at our own valuation. Manchester and Leeds may have shocking slums, but Manchester and Leeds do not perpetually run down the rest of England as seething in poverty and crime and place themselves on a pinnacle of perfection. We in Belfast have been doing this for several generations, and when a stranger comes, sees for himself, and tells us what he thinks of us, well, we should grin and bear it. If we insist on blessing ourselves, we cannot complain of others blaming us.
>
> In one respect Mr. Begbie has placed his finger upon a cankerous growth in the religious life of this city, the incessant preach-

ing of politics and denunciation of Popery in our pulpits. When the coal strike was at its most critical stage, the weekly prayer-meeting met to pray for Divine assistance in " the present grave crisis," but it was Home Rule that was the subject of the intercessions. Political sermons, Unionist Club church parades, anti-Home Rule religious conventions, what room have these left for spiritual growth or the uplifting of the masses ? Are there a dozen Protestant churches left in Belfast where a Liberal can worship without having his political principles attacked ? All honour to the exceptions, who really do minister to all sections of their flocks, who strive for the souls and not for the votes of their hearers, and who are more concerned with preaching the gospel of goodwill than in fanning the flames of religious hatred. But these exceptions are few, and, as Mr. Begbie points out, these men by abstaining from turning their pulpits into political platforms take their careers in their hands. It is not enough for them to remain neutral, to try to be pastors instead of politicians. Their very silence makes them marked men. This is the state into which the religious life of Belfast has fallen. Mr. Begbie has spoken no more than is true, and there is not an Ulster Liberal Protestant who will fail to corroborate his finding.

Belfast is built upon " slob," the foundations of the rich city are merely piles of timber driven into the marshy sludge of the river. I believe that the foundation of its prosperity is human slob, the flesh and blood sludge of sweated humanity ; and I believe that one day all this boastful prosperity will subside in ruin. How much slob there may be in the religion of Belfast I do not pretend to determine ; but I am very sure that this religion is not founded upon the rock.

" Will anyone," asked Benjamin Whichcote, " expect salvation from a Saviour that he will not imitate ? "

## CHAPTER XXII

### CONCLUSIONS

If I were an Irishman and lived in Belfast, I should be a Unionist —but not, the God of Sweetness and Light helping me, an Orangeman. I should be a Unionist in the same spirit and for the same reason as the young Socialist is a Unionist, of whom mention was made in the early pages of this book. I should be a Unionist in order to force for Belfast, by the strong hand of democratic England, taxation of the rich and social reformation for the poor.

And but for the obsession of a very arrogant, disfiguring, and entirely un-Christlike Protestantism—an artificially organized political religiousness—nine-tenths of the workmen in Belfast would be consistent Unionists of this character. Even as it is, the number of men who ignore the hypocrisy of politics disguised as religion, and who are clear-headed democrats and rational materialists, is very great and increases every day. Since the coming of hard-headed shipwrights from Scotland in the eighties—democrats who cared nothing at all about the religious feud of Ulster—intelligent workmen are ceasing to believe the silly calumny that Mr. Redmond will take their jobs and business from them and bestow both these blessings upon his Catholic supporters; but they refuse to believe—and I think they have wisdom—that the rule of Mr. Redmond in Dublin will be as fruitful with blessings for democracy in Belfast as the rule of Mr. Lloyd George in London.

No sensible man in Ireland can believe that an Irish Parliament will get quicker to the goal of Socialism than a British Parliament. An Irish Parliament will be Conservative. Save for a few members from the industrial quarters of Ulster, it will be untouched by the democratic spirit of modern Europe. It will be a Parliament representing before everything else the democracy of a landowning peasantry. I have no doubt at all in my mind that even if all the nations of the civilized world were to accept Socialism Ireland would remain Conservative, and Conservative as England herself has never been since the passing of the Reform Bill.

The real Ulster Difficulty lies in this natural conservatism of the Irish majority. Little or nothing will be done by an Irish Parliament, whose business will be to deal with natural conditions—little or nothing will be done to solve the difficulties of unnatural conditions existing in North-East Ulster. One might as well look to the British Parliament to spend itself on legislation for the small-holders of industrial England as expect an Irish Parliament to labour for the social betterment of the mechanics of agricultural Ireland. What the Belfast workman finds it difficult to realize is this, that he lives in unnatural conditions, that his existence is of no paramount importance to Ireland, and that the majority of his fellow-countrymen are determined to rescue themselves from a form of government which is unsuitable to people living in natural conditions.

English people are now so accustomed to regard legislation as the experimental remedies of social reformers attempting to deal with the diseases of unnatural conditions, that they cannot conceive of a legislation which would be entirely directed to the development and conservation of perfectly healthy and perfectly natural conditions. Legislation has ceased for us to be a wholesome food; it has become a patent medicine. It is no longer an evolution; it is a surgical operation. But Ireland is a country which has preserved natural life. Except for the destitution, the slums, the sweating, and the infant mortality of a corner in North-East Ulster, it is a country which pursues the way of primitive mankind—much nearer to the peasants of India in its manner of existence than to the scrofulous and anæmic inhabitants of our industrial towns. Ireland does not need, and she does not desire, the legislation of the Socialist, the Labour Party, and the advanced Liberal. She could hardly have a more congenial Prime Minister—this rebel Ireland—than Mr. Henry Chaplin, or Mr. Walter Long.

Now the natural condition of Irish humanity is at once the great attraction and the great instruction of the Irish question for modern England. We ourselves are committed, perhaps hopelessly committed, to competitive Commercialism. Our peasantry is, practically speaking, extinct. We are manufacturers. We live in slums. Our extremes of wealth and poverty, and the extent of our social problems, are unmatched in Europe. So complex and confusing is our condition that two clergymen of great intellectual abilities and undoubted sincerity, Bishop Gore and Canon Hensley Henson, come to blows in the columns of *The Times* over morals and economics. We are told, in the course of this clerical correspondence, that the idea of justice is alien to a discussion about wages; struggle for profits, it seems, must be left free to buy its labour in the cheapest market; there is no means for ascertaining what is a just wage—the term is absurd—we possess only a very obvious way of contriving to pay as little as possible.

For instance, I employ a gardener and pay him twenty shillings a week; a man out of work comes begging at my door and offers to take the gardener's place at fifteen shillings a week; six months later a man in more desperate straits begs to be taken as gardener at twelve shillings, at ten shillings, even at eight shillings a week. I must not say to myself, "The work is worth twenty shillings a week; a man cannot support himself in Christian decency on less." I must not listen to my conscience, to the moral side of my nature, when it says to me: "It is an infamy, worse than cheating, to take advantage of this man's hunger and bitter need." No; for to entertain such a notion would be to import morals into economics. Only a blundering sub-editor, enamoured of engaging headlines, could indulge a foolish taste for sentimentalism by a collocation of such discordant words as "Justice and Wages." Capital must buy its labour, where Misery buys its broken meat, in the cheapest market. On that power of our manufacturers to buy humanity at bottom prices is founded the safety, honour, and welfare of Great Britain's commerce.

To such a gospel we are now committed. It is perfectly logical, perfectly true, perfectly defensible. It may trouble the conscience of a few virtuous people, but it is the central fact of our modern existence. You can no more bring religion into the sphere of economics than you can bring a lighted candle into the region of a gas escape. Six weeks of Mr. Victor Grayson at Downing Street would bring the British Empire to ruin. No man of honest sense can believe that industrial England could survive such a preposterous experiment. And why is it so preposterous? Because the extreme Socialists are attempting to make normal ideas prevail in a community which has ceased to be normal. They are seeking to govern unnatural conditions by natural considerations. This is the very heart and centre of our national confusion.

Do we recognize that England has ceased to live its life under natural conditions? Do we realize that to pack men in conglomerate masses, to breed posterity out of all touch with nature, to make the day a torture of mechanic toil, and the night a pandemonium of public-house and blatant music-hall; do we realize that to be so expatriated from nature that even the instincts of maternity and motherhood have to be preached and taught to our women like a difficult lesson—do we realize that this is an effort of humanity to live clean contrary to the laws of nature?

It is of the utmost importance that we should confront this fact of modern industrialism. I do not argue that men and women in cities must be unhealthy, that children must grow to maturity without vigour and without enthusiasm, that urban humanity must be godless and immoral. That is not the question, and that is not of relative importance. My contention is that the inhabitants of a huge and crowded industrial town are not natural men and women, that the conditions of their existence are so foreign and contrary to natural conditions that their thoughts cease to be the thoughts of men and women living in the immemorial conditions of humanity —in a word, I contend that intellectually and spiritually an industrial population is an artificial and manufactured humanity.

When you consider that there are thousands of women on the eve of maternity working in factories that exacerbate the nervous system and imperil physical health; when you consider that death's annual toll of infants under one year of age is like the carnage of a military campaign; when you consider that little children in school have to be regularly inspected, like so many dotards, for defective eyesight and defective teeth; when you consider that the nourishment of the vast majority of these people is notoriously the worst possible kind of tinned or bottled dietary; when you consider that one of the most profitable trades of the country is the ceaseless manufacture of pre-digested foods and patent medicines; when you consider that by far the greatest number of families in England are now living without a garden, treading for ever on stone, walled in on every side by brick, shut out completely from the beauty and serenity of nature—so that even sunset is obscured by chimneys and the flare of artificial illumination puts out the light of the stars—when you consider these things you must come willingly or unwillingly, to the confession, which is so startling if its significance is perceived, that the life of an industrial population is unnatural and that the thoughts of such a population must also be unnatural. They are unconscious of the majesty of nature, unaware even of the mystery of their own bodies. A tired cynicism, a brutal depreciation of glory and enthusiasm, a harsh embittered contempt for wonder and reverence paralyses the noblest functions of these artificial minds. In the solitude of their souls such people are as different from natural man as the Thames of Wapping from the Thames of Marlow.

Consider, too, the state of things in the region of intellectual thought. The playwrights of civilization, and a considerable number of novelists and philosophers, devote themselves almost entirely and with a most fantastic seriousness to what civilization has termed the Marriage Problem.

The woman who refuses to bear children is the great figure of modern art. She is the rouged, frizzed, corseted, and scented Madonna in the temple of our chattering Materialism. She regards maternity through blackened eyes with a shuddering horror, and turns to adultery with a quiver of artistic satisfaction. The good man who marries a good woman, who sacrifices himself for posterity and finds in the sacrifice the enthusiasm of his life, cuts but a sorry if not a ridiculous figure on the modern stage. It is only to a music-hall audience that a man may appear with an infant in his arms, and then it is to degrade fatherhood and to set the atmosphere, that reeks with whisky and tobacco, rocking with hilarious laughter. The central companion of the adulteress on the modern stage is the smooth blackguard who breaks the sacred law of hospitality and coos his unholy way to the dishonour of his friend's wife, even, as in one notorious case, actually to the violation of his host's daughter —then to write a book about it!

Adultery has always had, like dirty stories, a morbid fascination for the backward individuals of an artificial state; but it has been reserved for a community so artificial and unnatural as our own to exalt the adulteress, to justify the seducer, and to make—not the universe, not God, not love, not righteousness, not science—but dirty-mindedness the intellectual occupation of its serious thinkers.

Take, also, the condition of mind which exists among those women of our cities who for the sake of getting a Parliamentary vote set at defiance the whole law of Christ and tread underfoot the very modesty of nature. A man tempted by hunger may break the law of Christ, may defy the criminal law, and we pity him, excuse him, and punish him; but we are asked not to excuse, but verily to admire, women who violate the most fundamental laws of humanity, who adjudge themselves superior to the teaching of Christ, who in cold blood and with calculation adopt violence as a method, who drag the modesty and beauty and self-effacement of womanhood through the mud of degradation—for the sake of a vote.

Take, again, the condition of public opinion. Men notorious for crime or rascality occupy unchallenged a prominent place in the national life. A swindler who enriched himself by the ruin of many thousands of people, and who bought himself a place in the country, where he made lackeys and sponges of the peasantry, has this line for his epitaph, "He was kind to the poor." And nobody laughs; nobody denounces the squirming sentimental hypocrisy of that unhallowed grave. A company promoter, who like a prostitute every day dresses himself attractively, and goes abroad smiling and captivating, and over the luncheon table of restaurants makes himself agreeable to rich old men for the sake of robbery—a man who in any natural state of existence would be put in the pond or hung from the nearest tree—may go in London unpunished by the law, continue his swindling in the eye of authority, and even be accepted by thousands of his fellow-countrymen as a hero of rational common sense. Of all the ministers of religion, tumbling over each other in London, there is no one to proclaim the scandal of this public apathy.

Authority in London also accepts as natural, as unalterable, a state of things which exists in no single city of Ireland—a procession, almost an army, of women parading the most central streets for the purpose of immorality, challenging the eyes of virtuous women with a mocking boldness, and startling pure and lovely children wellnigh out of their senses. This abomination, which the least virtuous village in England would regard as the triumph of hell, is considered in London, and in the great industrial cities, a natural evil.

A certain corner of Hyde Park has become the centre for a most atrocious and unspeakable vice; and neither the manhood of the city, nor the police, take steps to crush it out of existence. These things, we are told, exist everywhere; it is impossible to stop them.

Public opinion in England has suffered an enormous change since the coming of the industrial era. Once it was robust for virtue, a trifle truculent and boisterous perhaps, but always healthy, wholesome, downright and masculine. But with the coming of industrialism it lost vigour and slackened in its fibre. It is now little more than spasmodic sentimentalism. At one minute society empties its purse at the feet of General Booth, at the next it is giving bazaars in aid of the victims of a shipwreck, and at the next, as Mr. Masterman puts it, "shepherding its friends into drawing-room meetings to listen to some attractive speaker—an actor, a Labour member, a professional humorist—pleading for pity to the poor." However organized, it has not now even force enough to prevent women of virtue walking about the streets dressed so grotesquely, so indecorously, and so stupidly that an honest countryman must think them mad. The very street boys of London have lost the quickness of their eye and the energy of their mockery for ridiculous absurdity. People are afraid to express censure or to laugh at monstrosity. Not one man in ten thousand is strong enough publicly to express contempt for the folly and debasement of the times.

But I think one perceives more clearly than elsewhere the unreality of modern civilization in the works of literary reformers, both English and American. Books and plays are treated with a high seriousness that expose the vices and excesses of plutocracy, that draw lurid pictures of extravagance, luxury, and ostentation among a mere handful of people who have scrambled to the top of the swarming ant-heap of industrialism. Democratic politicians catch fire from these books and plays, and the platform as well as the stage, the newspaper columns as well as the libraries, are loud with scorn and denunciation of the rich.

Everyone living in contact with modern civilization is in a hurry; not only the Smart Set, but the prophets and teachers, are rushing to exhaust life. They have no time for deliberation. The ancient injunction, "Be still, and know that I am God," is scouted as absurd; the man in a motor-car does not even stop when he has knocked over a bicyclist or run his wheels over a child. The great thing now is not to pause, not to rest, not to be still, but to race like the wind. These literary and political reformers, for instance, seem incapable of the most elementary reflection. They do not see, apparently, that if plutocracy were abolished, if the wealth of these few people were distributed over the general field of national life, and if Socialism in fullest measure came to the rescue of civilization, humanity would be in just as perilous and calamitous a condition as it is at the present moment. It will still be, to quote Mr. Masterman again, "a complicated machine, which has escaped the control of all human volition, and is progressing towards no intelligible goal . . . some black windmill, with gigantic wings, rotating untended under the huge spaces of night."

Except in so far as the land laws have suffered the peasantry to rot, and have driven rural England into the slums of cities, the fault of all our misery lies at the door of democracy. The working-classes make England great or small. It is the soul of the working-classes that makes her righteous or infamous. It is the spirit of the working-classes that determines the tone and tendency of

English life. Plutocracy may scatter its money as it will, Aristocracy may be gracious or stupid, even Art and Literature may fall victims to ephemeral excitements and transitory crazes, losing all contact with the high and lofty interests of immortality ; but so long as democracy is virtuous, so long as democracy is conscious of reverence and wonder, so long as democracy honours motherhood and makes home-life the altar of the national religion, England will be great, civilization will be secure, and the blessing of God will rest upon the English people.

But democracy is ceasing to care for the things which make life beautiful and serene. Humility is out of fashion, and self-aggression is the law. Not to live simply, and healthfully, and gratefully, but to live richly, showily, and noisily is the passion of the industrial population. It is like a stampede in a moment of crisis. It is as if the ship of national life were sinking, and men, forgetting faith in God and hope of immortality, thrust women out of their way, crush children under their feet, and make for boats which will not live an hour in the sea of God's judgment. Money, not life, is the occupation of their thoughts. They are persuaded that pleasure can be bought, that rest is marked with a price, that peace is to be had in the market-place. They will not listen to the wisdom of the ages, they are impatient with the warning of history, they actually ignore and accuse of darkness the Light of the World. The symbol of democracy is the Lion of Force, not the meek and lowly Lamb of God.

And nothing else can be expected of an industrial democracy. The millions of England live no longer out of doors. They see nothing of nature's quiet. They experience nothing of nature's grandeur. They are shut up within walls for the long hours of their labour, and they go from their labour to a dark and sunless house in the slums. They have no experience of nature, no experience of home. Their wives toil in factories, or at sweated labour in a miserable kitchen ; their children are pale, querulous, and unlikeable ; the food they eat is ill-cooked and hideously set before them ; they have no gardens where they may dig, plant, and reap ; the rooms they inhabit are airless and dirty ; the beds they lie on are vile and unrestful. They awake to the clamour of the factory bell.

From the music-hall, where domestic life is degraded ; from the cinematograph exhibition, where crime and reckless adventure are exalted ; from the public-house, where poison is drunk and where boxing, football, dog-fighting, and horse-racing are discussed loudly and excitedly in a din of voices ; from the football match on Saturday afternoons, and the newspaper full of murders and divorces on Sunday—what can these people gather to elevate their minds and dignify their souls ?

And even, as is very often the case, where the women are clean, thrifty, and domestic, where the men are intelligent, temperate, and self-respecting, you find that their souls are almost always untouched by the grandeur and blessing of existence. They have little or no conception of the dignity of spiritual life. They toil that their daughters may not have to go out as domestic servants, and that their sons may pass competitive examinations and wear black coats for the rest of their days. Their holiday is spent on a shore so packed with humanity that you cannot see the sand. They pity the field labourers whom they see from the windows of their crowded railway carriage. To spend an hour in a wood, an hour in a field, an hour in exploring a hedgerow, would be a form of torture to them. They read novelettes that flatter aristocracy. They dress to look fashionable. They walk the streets to show themselves. They go to church because it is respectable.

The very best people in an industrial population suffer from the unnatural conditions of their lives. They are out of touch with Reality.

Mr. Healy said recently in the House of Commons: "You may be a great Empire, but we cannot afford you." It is true, morally as well as economically, that Ireland cannot afford Great Britain. Catholic Ireland desires natural conditions and conservative patience. She is in less hurry to exhaust life than "awakened" and modern China. She would develop her resources quietly and naturally. She is of opinion that existence is more important than wages. She has no ambition to be rich at the cost of peace, to gain the whole world and lose her soul. She believes that home-life is the centre of human life, that the spirit of the individual is indestructible and divinely immortal, that virtue is of immense importance, that communion with God is a reality and a blessing, that the foremost concern of every man, woman, and child—the concern infinitely more important than any conceivable advantage in the material world—is the spiritual life.

The spiritual life! How odd that phrase would sound in the public-houses of our industrial slums. Would it be understood? Would it have any more significance than a sonnet of Shakespeare? In Catholic Ireland—even among the most ignorant of the peasants, the most demoralized of the urban population—spiritual life is the supreme Reality.

If, then, I lived in rural Ireland I should be for Irish self-government. I should want to save my country from dragging at the heels of a rich, powerful, and sorely troubled nation committed to industrialism. I should fight to preserve the character of my own people, their simplicity, their natural conditions, their contentment, and their faith in God. And if I lived in Belfast, as I said before,

I should be a Unionist, a Unionist for the sake of England's purse and her genius for social legislation.

But I live in England, and here in England, writing the last pages of this book, I am conscious that the Irish question—rescued from the rival schools of Nationalists and Orangemen—presents an individual question to the mind of honest and disinterested men which admits of two contrary answers.

Is it possible, one asks oneself, to arrest the headlong and tumultuous course of modern industrialism? Is it possible for Ireland to make herself an oasis of tranquillity and spiritual peace in the sandstorm of materialism which is now raging across this desert of modern life? Is it not better for her to cling with all her might to England, trusting that the immense wealth, the unparalleled might, and the amazing luck of this tremendous neighbour may bring her safely through the storm, may land her at last in some unimagined millennium?

On the other hand, remembering the slums of Belfast and the beauty of Port-na-blah, one is tempted to cry out to England with all the energy of one's soul, that she has taken a wrong road, that ruin awaits her in the near distance, that at all hazards she must stop and get back as soon as possible to the path of nature.

It seems the most monstrous thing in the world to suggest that our great, mighty, and most glorious England should call a halt, should stop in her triumphant progress of conquest and dominion, should interrupt her work of solving social problems, to listen for a moment to some humble voice crying that her feet are on the way of ruin and calamity. As well might a vegetarian interrupt the mastication of roast beef at the Lord Mayor's Banquet with a chemical analysis of pea-nuts and lentils.

I will not presume to lift my voice and cry a halt. It may be that out of our present distress England is weaving some wondrous pattern of the Infinite Will. It may be that industrialism, and all the battling for material rewards, and all the struggle for mere animal existence among the millions of democracy, have a sublime significance, are in the moving light of divine revelation. Much in this fierce and awful civilization must perish, but some wonderful beauty may survive that will lighten for evermore the way of humanity. I can imagine such an emergence, though I cannot detect a shadow of its coming.

But I think it is wise for Ireland to pursue her own road. I am convinced that England has no legitimate right to coerce the soul and character of Ireland, to compel that little nation to march at her heels. And I believe that it is good for England to possess in her Empire, and close at her luxurious door, this modest, affectionate, and thrifty people who are struggling to live the spiritual life.

After all, the two nations are endeavouring to make two different experiments. England is seeking to live without relation to Nature. Ireland is seeking to live without relation to Materialism. Both endeavours are worth a student's while to watch; the contrast may have an infinite value for the philosophers of the next century. As Ireland has no right to prevent England from making her experiment, England has no right to prevent Ireland from making hers. And remember, it has been England's belief until quite recently that a bold and a free peasantry is essential to national greatness, that a rural population is of more concern to a State than an urban population. Ireland, on this matter, has not changed her mind. And England used to think—if her greatest poets and sages are to be trusted—that the home is the unit of the nation, that religion is the supreme law of the individual, and that it is impossible to serve both God and Mammon. On these matters, too, Ireland has not changed her mind.

England has changed her mind with the realization that it is possible not only to live, but even to create enormous wealth, in conditions which are unnatural. She has made her own Reality—a tremendous and most awe-inspiring Reality—and in contemplation of this immense Reality of her own creation, she has lost almost the knowledge of the older if less reputable Reality of nature. At any rate, she is indifferent to it. Her cities boast the increase of their herded humanity. Sanitation issues its challenges to Arcady. The Model Dwelling multiplies as the thatched cottage falls into ruin. And the Labour Party, monopolizing Parliament, has a mandate from every workman in the State, except the peasant.

One may almost say that England has lost her taste for nature—as a man loses his taste for a particular wine, a particular game. She is able to contemplate creation without wonder and without admiration. She is able to confront the tremendous thought of God without reverence and without misgiving. She is sceptical about immortality, and contemptuous of religious enthusiasm. She has ceased to be the poet of this beautiful earth and the priest of the immense universe which overshadows humanity; she has become the critic of natural law, the detective looking everywhere for the finger-prints of God to prove Him guilty of inferiority to human ideas. It may be, as one of her men of science has expressed it, that England's destiny is "to put the final question to the Universe with a solid passionate determination to be answered." But before the Universe surrenders to this bailiff's summons, England is certain to be the first of all European countries, the first of all peoples with a huge and complex civilization, to make the experiment of Socialism—some form of Socialism.

However wisely and quietly this experiment may be made,

Ireland—which will be the last of all nations to abandon Conservatism—has a right to be excluded from it, just as rich people have a right to make their investments abroad and to spend their winters in the south of France. And this, when all is said and done, is the spirit of Ireland's demand for self-government. She desires neither to live upon our bounty nor to share the perils of our legislative experiments. She claims her freedom to make her own destiny.

I am sure that Ireland will always be a small nation, and I hope that England may continue to be a great nation. I am as anxious to watch the experiment of England's attempt to live without relation to nature as Ireland's attempt to live without relation to materialism. But, on the whole, my sympathies are with Ireland. I think that Ireland is likely to be happier than England. I think her experiment is more beautiful than England's, and I think she will find it less difficult and troublesome to live outside materialism than England will find it easy to live outside natural conditions. And my book, I hope, may persuade all men in England able to look at the Irish question without the distorting frenzy of faction, to honour Ireland for her sense of nationality, to reverence her for the beauty and simplicity of her life, to be interested in her choice of natural simplicity, and to help her with all the power they possess to win that relative and restricted freedom, proposed by the present measure of Irish self-government, without which it is impossible for her to continue her experiment with safety and with self-respect.

## ON THE SWEATING OF BELFAST

THE following note appeared recently in the *Daily Chronicle*, answering three Belfast correspondents, Mr. Garrett Campbell, Mr. Cecil Pim, and Mr. J. H. Stirling, who resented some of my remarks on the linen industry :—

### OFFICIAL DISCLOSURES

We can assure Mr. Stirling that we have no desire to " throw mud in handfuls at Belfast." Our contention is that the conditions of labour in the textile trades of that city are very far from what they ought to be, and are in other towns in the United Kingdom. And, further, we contend that the attention of the workers is designedly distracted from all attempts at bettering their conditions of labour by talk about imaginary dangers to the unity of the Empire, and by a continual stirring up of the flames of religious bigotry.

As to the condition of things in the linen trade, no doubt Mr. Stirling has heard of the report of Dr. Bailie, the Medical Superintendent Officer of Health for Belfast. Dr. Bailie's soundness on the question of the Union is beyond suspicion. He was a

Unionist member of the corporation, and only resigned this position in order to take up the one he now holds.

Mr. Stirling speaks of the home-workers of Belfast as being "only a minute percentage of the whole industrial population." What does Dr. Bailie say on this point? He says that there are about 3700 out-workers* under inspection, but he goes on to show that this is very far from including all the out-workers in the town:

> Some employers seek to evade their responsibility under this section of the Act by ceasing to employ out-workers for a short period at February 1 and August 1, when the lists are due. And some attempts to fill in false or insufficient lists were discovered. One firm sent in a list having 80 per cent of the names and addresses given incorrectly, and an agent sent in a list giving only about 25 per cent of the workers known by the inspector to be employed by her.

And what does Dr. Bailie have to say about the wages earned by these out-workers?

> It is to be regretted that no improvement has been noted in the rate of payment given to out-workers in the city . . . which is still far too low. In the last week of December, for instance, a woman was observed embroidering small dots on cushion covers; there were 300 dots on each cushion, and for sewing these by hand she received the sum of 1d. SHE SAID THAT FOR A DAY'S WORK OF THIS KIND SHE WOULD HAVE DIFFICULTY IN MAKING 6d.
>
> Nor is this an exceptional case. Quite recently our inspector was shown handkerchiefs which were ornamented by a design in dots; these dots were counted, and it was found that the workers had to sew 384 dots for a penny. Comment is needless.
>
> BADLY PAID WORK
>
> Among the various kinds of badly paid work noticed may be mentioned:
>
> Children's pinafores (flounced and braided), 4½d. per dozen. Women's chemises, 7½d. per dozen. Women's aprons, 2½d. per dozen. Men's shirts, 10d. per dozen.
>
> From these very low rates of pay must be deducted the time spent in visiting the warehouses for work, the necessary upkeep of the worker's sewing-machine, and the price of the thread used in sewing, which is almost invariably provided by the worker. After these deductions are made, the amount left to the workers is so extremely small as to make one wonder if they

* "Out-workers" is the Belfast term for people who work in their own homes—home-workers.

are benefited by the work at all. Much the same scale of pay is found among the workers at the various processes of the linen trade, these workers constituting the larger proportion of the out-workers of Belfast. ONE PENNY PER HOUR IS THE ORDINARY RATE, AND IN MANY CASES IT FALLS BELOW THIS.

Work among the out-workers of Belfast continues to be complicated by the fact that much of the out-work done in the city in connection with the linen trade is not included in the trades listed as notifiable to the local authority. For this reason some of the employers do not and cannot be compelled to send in lists of their out-workers.

In face of this statement by Dr. Bailie, Mr. Stirling can hardly be justified in saying that "Belfast has been raked with a fine comb by the Socialists and Nationalists to find awful examples of the sweaters' tyranny." Nor can we follow him when he says that Sir Ernest Hatch, who is the chairman of the Committee appointed by the Board of Trade to inquire into the facts revealed by Dr. Bailie's report, "has certainly no bias in favour of the employers." Sir Ernest Hatch was for years a Unionist member of Parliament, and Mr. Stirling may rest assured that he will be fair to everybody.

### BELFAST v. OLDHAM

Mr. Garrett Campbell and Mr. Cecil Pim tell us that the average wage paid to able-bodied men in the linen mills of Belfast would be well above 25s. a week. This may or may not be true, but it may be pointed out that the number of able-bodied men employed is very few as compared with the total number of workers. In the last number of the *Labour Gazette* the total earnings of 18,309 persons engaged in all departments of the linen industry in Belfast in the week ending March 23 last are given, and they amount to £11,257, which is 12s. 3½d. a head.

If we turn to Oldham we find in the same week that 14,845 textile workers earned £15,820, or 21s. 4d. per head. But the workers in Oldham have a strong trade union behind them, and do not bother their heads about Lord Londonderry and Sir Edward Carson.

To the ordinary person it would seem that even if everything foretold came to pass after the Irish Parliament meets in Dublin, wages can hardly go below 1d. an hour and find your own thread and sewing-machine. Nor is it likely that even Mr. Redmond will be able to make some poor wretched creature sew more than 384 dots on a pocket-handkerchief for a penny.

WILLIAM BRENDON AND SON, LTD., PRINTERS, PLYMOUTH